Praise for *Saving Capitalism*

'A riveting guide to how our econon
become so badly flawed.'

Joseph Stiglitz

'Reich makes a very good case that widening inequality largely
reflects political decisions that could have gone in very different
directions ... *Saving Capitalism* is a very good guide to the state
we're in.'

Paul Krugman, *New York Review of Books*

'One of Reich's finest works, and is required reading for anyone who
has hope that a capitalist system can indeed work for the many, and
not just the few.'

Salon

'Arresting, thought-provoking ... Readily understandable language ... Powerful.'

Publishers Weekly

'Like any good teacher, Robert Reich knows that making a simple yet
crucial idea stick often takes much time and many presentations of
the concept ... In *Saving Capitalism*, Reich drives home a basic fact
that, if widely understood, could lift America from today's destruc-
tive political standoff.'

Chicago Tribune

'Reich has both the stature and eloquence to make a compelling
case ... Highly recommended to all readers ... Insightful.'

Library Journal, starred review

Praise for *Supercapitalism* (Icon Books, 2008)

'*Supercapitalism* is a grand debunking of the conventional wisdom
in the style of John Kenneth Galbraith ... Reich documents in lurid
detail the explosive growth of corporate lobbying expenditures and
campaign contributions since the 1970s. Today's presidential candidates should study his message carefully.'

New York Times

'A much-needed call for a reassessment of capitalism and recommendations for how to fix the mess we're in. An important book that needs to be read.'

Joseph Stiglitz

'Robert Reich's timely book should act as a wake-up call to the body politic.'

Tribune

'One of the most interesting books on political economy to appear in a long time.'

Financial Times

'*Supercapitalism* is a rounded and explicit discussion of how capitalist structures have stretched into the realm of democracy and eroded it.'

New Statesman

'Reich's book is fluently written, highly informative and a thoroughly absorbing read.'

Sunday Business Post

'The most original and honest criticism of the status quo that I have read for a long time.'

Literary Review

'Mr Reich argues that firms and financiers, from Wal-Mart to Wall Street, have caused such a dizzying gulf between rich and poor that the "common good" has disappeared and Americans have lost control of their democracy.'

Daily Telegraph

'There are many good reasons to read this book, not least the genuine importance of the issues under consideration.'

Spectator

'Robert Reich has done it again, offering a powerful new perspective on the predicaments in which we as Americans find ourselves. *Supercapitalism* highlights a new kind of social conflict – between ourselves as consumers and investors and ourselves as democratic citizens.'

Robert D. Putnam, author of *Bowling Alone*

SAVING
CAPITALISM

SAVING CAPITALISM

For the Many, Not the Few

Robert REICH

ICON

Published in the UK in 2016
by Icon Books Ltd, Omnibus Business Centre,
39–41 North Road, London N7 9DP
email: info@iconbooks.com
www.iconbooks.com

First published in the USA in 2015 by Alfred A. Knopf,
a Division of Penguin Random House LLC

Sold in the UK, Europe and Asia
by Faber & Faber Ltd, Bloomsbury House,
74–77 Great Russell Street,
London WC1B 3DA or their agents

Distributed in the UK, Europe and Asia
by Grantham Book Services,
Trent Road, Grantham NG31 7XQ

Distributed in Australia and New Zealand
by Allen & Unwin Pty Ltd,
PO Box 8500, 83 Alexander Street,
Crows Nest, NSW 2065

Distributed in South Africa
by Jonathan Ball, Office B4, The District,
41 Sir Lowry Road, Woodstock 7925

Distributed in India by Penguin Books India,
7th Floor, Infinity Tower – C, DLF Cyber City,
Gurgaon 122002, Haryana

ISBN: 978-178578-067-7

Typeset by North Market Street Graphics, Lancaster, PA
Designed by Maggie Hinders
Printed and bound in the UK by Clays Ltd, St Ives plc

In fond memory of John Kenneth Galbraith

There are two modes of invading private property; the first, by which the poor plunder the rich . . . sudden and violent; the second, by which the rich plunder the poor, slow and legal.

—JOHN TAYLOR, *An Inquiry into the Principles and Policy of the Government of the United States* (1814)

Contents

Preface to the British edition

Stagnant or declining wages for most, coupled with declining job security and widening inequality. Corporations, giant banks, and billionaires in control of a growing share of the economy and government. Rising populist agitation in the form of fierce xenophobia and anti-immigrant fervor.

Sound familiar? It's becoming the new political-economic normal in the United States, Britain, and elsewhere around the world. In this book I examine the connections between these phenomena, what they portend, and the critical choice they pose.

The standard explanation for the economic stresses that workers in Britain and the United States have endured over the last several decades focuses on globalization and technological displacement. While it's true that lower-paid workers abroad or computer-driven machines can now do many jobs more cheaply, these two factors by no means explain all that has happened.

In particular, they overlook the increasing concentration of political power in a corporate and financial elite that has been able to influence the rules by which the economy runs.

The ongoing debate between the political Left and Right over the merits of the so-called "free market" has diverted attention from the fact that the market in both our nations is organized differently from the way it was a half-century ago, and that its current organization is failing to deliver the widely shared prosperity and security it delivered then.

Such power is the main reason the compensation packages of the top executives of big companies have soared, that the wages and job prospects of recent college graduates have declined, and that the middle classes in both Britain and the United States have less employment security than they had decades ago.

To take but one example, our corporate and financial elites have enlarged and extended intellectual property rights—patents, trademarks, and copyrights—thereby increasing the profits of corporations engaged in the production of pharmaceuticals, high technology, biotechnology, and entertainment. Those profits have come at the expense of higher prices for average consumers—a portion of whose incomes have thereby been redistributed upwards to top executives and major shareholders.

Many corporations have also gained sufficient market power to set their prices higher than they would be under normal competitive circumstances. In the United States, such corporations include giant food processors, airlines, Internet service providers, health insurers, and high-tech companies owning software platforms now de facto industry standards (Amazon, Facebook, and Google). Such market power translates into higher profits, propelled by a redistribution from average consumers to top executives and major shareholders.

Laws governing bankruptcy have been altered to the further advantage of large corporations and financial institutions. In the United States, a wealthy individual can use bankruptcy to shield his fortune from investments that have gone badly, and a corporation can use bankruptcy to abrogate labor contracts. But former students who have borrowed for their education and are having difficulty repaying what they owe, or homeowners who are caught in the downdraft of a major recession and cannot meet their mortgage payments, are not allowed to reorganize their debts under bankruptcy. Here again, the consequence is a hidden redistribution upward.

At the same time, major corporations and financial institutions in both our nations have used their political influence to prevent the wages of most workers from rising in tandem with productivity gains. Trade agreements have encouraged companies to outsource jobs abroad, even while enlarging the protections accorded these corporations' intellectual property and financial assets abroad. Government budgets in Britain and the United States have emphasized debt reduction over job creation, thereby further undermining the bargaining power of average workers. Diminished safety nets and labor protections in both nations have added to the job insecurities of average workers, and therefore their willingness to accept lower wages.

Corporate and financial power is also reflected in the decline of labor unions in Britain and the United States. Fifty years ago, when General Motors was the largest employer in America, the typical GM worker earned $35 an hour in today's dollars. By 2014, America's largest employer was Walmart, and the typical entry-level Walmart worker earned about $9 an hour. That's largely because GM workers a half-century ago had a powerful union behind them, while Walmart workers have no union at all. Walmart has blocked all attempts at unionization. The pattern is much the same across the U.S. economy: In the 1950s, a third of all private-sector workers in America belonged to a union; now, fewer than 7 percent do.

It should not be surprising that corporate profits have increased as a portion of the total U.S. economy while the share going to wages has declined. In both the U.S. and in Britain, people whose incomes derive directly or indirectly from profits—corporate executives, Wall Street traders, and shareholders—have done exceedingly well. People dependent primarily on wages have not.

Britain has not moved as far toward American-style oligarchic capitalism, to be sure, but Britain is following America's dubious lead. Markets do not exist without rules. When large corporations, major banks, and the very rich gain the most influence over those rules, market outcomes begin to favor them—further adding to their wealth and their political influence. Unaddressed and unstopped, this vicious cycle accelerates.

Britain, beware. This trend is not sustainable, economically or politically. No economy can maintain positive momentum without the purchasing power of a large and growing middle class—one reason why, six full years into an economic recovery, the U.S. economy is barely back to where it was before succumbing to the Great Recession. Meanwhile, a large portion of the American electorate, having worked hard but seen no wage gains for many years, has grown angry and frustrated—fueling a nationalist revolt against the prevailing establishment and against convenient scapegoats such as immigrants. Political economies that bestow most gains on small groups at the top are inherently unstable.

The real question is not whether Britain and the United States will move toward a capitalism that works for the many rather than the few. Both of our nations will have to. The question is whether this change will occur through democratic reforms or by means of authoritarian mandates. Such, I believe, is the choice our two nations—the leading forces of capitalism in the nineteenth and twentieth centuries, respectively—will face in coming years.

Robert Reich
Berkeley, California
December 2015

Introduction

Do you recall a time when the income of a single schoolteacher or baker or salesman or mechanic was enough to buy a home, have two cars, and raise a family? I do. In the 1950s, my father, Ed Reich, had a shop on the main street of a nearby town, in which he sold women's clothing to the wives of factory workers. He earned enough for the rest of us to live comfortably. We weren't rich but never felt poor, and our standard of living rose steadily through the 1950s and 1960s.

That used to be the norm. For three decades after World War II, America created the largest middle class the world had ever seen. During those years the earnings of the typical American worker doubled, just as the size of the American economy doubled. Over the last thirty years, by contrast, the size of the economy doubled again but the earnings of the typical American went nowhere.

Then, the CEOs of large corporations earned an average of about twenty times the pay of their typical worker. Now they get substantially over two hundred times. In those years, the richest 1 percent of Americans took home 9 to 10 percent of total income; today the top 1 percent gets more than 20 percent.

Then, the economy generated hope. Hard work paid off, education was the means toward upward mobility, those who contributed most reaped the largest rewards, economic growth created more and better jobs, the living standards of most people improved throughout their working lives, our children would enjoy better lives than we had, and the rules of the game were basically fair.

But today all these assumptions ring hollow. Confidence in the economic system has declined sharply. The apparent arbitrariness and unfairness of the economy have undermined the public's faith in its basic tenets. Cynicism abounds. To many, the economic and political systems seem rigged, the deck stacked in favor of those at the top.

The threat to capitalism is no longer communism or fascism but a steady undermining of the trust modern societies need for growth and stability. When most people stop believing they and their children have a fair chance to make it, the tacit social contract societies rely on for voluntary cooperation begins to unravel. In its place comes subversion, small and large—petty theft, cheating, fraud, kickbacks, corruption. Economic resources gradually shift from production to protection.

We have the power to change all this, re-creating an economy that works for the many rather than the few. Contrary to Karl Marx, there is nothing about capitalism that leads inexorably to mounting economic insecurity and widening inequality. The basic rules of capitalism are not written in stone. They are written and implemented by human beings. But to determine what must be changed, and to accomplish it, we must first understand what has happened and why.

For a quarter century, I've offered in books and lectures an explanation for why average working people in advanced nations like the United States have failed to gain ground and are under increasing economic stress: Put simply, globalization and technological change have made most of us less competitive. The tasks we used to do can now be done more cheaply by lower-paid workers abroad or by computer-driven machines.

My solution—and I'm hardly alone in suggesting this—has

been an activist government that raises taxes on the wealthy, invests the proceeds in excellent schools and other means people need to get ahead, and redistributes to the needy. These recommendations have been vigorously opposed by those who believe the economy will function better for everyone if government is smaller and if taxes and redistributions are curtailed.

While the explanation I have offered for what has happened is still relevant, I've come to believe it overlooks a critically important phenomenon: the increasing concentration of political power in a corporate and financial elite that has been able to influence the rules by which the economy runs. And the governmental solutions I have propounded, while I think still useful, are in some ways beside the point, because they take insufficient account of the government's more basic role in setting the rules of the economic game. Worse yet, the ensuing debate over the merits of the "free market" versus an activist government has diverted attention from several critical issues: how the market has come to be organized differently from the way it was a half century ago, why its current organization is failing to deliver the widely shared prosperity it delivered then, and what the basic rules of the market should be.

I have come to think that the diversion of attention away from these issues is not entirely accidental. Many of the most vocal proponents of the "free market"—including executives of large corporations and their ubiquitous lawyers and lobbyists, denizens of Wall Street and their political lackeys, and numerous multimillionaires and billionaires—have for many years been actively reorganizing the market for their own benefit and would prefer these issues not be examined.

It is my intention in this book to put these issues front and center. My argument is straightforward. As I will elaborate in Part I, markets depend for their very existence on rules governing property (what can be owned), monopoly (what degree of market power is permissible), contracts (what can be exchanged and under what terms), bankruptcy (what happens when purchasers can't pay up), and how all of this is enforced.

Such rules do not exist in nature. They must be decided upon, one way or another, by human beings. These rules have been altered over the past few decades as large corporations, Wall Street, and wealthy individuals have gained increasing influence over the political institutions responsible for them.

Simultaneously, centers of *countervailing* power that between the 1930s and late 1970s enabled America's middle and lower-middle classes to exert their own influence—labor unions, small businesses, small investors, and political parties anchored at the local and state levels—have withered. The consequence has been a market organized by those with great wealth for the purpose of further enhancing their wealth. This has resulted in ever-larger upward pre-distributions *inside* the market, from the middle class and poor to a minority at the top. Because these pre-distributions occur inside the market, they have largely escaped notice.

In Part II, I show what this has meant for the resulting distribution of income and wealth in society. The meritocratic claim that people are paid what they are worth in the market is a tautology that begs the questions of how the market is organized and whether that organization is morally and economically defensible. In truth, income and wealth increasingly depend on who has the power to set the rules of the game.

As I will show, CEOs of large corporations and Wall Street's top traders and portfolio managers effectively set their own pay, advancing market rules that enlarge corporate profits while also using inside information to boost their fortunes. Meanwhile, the pay of average workers has gone nowhere because they have lost their aforementioned countervailing economic power and political influence. The simultaneous rise of both the working poor and non-working rich offers further evidence that earnings no longer correlate with effort. The resulting skewed pre-distribution of income to the top *inside* the market has generated demands for larger downward redistributions outside the market through taxes and transfer payments to the poor and lower-middle class, but such demands have simply added fuel to the incendiary debate over government's size.

As I elaborate in Part III, the solution is not to create more or less government. The problem is not the size of government but whom the government is *for*. The remedy is for the vast majority to regain influence over how the market is organized. This will require a new countervailing power, allying the economic interests of the majority who have not shared the economy's gains. The current left-right battle pitting the "free market" against government is needlessly and perversely preventing such an alliance from forming.

As I will explain, the biggest political divide in America in years to come will not be between the Republican and Democratic parties. It will be between the complex of large corporations, Wall Street banks, and the very rich that has fixed the economic and political game to their liking, and the vast majority who, as a result, find themselves in a fix. My conclusion is that the only way to reverse course is for the vast majority who now lack influence over the rules of the game to become organized and unified, in order to re-establish the countervailing power that was the key to widespread prosperity five decades ago.

While this book focuses on the United States, the center of global capitalism, the phenomena I describe are increasingly common to capitalism as practiced elsewhere around the world, and I believe the lessons drawn from what has occurred here are as relevant to other nations. Although global businesses are required to play by the rules of the countries where they do business, the largest global corporations and financial institutions are exerting growing influence over the makeup of those rules wherever devised. And the growing insecurities and cumulative frustrations of average people who feel powerless in the face of economies (and market rules) that are not working for them are generating virulent nationalist movements, sometimes harboring racist and anti-immigrant sentiments, as well as political instability in even advanced nations around the globe.

.   .   .

I believe that if we dispense with mythologies that have distracted us from the reality we find ourselves in, we can make capitalism work for most of us rather than for only a relative handful. History provides some direction as well as some comfort, especially in America, which has periodically readapted the rules of the political economy to create a more inclusive society while restraining the political power of wealthy minorities at the top. In the 1830s, the Jacksonians targeted the special privileges of elites so that the market system would better serve ordinary citizens. In the late nineteenth and early twentieth centuries, progressives enacted antitrust laws to break up the giant trusts, created independent commissions to regulate monopolies, and banned corporate political contributions. In the 1930s, New Dealers limited the political power of large corporations and Wall Street while enlarging the countervailing power of labor unions, small businesses, and small investors.

The challenge is not just economic but political. The two realms cannot be separated. Indeed, the field on which I draw in this book used to be called "political economy"—the study of how a society's laws and political institutions relate to a set of moral ideals, of which a fair distribution of income and wealth was a central topic. After World War II, under the powerful influence of Keynesian economics, the focus shifted away from these concerns and toward government taxes and transfers as means of both stabilizing the business cycle and helping the poor.* For many decades this formula worked. Rapid economic growth gen-

---

* The emergence of economics as a discipline distinct from political economy began in 1890 with the publication of Alfred Marshall's *Principles of Economics*. The new discipline sought to identify abstract variables applicable to all systems of production and exchange and paid little or no attention to the distribution of those resources or to a specific society's legal and political institutions. The study both of economics and of many other aspects of society thereafter began shifting from historically specific political, moral, and institutional relationships to more universal and scientific "laws." John Maynard Keynes's *General Theory of Employment, Interest, and Money* (1936) dominated American economic policy from the end of World War II until the late 1970s.

erated widespread prosperity, which in turn created a buoyant middle class. Countervailing power fulfilled its mission. We did not have to attend to the organization of the political economy or be concerned about excessive economic and political power at its highest rungs. Now, we do.

In a sense, then, this book harkens back to an earlier tradition of inquiry and a longer-lived concern. The book's optimism is founded precisely in that history. Time and again we have saved capitalism from its own excesses. I am confident we will do so again.

PART I

The Free Market

1

The Prevailing View

It usually occurs in a small theater or a lecture hall. Someone introduces me and then introduces a person who is there to debate me. My debate opponent and I then spend five or ten minutes sparring over the chosen topic—education, poverty, income inequality, taxes, executive pay, middle-class wages, climate change, drug trafficking, whatever. It doesn't matter. Because, with astounding regularity, the debate soon turns to whether the "free market" is better at doing something than government.

I do not invite this. In fact, as I've already said and will soon explain, I view it as a meaningless debate. Worse, it's a distraction from what we should be debating. Intentional or not, it deflects the public's attention from what's really at issue.

Few ideas have more profoundly poisoned the minds of more people than the notion of a "free market" existing somewhere in the universe, into which government "intrudes." In this view, whatever inequality or insecurity the market generates is assumed to be the natural and inevitable consequence of impersonal "market forces." What you're paid is simply a measure of what you're worth in the market. If you aren't paid enough to live on, so be it. If others rake in billions, they must be worth it. If millions of people are unemployed or their paychecks are shrinking or they have to work two or three jobs and have no idea what they'll be earning next month or even next week, that's unfortunate but it's the outcome of "market forces."

According to this view, whatever we might do to reduce inequality or economic insecurity—to make the economy work for most of us—runs the risk of distorting the market and causing it to be less efficient, or of producing unintended consequences that may end up harming us. Although market imperfections such as pollution or unsafe workplaces, or the need for public goods such as basic research or even aid to the poor, may require the government to intervene on occasion, these instances are exceptions to the general rule that the market knows best.

The prevailing view is so dominant that it is now almost taken for granted. It is taught in almost every course on introductory economics. It has found its way into everyday public discourse. One hears it expressed by politicians on both sides of the aisle.

The question typically left to debate is how much intervention is warranted. Conservatives want a smaller government and less intervention; liberals want a larger and more activist government. This has become the interminable debate, the bone of contention that splits left from right in America and in much of the rest of the capitalist world. One's response to it typically depends on which you trust most (or the least): the government or the "free market."

But the prevailing view, as well as the debate it has spawned, is utterly false. There can be no "free market" without government. The "free market" does not exist in the wilds beyond the reach of civilization. Competition in the wild is a contest for survival in which the largest and strongest typically win. Civilization, by contrast, is defined by rules; rules create markets, and governments generate the rules. As the seventeenth-century political philosopher Thomas Hobbes put it in his book *Leviathan:*

[in nature] there is no place for industry, because the fruit thereof is uncertain: and consequently no culture of the earth; no navigation, nor use of the commodities that may be imported by sea; no commodious building; no instruments of moving and removing such things as require much force; no knowledge of the face of the earth; no account of time; no arts; no letters; no society; and which is worst of all, continual fear, and danger of violent death; and the life of man, solitary, poor, nasty, brutish, and short.

A market—any market—requires that government make and enforce the rules of the game. In most modern democracies, such rules emanate from legislatures, administrative agencies, and courts. Government doesn't "intrude" on the "free market." It creates the market.

The rules are neither neutral nor universal, and they are not permanent. Different societies at different times have adopted different versions. The rules partly mirror a society's evolving norms and values but also reflect who in society has the most power to make or influence them. Yet the interminable debate over whether the "free market" is better than "government" makes it impossible for us to examine who exercises this power, how they benefit from doing so, and whether such rules need to be altered so that more people benefit from them.

The size of government is not unimportant, but the rules for how the free market functions have far greater impact on an economy and a society. Surely it is useful to debate how much government should tax and spend, regulate and subsidize. Yet these issues are at the margin of the economy, while the rules *are* the economy. It is impossible to have a market system without such rules and without the choices that lie behind them. As the economic historian Karl Polanyi recognized, those who argue for "less government" are really arguing for a *different* government— often one that favors them or their patrons.* "Deregulation" of

---

* In his book *The Great Transformation* (1944) Polanyi argued that the market economy and the nation-state should be viewed as a single man-made system he called the "Market Society." In his view, the coming of the modern nation-state and the modern capitalist economies it fostered altered human consciousness, from one based on reciprocity and redistribution to one based on utility and self-interest.

the financial sector in the United States in the 1980s and 1990s, for example, could more appropriately be described as "reregulation." It did not mean less government. It meant a different set of rules, initially allowing Wall Street to speculate on a wide assortment of risky but lucrative bets and permitting banks to push mortgages onto people who couldn't afford them. When the bubble burst in 2008, the government issued rules to protect the assets of the largest banks, subsidize them so they would not go under, and induce them to acquire weaker banks. At the same time, the government enforced other rules that caused millions of people to lose their homes. These were followed by additional rules intended to prevent the banks from engaging in new rounds of risky behavior (although in the view of many experts, these new rules are inadequate).

The critical things to watch out for aren't the rare big events, such as the 2008 bailout of the Street itself, but the ongoing multitude of small rule changes that continuously alter the economic game. Even a big event's most important effects are on how the game is played differently thereafter. The bailout of Wall Street created an implicit guarantee that the government would subsidize the biggest banks if they ever got into trouble. This, as I will show, gave the biggest banks a financial advantage over smaller banks and fueled their subsequent growth and dominance over the entire financial sector, which enhanced their subsequent political power to get rules they wanted and avoid those they did not.

The "free market" is a myth that prevents us from examining these rule changes and asking whom they serve. The myth is therefore highly useful to those who do not wish such an examination to be undertaken. It is no accident that those with disproportionate influence over these rules, who are the largest beneficiaries of how the rules have been designed and adapted, are also among the most vehement supporters of the "free market" and the most ardent advocates of the relative superiority of the market over government. But the debate itself also serves their goal of distracting the public from the underlying realities of how the rules are generated and changed, their own power over this process, and the extent to which they gain from the results. In other words, not only do these "free market" advocates want the public to agree with them about the superiority of the market but also about the central importance of this interminable debate.

They are helped by the fact that the underlying rules are well hidden in an economy where so much of what is owned and traded is becoming intangible and complex. Rules governing intellectual property, for example, are harder to see than the rules of an older economy in which property took the tangible forms of land, factories, and machinery. Likewise, monopolies and market power were clearer in the days of giant railroads and oil trusts than they are now, when a Google, Apple, Facebook, or Comcast can gain dominance over a network, platform, or communications system. At the same time, contracts were simpler to parse when buyers and sellers were on more or less equal footing and could easily know or discover what the other party was promising. That was before the advent of complex mortgages, consumer agreements, franchise systems, and employment contracts, all of whose terms are now largely dictated by one party. Similarly, financial obligations were clearer when banking was simpler and the savings of some were loaned to others who wanted to buy homes or start businesses. In today's world of elaborate financial instruments, by contrast, it is sometimes difficult to tell who owes what to whom, or when, or why.

Before we can understand the consequences of all of this for modern capitalism, it is first necessary to address basic questions about how government has organized and reorganized the market, what interests have had the most influence on this process, and who has gained and who has lost as a result. To do so, we must examine the market mechanism in some detail.

2

The Five Building Blocks
of Capitalism

In order to have a "free market," decisions must be made about

- PROPERTY: what can be owned
- MONOPOLY: what degree of market power is permissible
- CONTRACT: what can be bought and sold, and on what terms
- BANKRUPTCY: what happens when purchasers can't pay up
- ENFORCEMENT: how to make sure no one cheats on any of these rules

You might think such decisions obvious. Ownership, for example, is simply a matter of what you've created or bought or invented, what's *yours*.

Think again. What about slaves? The human genome? A nuclear bomb? A recipe? Most contemporary societies have decided you can't own these things. You can own land, a car, mobile devices, a home, and all the things that go into a home. But the most important form of property is now intellectual property—new designs, ideas, and inventions. What exactly counts as intellectual property, and how long can you own it?

Decisions also underlie what degree of market power is permissible—how large and economically potent a company or small group of firms can become, or to what extent dominance over a standard platform or search engine unduly constrains competition.

Similarly, you may think buying and selling is simply a matter of agreeing on a price—just supply and demand. But most societies have decided against buying and selling sex, babies, and votes. Most don't allow the sale of dangerous drugs, unsafe foods, or deceptive Ponzi schemes. Similarly, most civilized societies do not allow or enforce contracts that are coerced or that are based on fraud. But what exactly does "coercion" mean? Or even "fraud"?

Other decisions govern unpaid debts: Big corporations can use bankruptcy to rid themselves of burdensome pension obligations to their employees, for example, while homeowners cannot use bankruptcy to reduce burdensome mortgages, and former students cannot use it to reduce burdensome debts for higher education.

And we rely on decisions about how all these rules are enforced—the priorities of police, inspectors, and prosecutors; who can participate in government rule making; who has standing to sue; and the outcomes of judicial proceedings.

Many of these decisions are far from obvious and some of them change over time, either because social values change (think of slavery), technologies change (patents on novel arrangements of molecules), or the people with power to influence these decisions change (not just public officials, but the people who got them into their positions).

These decisions don't "intrude" on the free market. They constitute the free market. Without them there is no market.

What guides these decisions? What do the people who make the rules seek to achieve? The rules can be designed to maximize efficiency (given the current distribution of income and wealth in society), or growth (depending on who benefits from that growth and what a society is willing to sacrifice to achieve it, such as fouling the environment), or fairness (depending on prevailing norms about what constitutes a fair and decent society); or they can be designed to maximize the profits of large corporations and big banks, and the wealth of those already very wealthy.

If a democracy is working as it should, elected officials, agency heads, and judges will be making the rules roughly in accordance with the values of most citizens. As philosopher John Rawls has suggested, a fair choice of rule would reflect the views of the typical citizen who did not know how he or she would be affected by its application. Accordingly, the "free market" would generate outcomes that improved the well-being of the vast majority.

But if a democracy is failing (or never functioned to begin with), the rules might instead enhance the wealth of a comparative few at the top while keeping almost everyone else relatively poor and economically insecure. Those with sufficient power and resources would have enough influence over politicians, regulatory heads, and judges to ensure that the "free market" worked mostly on their behalf.

This is not corruption as commonly understood. In the United States, those with power and resources rarely directly bribe public officials in order to receive specific and visible favors, such as advantageous government contracts. Instead, they make campaign contributions and occasionally hold out the promise of lucrative jobs at the end of government careers. And the most valuable things they get in exchange are market rules that seem to apply to everyone and appear to be neutral, but that systematically and disproportionately benefit them. To state the matter another way, it is not the unique and perceptible government "intrusions" into the market that have the greatest effect on who wins and who loses; it is the way government organizes the market.

Power and influence are hidden inside the processes through which market rules are made, and the resulting economic gains and losses are disguised as the "natural" outcomes of "impersonal market forces." Yet as long as we remain obsessed by the debate over the relative merits of the "free market" and "government," we have little hope of seeing through the camouflage.

Before examining each of the five building blocks of capitalism separately, it is useful to see how political power shapes all of them and why market freedom cannot be understood apart from how such power is exercised, and by whom.

3

Freedom and Power

As income and wealth have concentrated at the top, political power has moved there as well. Money and power are inextricably linked. And with power has come influence over the market mechanism. The invisible hand of the marketplace is connected to a wealthy and muscular arm.

It is perhaps no accident that those who argue most vehemently on behalf of an immutable and rational "free market" and against government "intrusion" are often the same people who exert disproportionate influence over the market mechanism. They champion "free enterprise" and equate the "free market" with liberty while quietly altering the rules of the game to their own advantage. They extol freedom without acknowledging the growing imbalance of power in our society that's eroding the freedoms of most people.

In 2010, a majority of the Supreme Court of the United States decided in *Citizens United v. Federal Election Commission* that corporations are people under the First Amendment, entitled to freedom of speech. Therefore, said the court, the Bipartisan Campaign Reform Act of 2002 (commonly referred to as the McCain-Feingold Act), which had limited spending by corporations on political advertisements, violated the Constitution and was no longer the law of the land.

Yet as a practical matter, freedom of speech is the freedom to be heard, and most citizens' freedom to be heard is reduced when those who have the deepest pockets get the loudest voice. Nowhere did the five members in the majority acknowledge the imbalance of power between big corporations increasingly willing to finance vast political advertising campaigns and ordinary citizens. In practice, therefore, the freedom of speech granted by the court to corporations would drown out the speech of regular people without those resources.

In the first decades of the twentieth century, the court was similarly blind to the realities of power. Conservatives on the court struck down laws enacted to protect the freedom of workers to organize and bargain collectively. In *Carter v. Carter Coal Company* (1936), the court's majority ruled that collective bargaining was "an intolerable and unconstitutional interference with personal liberty and private property . . . a denial of rights safeguarded by the due process clause of the Fifth Amendment." Yet without collective bargaining, workers weren't free to negotiate their terms of employment; if they wanted a job, they had to accept whatever terms were dictated by the big businesses that dominated the economy. By elevating "personal liberty and private property" over the freedom of workers to band together to achieve better terms, the court tipped the Constitution in the direction of the powerful. *Carter* was subsequently overruled, but the ideology behind it lives on.

Now, as economic and political power have once again moved into the hands of a relative few large corporations and wealthy individuals, "freedom" is again being used to justify the multitude of ways they entrench and enlarge that power by influencing the rules of the game. These include escalating campaign contributions, as well as burgeoning "independent" campaign expenditures, often in the form of negative advertising targeting candidates whom they oppose; growing lobbying prowess, both in Washington and in state capitals; platoons of lawyers and paid experts to defend against or mount lawsuits, so that courts interpret the laws in ways that favor them; additional lawyers and experts to push their agendas in agency rule-making proceedings; the prospect of (or outright offers of) lucrative private-sector jobs for public officials who define or enforce the rules in ways that benefit them; public relations campaigns designed to convince the public of the truth and wisdom of policies they support and the falsity and deficiency of policies they don't; think tanks and sponsored research that confirm their positions; and ownership of, or economic influence over, media outlets that further promote their goals.

Under these circumstances, arguments based on the alleged superiority of the "free market," "free enterprise," "freedom of contract," "free trade," or even "free speech" warrant a degree of skepticism. The pertinent question is: Whose freedom?

The expanding freedom of corporations to do what they want may theoretically enlarge the economic pie for everyone. But in recent years the major consequence of such freedom has been to give bigger slices to the top executives of large corporations and Wall Street banks, and their shareholders, and smaller slices to almost everyone else. Another consequence has been to reduce the freedoms of ordinary working people in the workplace. The supposed freedom of contract is a cruel joke to workers who have no alternatives but to agree to terms mandating arbitration of all grievances before an arbiter chosen by the company, thereby forcing employees to give up their constitutional right to a trial. A corporation that monitors its employees' every motion from the minute they check in to the minute they check out, even limiting bathroom breaks to six minutes a day, may be a model of free enterprise, but it does not contribute to the liberty of the people working for it.

"Free enterprises" designed to maximize shareholder returns have been known to harm the environment, endanger the health and safety of consumers and others, and defraud investors. Even when such actions are illegal, some corporations have chosen to defy the law when the risks and costs of getting caught are less than the profits to be made. The list of enterprises that in recent years have made such a calculation, wittingly or unwittingly—including BP, Halliburton, Citigroup, and General Motors—makes clear that corporate power will infringe on individual liberties if the potential financial returns are sufficiently high.

The freedom of enterprises to monopolize a market likewise reduces the freedom of consumers to choose. Allowing Internet service providers to reduce or eliminate competition, for example, has made Internet service in the United States more expensive than in any other rich country. Permitting drug companies to prolong their patents by paying generic producers to delay lower-cost versions has kept drug prices higher in the United States than in Canada or Europe. Most of us remain "free" in the limited sense of not being coerced into purchasing Internet services or drugs. We can choose to do without them. But this is a narrow view of freedom.

Similarly, those who view the global economy as presenting a choice between "free trade" and "protectionism" overlook the centrality of power in determining what is to be traded and how. Since all nations' markets depend on political decisions about how their markets are organized, as a practical matter "free trade" agreements entail complex negotiations about how different market systems will be integrated. "Free trade" with China, for example, doesn't simply mean more trade, because China's market is organized quite differently from that of the United States. The real issues involve such things as the degree of protection China will give the intellectual property of American-based corporations, how China will treat the assets of U.S.-based investment banks, and the access of China's state-run enterprises to the American market. In such negotiations the interests of big American-based corporations and Wall Street banks have consistently trumped the interests of average working Americans, whose wages are considered less worthy of protection than, say, an American company's intellectual capital or a Wall Street bank's financial assets. The United States has never sought to require, for example, that trading partners establish minimum wages equal to half their median wages.

In all these respects, freedom has little meaning without reference to power. Those who claim to be on the side of freedom while ignoring the growing imbalance of economic and political power in America and other advanced economies are not in fact on the side of freedom. They are on the side of those with the power.

A close examination of each building block of the market will make this apparent.

4

The New Property

Private property is the most basic building block of free-market capitalism. In the conventional debate it's contrasted with government ownership, or socialism. What is left out of that debate are the myriad ways government organizes and enforces property rights and who has the most influence over those decisions.

Private property has obvious advantages over common ownership. A half century ago the American environmentalist Garrett Hardin warned of the "tragedy of the commons," by which individuals, acting rationally but selfishly, deplete a common resource—allowing their cattle to overgraze the town common, for example. When property is privately held, on the other hand, rational owners take care to avoid depletion, investing in fertilizer and irrigation. There are many other examples. To my knowledge, no customer has ever washed a rental car.

But the debate over private versus public ownership obscures basic decisions about the rules governing private property: What can be owned, on what condition, and for how long? Some of these are profoundly moral issues. They are also, inevitably, political, because their answer depends on the distribution of power in society.

Three centuries ago, it was common for people to own other

people. As historian Adam Hochschild has noted, by the end of the eighteenth century well over three-quarters of all people alive in the world were in bondage of one kind or another, as slaves or serfs. In parts of the Americas and Africa, slaves far outnumbered free persons.

Slavery rested on the political power of slave owners and traders to maintain slavery as a form of property. The Republican Party in the United States was founded in the 1850s in direct opposition to wealthy slaveholders and those Democrats who asserted that ownership of slaves was a property right protected by the Constitution. Yet within fifteen years, politics and power shifted. Slavery was banned in America in 1865 with the passage of the Thirteenth Amendment to the Constitution. By the end of the nineteenth century slavery was outlawed almost everywhere in the world. But not entirely. It was not officially banned in Mauritania until 1981. And it still continues, illegally, in many places around the world. Even in twenty-first-century America, an estimated 100,000 children are enslaved in the sex trade.

Other than slaves, the most valuable form of property in the nineteenth century was land. Yet even landownership was based on social norms as well as political power. In England, vast tracts were locked away in an aristocracy that handed them down from generation to generation, allowing tenants to farm them. In America, by contrast, a series of laws, beginning with the Land Ordinance of 1785 through the Homestead Act of 1862, made frontier land available to potential settlers rather than to political elites. (In most Latin American countries, frontier lands went to the politically powerful.) But America's white settlers had political power behind them, too. The United States gave them right to the land, and the U.S. military fought native Americans to secure it.

As land prices escalated through the nineteenth century, those who owned large tracts saw their wealth increase dramatically even if they did nothing but rent the land. Land values were increasing simply because land was becoming scarce.

Henry George, in his book *Progress and Poverty* (1879), described progress that pushed up land prices as "an immense wedge being forced, not underneath society, but through society. Those who are above the point of separation are elevated, but those who are below are crushed down." The book sold two million copies, but George's proposal for a steep tax on land that would recapture for society most of a landowner's capital gains went nowhere.

Then came another economic and political shift, as factories and machines transformed America and other advanced economies from agriculture to industry. Within a few decades, most Americans no longer owned or even rented the property that supplied their livelihoods. They were employees. And the critical question about property then moved to the freedom of workers to organize in order to gain a larger share of the income resulting from the combination of their labors with the factories and machines, versus the owners' "liberty of contract."

Even the modern corporation, and its ownership, is part of the property mechanism—a consequence of particular decisions by legislatures, agencies, and courts that people who invest in the corporation are entitled to a share of its profits and that their personal property beyond those investments is protected if the corporation can't pay its debts. The "free market" doesn't dictate this. Property and contract rules do. Yet the idea that shareholders are a corporation's only owners, and therefore that the sole purpose of the corporation is to maximize the value of their investments, appears nowhere in the law. In fact, in the first three decades following World War II, corporate managers saw their job as balancing the claims of investors, employees, consumers, and the public at large. The large corporation was in effect "owned" by everyone with a stake in how it performed. The notion that only shareholders count emerged from a period in the 1980s when corporate raiders demanded managers sell off "underperforming" assets, close factories, take on more debt, and fire employees in order to maximize shareholder returns.

The rules governing private property are constantly being contested and adapted, sometimes in big ways (banning slavery) but often in small ways barely noticeable to anyone not directly involved. What looks like government regulation is sometimes better understood as the creation of a property right. For example, before 1978, airlines with overbooked flights simply bumped their excess passengers arbitrarily. After many complaints, the Civil Aeronautics Board (which then regulated airlines) began requiring airlines to treat each seat as the property of the passenger who booked it. That way, airlines with overbooked flights would have to "buy" the excess seats back by offering whatever inducement was necessary to get the right number of passengers to give up their "property" voluntarily.

Scarce resources often depend on property rights to encourage conservation and investment in technologies that could reduce future scarcity and help ensure that those who need them can get them. By 2015, several water districts in California, facing acute shortages because of drought conditions, turned water into a form of property whose cost depended on usage—starting low for a basic allocation covering families' essential needs and rising rapidly with volume so that people do not mindlessly refill their swimming pools. The same approach could be taken with the environment as a whole—a scarce resource on a global scale. Ideally, the right to emit carbon dioxide into the atmosphere would be treated as a form of property whose price continued to rise over time. Polluters could buy and trade it, so it would be used where most needed. This would also give them a strong incentive to minimize their emissions immediately and devise innovative ways of reducing them further. Such property rights require that government determines how they are to be allocated initially, by what criteria, and how they are to be traded. If necessities such as clean air and water simply go to the highest bidders, income and wealth disparities can result in wildly unfair outcomes. Government must also monitor and enforce any such system.

.　　.　　.

The underlying mechanisms that define property become even more complicated when property takes the form of strands of genetic material, or combinations of molecules, or gigabits of software code, or, more generally, information and ideas. This sort of property doesn't exist in one unique place and time. It can't be weighed or measured concretely. And most of the cost of producing it goes into discovering it or making the first copy. After that, the additional production cost is often zero. Yet such intellectual property is the key building block of the new economy, and without government decisions over who can own what aspects of it, and on what terms, the new economy could not exist.

Here, the tragedy of the commons poses a particularly vexing dilemma. Unless discoverers and inventors can own what they discover and invent, and make money by selling or licensing it, many won't put in the effort in the first place. Some might do it for free because of the thrill of discovery, or fame, or simply having others use these new items—creators of all sorts post on the Internet free of charge. But free labor won't pay the rent, and an economy cannot be based entirely on it, so some property rights are necessary. Yet once the discovery or invention has been made, the public will benefit most by having full access to it at no more than the cost of replicating it—which is often near zero. Why should a company that creates a blockbuster drug that can be reproduced for pennies earn billions while many who would benefit from it cannot afford it?

What's the proper balance between giving would-be inventors enough ownership that they're motivated to invent and giving the public affordable access to their discoveries? Here again, it's not a matter of the "free market" versus the government. Legislatures, courts, and administrative agencies must decide.

One way of dealing with the dilemma is to give inventors a temporary monopoly—a property right that disappears after a certain length of time. The framers of the Constitution contemplated this, authorizing Congress to grant patents and copyrights "to promote the Progress of Science and useful Arts, by securing for limited Times to Authors and Inventors the exclusive Right to their respective Writings and Discoveries." But they did not decide precisely what could be patented or for how long because they had no way of knowing what would be invented. The first patent law in America, enacted in 1790, simply said patents could be obtained for "any useful art, manufacture, engine, machine, or device, or any improvement thereon not before known or used," and its duration would be fourteen years. Since then, Congress has extended patent protection to twenty years (for applications filed after 1995), but the real battles have been over what is "new and useful." The Patent and Trademark Office makes these determinations on a case-by-case basis; another office handles copyrights on literary works.

Those who disagree with Patent Office decisions can appeal them to a special court set up for the purpose and take their cases all the way to the Supreme Court if the court is willing to hear them. As inventions have become ever more complex, patent litigation—typically legal fights between those who are granted patents and competitors who believe the patents unjustifiably infringe on patents they already own, or who believe no patent should have been awarded—has increased in volume and duration. By the second decade of the twenty-first century, the U.S. Patent and Trademark Office had almost ten thousand employees, most of them based in a five-building headquarters in Alexandria, Virginia, and the federal courts included a special court of appeals to hear patent cases. Most patents are for software and deal with highly technical issues regarding what is new or has already been discovered. Some applications merely describe ideas or concepts that will be turned into software. Amazon, for example, received a patent for the concept of "one-click checkout." In 2014, Apple received a patent based on the idea of offering author autographs on e-books.

Strong and enduring property rights provide incentives to invest and innovate, but they also raise consumer prices. Importantly, the economic power of those who possess these rights often translates into political and legal power to make them even stronger and more enduring.

An entire legal industry has developed around defending patents or suing for patent infringement. Big high-tech companies often dedicate small armies of lawyers to the task. In 2013, Congress rejected a proposal that would have allowed the Patent Office to expedite its review of questionable software patents, often filed by big companies to lay claim to vast areas of possible invention. Among the corporations whose lobbyists successfully blocked the proposal: IBM and Microsoft.

The biggest technology companies are spending billions accumulating patent portfolios and then suing and countersuing one another. By purchasing Motorola Mobility for $12.5 billion in 2012, for example, Google gained ownership of seventeen thousand patents, many of which would serve as valuable ammunition in the smartphone patent wars that Google, Samsung, and Apple were waging against one another. As White House intellectual property advisor Colleen Chien noted in 2012, Google and Apple have been spending more money acquiring and litigating over patents than on doing research and development.

Again, the underlying issue here has nothing to do with whether one prefers the "free market" or government. The question is how government defines property rights, what that process entails, and who has the most power to determine its outcomes.

America spends far more on medications per person than does any other developed country, even though the typical American takes fewer prescription drugs than the typical citizen of other advanced nations. Of the $3.1 trillion America spent on health in 2014, drugs accounted for 10 percent of the total. Government pays some of this tab through Medicare, Medicaid, and subsidies under the Affordable Care Act. We pick up the tab indirectly through our taxes. We pay the rest directly, through copayments, deductibles, and premiums.

Drug prices are high in America partly because, while other governments set wholesale drug prices in their countries, the law bars the U.S. government from using its considerable bargaining power to negotiate lower costs. But the bigger reason drug prices are so high in America is that drugs are patented—and those temporary monopolies often last beyond when the patents are supposed to run out (now twenty years); I will explain why in a moment.

The Patent Office and the courts initially decided that products from nature couldn't be patented. That's why early vaccines, using viruses to build up the human body's immunity, couldn't become the private property of drug companies. It also explains why drug manufacturers were slow to invest in research necessary to come up with new vaccines.

But in the 1990s, the rules changed. Pharmaceutical companies were allowed to patent the processes they used to manufacture vaccines and other products from nature. As a result, the number of applications for patents on vaccines soared tenfold to more than ten thousand. Not surprisingly, vaccine prices also took off. In 2013, Pfizer raked in nearly $4 billion on sales of the Prevnar 13 vaccine, which prevents diseases caused by pneumococcal bacteria, from ear infections to pneumonia—for which Pfizer was the only manufacturer.

Many lifesaving drugs continue to be made by only one company long after the original patent expires. In part, that's because the Patent Office often renews patents on the basis of small and insignificant changes to the original drugs that technically make them new and therefore patentable. The office is not required to weigh the financial burdens its decisions impose on customers. And pharmacies cannot substitute generic versions of a brand-name drug when it has changed in even the most minor of ways. For example, Forest Laboratories announced in February 2014 it would stop selling the existing tablet form of Namenda, its widely used drug to treat Alzheimer's, in favor of new, extended-release capsules called Namenda XR. The capsules were simply a reformulated version of the tablet, but even that minor change prevented pharmacists from substituting generic versions of the tablet, whose patent was about to run out. "Product hopping" like this keeps profits flowing to the pharmaceutical companies but costs consumers and health insurers a bundle.

Many drugs that are available over the counter in other countries can be bought only by prescription in the United States, and the drug companies aggressively market these brands long after the patents have expired so that patients ask doctors to prescribe them. America is one of the few advanced nations that allow direct advertising of prescription drugs to consumers.

It is illegal for Americans to shop at foreign pharmacies for cheaper versions of the same drugs sold in the United States, either branded or generic. In 2012, Congress authorized U.S. Customs to destroy any such medications. The ostensible reason is to protect the public from dangerous counterfeit drugs. But for at least a decade before then, during which time tens of millions of prescriptions were filled over the Internet, no case was reported of Americans having been harmed by medications bought online from a foreign pharmacy. The real reason for the ban is to protect the profits of U.S. pharmaceutical companies, which lobbied intensely for it. Yet the real threat to the public's health is drugs priced so high that an estimated fifty million Americans—more than a quarter of them with chronic health conditions—did not fill their prescriptions in 2012, according to the National Consumers League.

The law allows pharmaceutical companies to pay doctors for prescribing their drugs. Over a five-month period in 2013, doctors received some $380 million in speaking and consulting fees from drug companies and device makers. Some doctors pocketed over half a million dollars each, and others received millions of dollars in royalties from products they had a hand in developing. Doctors claim these payments have no effect on what they prescribe. But why would pharmaceutical companies shell out all this money if it did not provide them a healthy return on their investment?

Drug companies pay the makers of generic drugs to delay their cheaper versions. These so-called pay-for-delay agreements, perfectly legal, generate huge profits both for the original manufacturers and for the generics—profits that come from consumers, from health insurers, and from government agencies paying higher prices than would otherwise be the case. The tactic costs Americans an estimated $3.5 billion a year. Europe doesn't allow these sorts of payoffs. The major American drugmakers and generics have fought off any attempts to stop them.

The drug companies claim they need these additional profits to pay for researching and developing new drugs. Perhaps this is so. But that argument neglects the billions of dollars drug companies spend annually for advertising and marketing—often tens of millions of dollars to promote a single drug. They also spend hundreds of millions every year lobbying. In 2013, their lobbying tab came to $225 million, which was more than the lobbying expenditures of America's military contractors. In addition, Big Pharma spends heavily on political campaigns. In 2012 it shelled out more than $36 million, making it one of the biggest political contributors of all American industries.*

The average American is unaware of this system—the patenting of drugs from nature, the renewal of patents based on insignificant changes, the aggressive marketing of prescription drugs, bans on purchases from foreign pharmacies, payments to doctors to prescribe specific drugs, and pay-for-delay—as well as the laws and administrative decisions that undergird all of it. Yet, as I said, because of this system, Americans pay more for drugs, per person, than citizens of any other nation on earth. The critical question is not whether government should play a role. Without government, patents would not exist, and pharmaceutical com-

---

* The amount of money industry spends directly on political contributions, although substantially more than industry spent before the 1980s in real terms, is still typically small compared to what it spends on lobbying, litigating, and otherwise seeking to influence policymakers. And all such expenditures, together, are far smaller than the gains they expect from such tactics. This is because businesses spend only what they need to spend to achieve their desired ends. And due to the decline of countervailing power, which I will discuss later, they can get what they want at bargain-basement prices.

panies would have no incentive to produce new drugs. The issue is *how* government organizes the market. So long as big drug-makers have a disproportionate say in those decisions, the rest of us pay through the nose.

The story with copyrights—applied to works of art and music—is similar. So is the underlying dilemma of how much of a property right to give creators so they have adequate inducement to toil away, while not denying society inexpensive or free access to works that cost little or nothing to reproduce. But here again, the creators (usually in the form of large corporations or trusts that have come to own the copyrights) consistently want more—and have always gotten it. The result has been more money for them and higher cost and less access for the rest of us. And as their profits have increased, so has their political clout for the next round.

When the nation was founded, copyrights covered only "maps, charts, and books" and gave the author the exclusive right to publish for fourteen years, which could be renewed once, for a maximum term of twenty-eight years. In 1831, the maximum was increased to forty-two years. In 1909, Congress again extended the maximum, this time to fifty-six years, where it remained for the next half century. Then, beginning in 1962, Congress extended the maximum eleven more times. In 1976, Congress extended it to the life of the author plus an additional fifty years. The creator did not even have to seek renewal. If the creation emerged from a corporation, the copyright lasted seventy-five years. (This change operated retroactively, so any work still under corporate copyright in 1978, when the new law took effect, was eligible for an additional nineteen years of protection.)

In 1998, Congress added twenty years on top of all this—to ninety-five years from the first publication, in the case of corporate owners. The Copyright Term Extension Act of 1998 was also known around Washington as the Mickey Mouse Protection Act because it was basically about Mickey. Walt Disney had created

Mickey in 1928, so under the prevailing seventy-five-year corporate limit Mickey would move into the public domain in 2003. Pluto, Goofy, and the rest would become public shortly thereafter. That would mean big revenue losses for the Disney Corporation. Accordingly, Disney lobbied Congress intensively to extend copyright protection for another twenty years, as did Time Warner, which held copyrights on many twentieth-century films and musical scores, along with the heirs of dead songwriters George and Ira Gershwin. They got what they wanted. Most of those old copyrights are now scheduled to expire in 2023. It seems a safe bet that before that year, copyrights will be extended yet again. Moreover, copyrights now cover almost all creative works, including computer programs, and give owners (now, usually large corporations) rights over all derivative work that might be generated by the original.

As a result, much of the creative output of the last century—not just Mickey Mouse and other Disney characters but many of the icons of the twentieth century, including Superman and Dick Tracy; a treasure trove of movies, among them *Gone with the Wind* and *Casablanca;* the last century's great outpouring of music, including George Gershwin's "Rhapsody in Blue" and Bob Dylan's "Blowin' in the Wind"; and masterpieces of literature, such as the works of Faulkner and Hemingway—have been locked away for an additional two decades. Here again, the result is higher corporate profits, higher costs to consumers, and less access for everyone. The reason more printed books are available on Amazon.com from the 1880s than from the 1980s, for example, is that anyone is free to republish books from the earlier era.

This reorganization of the market will not spur more creativity from Walt Disney or the brothers Gershwin, since they are no longer with us. It is doubtful the reorganization will even give added incentive to writers and artists now alive, who will have to be dead for seventy years, rather than fifty, before their works move into the public domain. Ironically, many of Disney's original creations drew heavily on characters and stories that had become classics, such as Aladdin, the Little Mermaid, and Snow White, because they had long been in the public domain. But the public domain is now far smaller.

Meanwhile, the large corporate owners of copyrights aggressively fight in court to extend their ownership to anything that might be considered derivative of their long-extended copyrights, adding to their bottom lines and their economic clout but presenting insurmountable barriers for individual creators, including computer programmers, who might have an idea that turns out to be too close to one already owned. As a result, big players continue to win while the rest of us lose, because they can pour so much money into these market-defining decisions.

In sum, property—the most basic building block of the market economy—turns on political decisions about what can be owned and under what circumstances. Due to the increasing wealth and political influence of large corporations, as well as the subtlety and complexity of the contours of intellectual property, these political decisions have tended to enlarge and entrench that wealth and power. The winners are adept at playing this game. The rest of us, lacking such influence and unaware of its consequences, often lose out. As we bicker over whether we prefer the "free market" to government, the game continues and the winnings accumulate.

5

The New Monopoly

The second building block of a market economy follows directly from the first. Businessmen and -women need some degree of market power in order to be induced to take the risks of starting new businesses. If any rival could swiftly and effortlessly take away any other business's competitive advantage, there would be no reason for any business to invest in the first place. The question of how much market power is desirable therefore poses a trade-off similar to that presented by rules about property, including intellectual property. Substantial market power provides strong incentives to invest and innovate but also raises consumer prices. Such power can also translate into political power, distorting markets further in favor of those who possess it. What's the "best" trade-off? Such decisions typically are buried within antitrust or antimonopoly laws, as enforced by administrative agencies and interpreted by prosecutors and courts.

Here again, the underlying issue has nothing to do with a hypothetical choice between the "free market" and government. Decisions must be made about whether a particular company or group of companies has "excessive" market power. The important question is how such decisions are made and influenced. Many of the corporations that have gained dominance over large swaths of the economy in recent years have done so by extending their domains of intellectual property; expanding their owner-ship of natural monopolies, where economies of scale are critical; merging with or acquiring other companies in the same market; gaining control over networks and platforms that become indus-try standards; or using licensing agreements to enlarge their dominance and control. Such economic power has simultane-ously increased their influence over government decisions about whether such practices should be allowed.

All this has hobbled smaller businesses. Contrary to the con-ventional view of an American economy bubbling with innova-tive small companies, the reality is quite different. Intellectual property, network effects, natural monopolies, expensive R&D, fleets of lawyers to litigate against potential rivals, and armies of lobbyists have created formidable barriers to new entrants. This is one major reason the rate at which new businesses have formed in the United States has slowed markedly in recent years. Between 1978 and 2011, as the new giants gained control, that rate was halved, according to a Brookings Institution study released in May 2014. The decline transcends the business cycle; neither the expansions of the late 1990s and early 2000s, nor the recessions of 2001 and 2008–09, seem to have had any effect on the downward trend. And that trend has been immune to which party has occu-pied the White House or controlled Congress (see figure 1).

The continued dominance of the new giants is by no means assured. A new entrant with a far better idea could nibble away at one of the giant's markets, although the giant would probably buy the new entrant before incurring any substantial damage. An aggressive enforcer of antitrust laws could win a court victory that forced the giant to relinquish market share, although the giant's army of litigators would probably halt any such assault, and its legislative allies would discourage the assault to begin with. The more likely threat to one of the giants comes from another giant seeking to expropriate its market.

The positions of the new giants are remarkably strong because

FIGURE 1. THE U.S. ECONOMY HAS BECOME LESS ENTREPRENEURIAL OVER TIME
Firm Entry and Exit Rates in the United States, 1978–2011

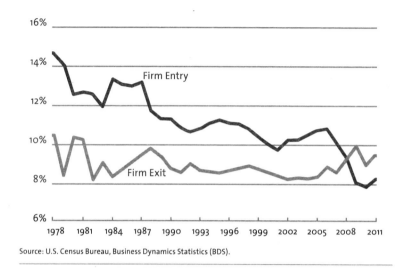

Source: U.S. Census Bureau, Business Dynamics Statistics (BDS).

they have perfected ways to use their profits to entrench their economic and political power. They herald the "free market" as they busily shape it to their advantage. They are the kingpins of the new economy, and average Americans are paying the price.

Consider that by 2014, the United States had some of the highest broadband prices among advanced nations, and the slowest speeds. The average peak Internet connection speed in America was nearly 40 percent slower than that of Hong Kong or South Korea. And many lower-income Americans had no high-speed access at all in their homes because they couldn't afford it. The costs are so high and the service so bad because the vast majority of Americans have to rely on their local cable monopoly in order to connect. Cable companies have tubes in the ground that are slower than fiber-optic cable. When it comes to fiber connections, the United States is behind Sweden, Estonia, South Korea, Hong Kong, Japan, and most other developed countries, putting us twenty-eighth worldwide in terms of speed of Internet access and twenty-third in terms of cost.

For example, 100 percent of the inhabitants of Stockholm, Sweden, have high-speed service in their homes that costs no more than twenty-eight dollars a month. Stockholm built fiber lines and leased them out to private operators. That resulted in intense competition among operators, low prices, and universal coverage. The project quickly recouped its costs and by 2014 was bringing millions of dollars of revenue to the city.

What's stopping American cities from doing the same? Cable operators with deep pockets and lots of political influence. They exemplify the new monopolists. They pay millions of dollars a year to cities in video franchise fees in order to retain their monopoly, and millions more to lobbyists and lawyers to ensure cities don't stray. They have successfully pushed twenty states to enact laws prohibiting cities from laying fiber cables. In 2011, John Malone, chairman of Liberty Global, the largest cable company in the world, admitted that when it comes to high-capacity data connections in the United States, "Cable's pretty much a monopoly now." Indeed, by 2014 more than 80 percent of Americans had no choice but to rely on one single cable company for high-capacity wired data connections to the Internet. Since none of the cable companies face real competition, they have no incentive to invest in fiber networks or even to pass along to consumers the lower prices their large scale makes possible.

One city that has bucked the trend is Chattanooga, Tennessee, which built its own fiber-optic network. In less than a minute, the lucky inhabitants of Chattanooga can download a two-hour movie that takes nearly a half hour to download with a typical high-speed broadband connection. But the cable operators are fighting back. By 2014, Comcast, one of the nation's largest cable operators, had twice sued the city-owned utility and was spending millions on a PR campaign aimed at discrediting the publicly run service.

Here again, the issue has nothing to do with choosing the "free market" or government. Whoever lays the cable has a monopoly, because no one else has an economic incentive to lay new cables. The real issue is how that monopoly is organized. As noted, Stockholm stimulated competition in the private sector. Comcast and other American cable companies face little or no competition and are consolidating their power even further. Cable broadband might eventually face competitors, such as upgraded DSL from telephone companies, next-generation wireless, and very-high-speed fiber like that being supplied to a few cities by Google. But none of these alternatives is likely to be available for some time, and most cities lack the money and expertise for Google fiber. Put simply, cable is the only game in town—and cable operators intend to keep it that way.

Comcast and other cable operators spend millions of dollars each year lobbying and contributing to political campaigns (in 2014, Comcast ranked thirteenth of all corporations and organizations reporting lobbying expenditures and twenty-eighth for campaign donations). They also provide jobs to officials who make these sorts of decisions. Michael Powell, who chaired the Federal Communications Commission (FCC) in 2002, subsequently became head of the cable industry's lobbying group. (The National Cable and Telecommunications Association ranked twelfth in lobbyist spending in 2014.)

Comcast is also one of Washington's biggest revolving doors. Of its 126 lobbyists in 2014, 104 had worked in government before joining Comcast. Former FCC member Meredith Attwell Baker, for example, went to work for Comcast four months after voting to approve Comcast's bid for NBCUniversal in 2011 (she subsequently went to work for the industry's lobbying group). Comcast's in-house lobbyists include several former chiefs of staff to Senate and House Democrats and Republicans as well as a former commissioner of the FCC.

I'm not suggesting anyone has acted illegally. To the contrary: CEOs believe they are supposed to maximize shareholder returns, and one means of accomplishing that goal is to play the political game as well as it possibly can be played and field the largest and best legal and lobbying teams available. Trade associations see their role as representing the best interests of their corporate members, which requires lobbying ferociously, raising as much money as possible for political campaigns of pliant lawmakers, and even offering jobs to former government officials. Public officials, for their part, perceive their responsibility as acting in the public interest. But the public interest is often understood as emerging from a consensus of the organized interests appearing before them. The larger and wealthier the organization, the better equipped its lawyers and its experts are to assert what's good for the public. Any official who once worked for such an organization, or who suspects he may work for one in the future, is prone to find such arguments especially persuasive.

Inside the mechanism of the "free market," the economic and political power of the new monopolies feed off and enlarge each other.

Monsanto, the giant biotech corporation, owns the key genetic traits in more than 90 percent of the soybeans planted by farmers in the United States and 80 percent of the corn. Its monopoly grew out of a carefully crafted strategy. It patented its own genetically modified seeds, along with an herbicide that would kill weeds but not soy and corn grown from its seeds. The herbicide and herbicide-resistant seeds initially saved farmers time and money. But the purchase came with a catch that would haunt them in the future: The soy and corn that grow from those seeds don't produce seeds of their own. So every planting season, farmers have to buy new seeds. In addition, if the farmers have any seeds left over, they must agree not to save and replant them in the future. In other words, once hooked, farmers have little choice but to become permanent purchasers of Monsanto seed. To ensure its dominance, Monsanto has prohibited seed dealers from stocking its competitors' seeds and has bought up most of the small remaining seed companies.

Not surprisingly, in less than fifteen years, most of America's commodity crop farmers have become dependent on Monsanto. The result has been higher prices far beyond the cost-of-living rise. Since 2001, Monsanto has more than doubled the price of corn and soybean seeds. The average cost of planting one acre of soybeans increased 325 percent between 1994 and 2011, and the price of corn seed rose 259 percent. Another result has been a radical decline in the genetic diversity of the seeds we depend on. This increases the risk that disease or climate change might wipe out entire crops for years, if not forever. A third consequence has been the ubiquity of genetically modified traits in our food chain.

At every stage, Monsanto's growing economic power has enhanced its political power to shift the rules to its advantage, thereby adding to its economic power. Beginning with the Plant Variety Protection Act of 1970, and extending through a series of court cases, Monsanto has gained increased protection of its intellectual property in genetically engineered seeds. It has successfully fought off numerous attempts in Congress and in several states to require labeling of genetically engineered foods or to protect biodiversity. It has used its political muscle in Washington to fight moves in other nations to ban genetically engineered seed.

To enforce and ensure dominance, the company has employed a phalanx of lawyers. They've sued other companies for patent infringement and sued farmers who want to save seed for replanting. Monsanto's lawyers have also prevented independent scientists from studying its seeds, arguing that such inquiries infringe the company's patents. You might think Monsanto's overwhelming market power would make it a target of antitrust enforcement. Think again. In 2012, it succeeded in putting an end to a two-year investigation by the antitrust division of the Justice Department into Monsanto's dominance of the seed industry.

Monsanto has the distinction of spending more on lobbying—nearly $7 million in 2013 alone—than any other big agribusiness. And Monsanto's former (and future) employees frequently inhabit top posts at the Food and Drug Administration and the

Agriculture Department, they staff congressional committees that deal with agriculture policy, and they become advisors to congressional leaders and at the White House. Two Monsanto lobbyists are former congressman Vic Fazio and former senator Blanche Lincoln. Even Supreme Court justice Clarence Thomas was at one time an attorney for Monsanto. Monsanto, like any new monopoly, has strategically used its economic power to gain political power and used its political power to entrench its market power.

It's useful to view the strategy of the new monopolists as integrating economic and political dominance. They acquire key patents and then spend vast sums protecting them and charging others with patent infringement. In addition, they use mandatory licensing agreements to require potential competitors to use whole lines of their products and prevent customers from using competing products, thereby creating de facto industry standards. Favorable court rulings, advantageous laws, and administrative decisions to forgo antitrust lawsuits or bring them against competitors extend these de facto standards to entire sectors of the economy.

Monsanto's genetically engineered seeds offer one example, but other examples abound in high tech, where a handful of companies—Google, Apple, Facebook, Twitter, Amazon, and Alibaba—are busily creating patented systems that are becoming worldwide standards and network platforms. The more people use the standard or platform, the more useful it becomes. When enough people adopt it, others have no choice but to adopt it as well.

For example, if you want Apple's increasingly popular iPhone or other hardware, you have to accept its software. Although other developers can run their apps on Apple devices, Apple's own software often runs more smoothly. Google's Chrome browser doesn't work as fast on Apple hardware as does Apple's own free browser, Safari. And Safari is the only browser that functions as a default on Apple hardware. That's because Apple doesn't give other software developers access to the accelerated Nitro Java-Script engine that runs its software. Apple says it wants to ensure consumers a seamless experience, so its software is perfectly integrated with its hardware. More likely, Apple wants full control so that its software becomes as much of a standard for consumers as its iPhone and other hardware.

Will the federal government sue Apple for violating antitrust law, as it did in the 1990s when it accused Microsoft of illegally bundling its popular Windows operating system with its Internet Explorer browser in order to create the de facto industry standard? (Microsoft settled the case by agreeing to share its application programming interfaces with other companies.) That seems unlikely. Technically, Apple does allow other companies' software to run on its hardware. But just in case, Apple has a formidable team of lawyers ready to spend whatever it takes to prevail in such a lawsuit. And it is no accident that Apple—along with Google, Facebook, Microsoft, and Amazon—maintains a platoon of lobbyists in Washington. (In 2013, Apple spent $3,370,000 on lobbying; Amazon, $3,456,000; Facebook, $6,430,000; Microsoft, $10,490,000; and Google, $15,800,000, according to the Center for Responsive Politics. By 2014 Google had become the largest corporate lobbyist in the United States.)

In 2012, the staff of the Federal Trade Commission's Bureau of Competition submitted to the commissioners a 160-page analysis of Google's dominance of the search market, and recommended suing Google for "conduct . . . that will result in real harm to customers and to innovation." It is unusual for the commissioners not to accept staff recommendations, but in this instance they decided against suing Google. They did not explain why, but a plausible explanation is Google's increasing political clout. By contrast, Europe's antitrust regulator filed charges against Google in 2015.

Whether it is Apple's mobile hardware and related software, Google's search engine and content, Twitter's tweets, Facebook's connections, Amazon's shopping platform, or Alibaba's shopping exchange, huge revenues come from owning a standard platform. To be sure, such platforms can sometimes make it easier for innovators to introduce their apps or books or videos or whatever other content they want to showcase. But the real power and profits lie with the owners of the platform rather than with the innovators who make use of it. And as that power and those profits increase, the innovators who depend on it have less and less bargaining leverage to negotiate good prices for their contributions. Since it costs almost nothing to sell more units, these new monopolists can keep out (or buy out) potential competitors and gain almost complete control—along with the profits and the legal and political leverage control brings.

A handful of giant corporations are reaping the rewards of such network effects. The larger their networks become, the more data they collect, and therefore the more effective and powerful they become. Consumers may be satisfied with the results, but they will never know what innovations have been squelched or stymied, how much more they are paying than they would otherwise, and how the rules of the game are being changed to the advantage of the owners of the standard platforms.

By 2014, for example, Google and Facebook were the first stops for most Americans seeking news, while Internet traffic to many of the nation's preeminent news organizations—national newspapers, network television, news-gathering agencies—had fallen well below 50 percent. The newer the media company, such as BuzzFeed, the more likely it was to rely on Google's or Facebook's platforms to attract viewers or readers. All this has given Google and Facebook unprecedented economic and political power over these critical networks. Meanwhile, rather astoundingly, Amazon has become the first stop for almost a third of all American consumers looking to buy *anything*. Despite an explosion in the number of websites over the last decade, page views have become far more concentrated. While in 2001, the top ten websites accounted for 31 percent of all page views in America, by 2010 the top ten accounted for 75 percent. Talk about power.

In 2014, Amazon, already accounting for half of all book sales in the United States, delayed or stopped delivering books published by Hachette, the nation's fourth-largest publisher, because it wanted better terms from Hachette (purportedly 50 percent of revenues from sales of e-books rather than 30 percent). Amazon said this was only fair: It accounted for 60 percent of Hachette's e-book sales in the United States, and Hachette was making more money on digital sales than on its sales of physical books, so why shouldn't Amazon have its due? Yet Amazon had so much power over the book publishing industry that it could take a loss on each book it sold in order to gain further market share for its Kindle e-reader, introduced in 2007. With a large enough share of the publishing market, it could then dictate its own terms—as it was seeking to do with Hachette. Amazon eventually agreed that Hachette could set its own prices for e-books, but Amazon showed the industry it was not reluctant to use its power if publishers failed to cooperate. Large retailers including Borders were already gone, Barnes & Noble was perilously weak, and thousands of smaller bookstores had closed. Amazon was also publishing books itself. How long would it be before Amazon put publishers out of business, too? How many years before it replaced books with downloads from a gigantic digital library in the cloud? How long, in other words, before Amazon had so much power that it was able to abuse it?

Undoubtedly, Amazon allows consumers to save money and enjoy the convenience of online shopping. And its platform allows more authors to market their books directly to readers. But by contributing to the demise of booksellers and possibly publishers as well, Amazon has enhanced its economic power relative to every other actor, including authors. If authors don't agree to the price Amazon dictates, they may have few if any other avenues for getting their works to potential readers. In this way, Amazon may end up limiting the marketplace of ideas, just as Google and Facebook have chokeholds on the news—analogous to the way Monsanto's seeds have reduced biodiversity in our food supply.

Moreover, as Amazon's economic power increases, so does its

political clout. Decisions have to be made about how the market is organized, and Amazon has excelled at using its power to shape the rules. In 2012 Amazon quietly pushed the Justice Department to sue five major publishers and Apple for illegally colluding to raise the price of e-books, yet in 2014 the department didn't question Amazon's tactics for squeezing better terms from publishers. (Perhaps it was pure coincidence, but in September 2014, as *The New York Times's Bits* blog pointed out, Amazon was treating two Hachette books quite differently, shipping Daniel Schulman's *Sons of Wichita,* a profile of the Koch brothers, over a two- to three-week interval but promising to get Republican House Budget Committee chair Paul Ryan's *The Way Forward* into readers' hands in just two days.) Other nations have laws protecting their bookstores and publishers. In France, for example, no seller can offer more than 5 percent off the cover price of new books, with the result that books cost about the same wherever you buy them in France, even online. The French government classifies books as an "essential good," along with electricity, bread, and water.

But America is hurtling toward a very different kind of market, shaped by Amazon. The firm's annual lobbying expenditures have grown from $1.3 million in 2008 to $2.5 million in 2012 and $4 million in 2014. In 2013, the firm beefed up its presence in Washington still further when its CEO, Jeff Bezos, purchased the venerable *Washington Post.*

Unlike the old monopolists, who controlled production, the new monopolists control networks. Antitrust laws often busted up the old monopolists. But the new monopolists have enough influence to keep antitrust at bay.

By 2014, Wall Street's five largest banks held about 45 percent of America's banking assets, up from about 25 percent in 2000. They held a virtual lock on taking companies public, played key roles in the pricing of commodities, were involved in all major U.S. mergers and acquisitions and many overseas, and were responsible for most of the trading in derivatives and other complex financial instruments. Wall Street's biggest banks offered the largest financial rewards and fattest bonuses, attracted the most talent, oversaw the biggest pools of money, and effectively controlled the fastest-growing sector of the entire U.S. economy. Between 1980 and 2014, the financial sector grew six times as fast as the economy overall.

Here again, economic prowess and political power feed on each other. As the big banks have gained dominance over the financial sector, they've become more politically potent. They are major sources of campaign funds for both Republican and Democratic candidates. In the 2008 presidential campaign, the financial sector ranked fourth among all industry groups giving to then-candidate Barack Obama and the Democratic National Committee, according to the nonpartisan Center for Responsive Politics. Obama reaped far more in contributions—roughly $16.6 million—from Wall Street than did his Republican opponent, John McCain, at $9.3 million. The employees of Goldman Sachs were Obama's leading source of campaign donations from a single corporate workforce. In the presidential campaign of 2012, Wall Street's contributions went mainly to Mitt Romney.

Wall Street also supplies personnel for key economic posts in Republican and Democratic administrations and provides lucrative employment to economic officials when they leave Washington. The Treasury secretaries under Bill Clinton and George W. Bush, Robert Rubin and Henry Paulson, Jr., respectively, had each chaired Goldman Sachs before coming to Washington, and Rubin returned to the Street thereafter. Before becoming Barack Obama's secretary of the Treasury during the Wall Street bailout, Timothy Geithner had been handpicked by Rubin to be president of the Federal Reserve Bank of New York; when Geithner left the Obama administration he returned to the Street. Former Republican House majority leader Eric Cantor was for many years one of the Street's strongest advocates in Congress. As a member of the House Financial Services Committee charged with overseeing Wall Street, he fought for the bailout of the Street, to retain the Street's tax advantages and subsidies, and to water down the Dodd-Frank financial reform legislation. In September 2014, just two weeks after resigning from the House, Cantor joined the Wall Street investment bank of Moelis & Company, as vice chairman and managing director, starting with a $400,000 base salary, $400,000 initial cash bonus, and $1 million in stock. Cantor would run the firm's Washington office, presumably opening doors and keeping the congressional largesse flowing. Cantor explained, "I have known Ken [the bank's CEO] for some time and . . . followed the growth and success of his firm." Exactly. They had been doing business together for years. The well-worn path from Washington to Wall Street had rarely been as clear, nor the entrenched culture of mutual behind-kissing as transparent.

In the decades leading up to the near financial meltdown of 2008, the biggest banks had already grown much larger and more profitable by persuading Congress and presidential administrations to dismantle many of the laws and rules that had been enacted in the wake of the Great Crash of 1929 to prevent big banks from making excessively risky bets. Then, after their risky behavior precipitated the crash of 2008 and they were bailed out by American taxpayers, they became even larger and more powerful—with so much clout they could water down new rules intended to prevent further crises.

Along the way, Wall Street's major players have cooperated and colluded to enlarge their profits. In 2014, for example, three leading private-equity firms—Kohlberg Kravis Roberts, the Blackstone Group, and TPG—agreed to pay the government a combined $325 million to settle accusations that they colluded to drive down the price of corporate takeover targets. Evidence showed that when Blackstone had its eye on a company, Hamilton E. James, its president, wrote to George Roberts of KKR, "We would much rather work with you guys than against you. Together we can be unstoppable but in opposition we can cost each other a lot of money." Roberts responded, "Agreed."

For an example of collusion on a grander scale, consider the so-called Libor scandal, which at this writing continues to be investigated. Libor (short for "London interbank offered rate") is the benchmark interest rate for trillions of dollars of loans worldwide—compiled by averaging the rates at which the major banks say they borrow. Evidence shows that bankers have manipulated Libor, enabling them to place bets in the global financial casino armed with inside information on what the market is really predicting. The scandal initially focused on one bank headquartered in Britain, Barclays, but Barclays couldn't have rigged Libor alone. In fact, Barclays's defense is that every major bank has fixed Libor in the same way, and for the same reason.

Wall Street's new monopolists rig financial markets for their own benefit. And again, the rest of us pick up the tab.

The health care sector accounts for nearly a fifth of the U.S. economy, and here we see a similar pattern. Even before the Affordable Care Act was on the drawing board, health insurers, hospitals, and hospital systems were already merging into larger and larger entities. Insurers had long nurtured strong political ties. In 1945, they wangled from Congress an exemption to the antitrust laws—allowing them to fix prices, allocate markets, and collude over the terms of coverage—on the assumption that they'd be regulated by state insurance commissioners. But by the 1980s they had outgrown state regulation; they were consolidating into a few large national firms, operating across many different states. That gave them even more clout in Washington.

The consolidation also gave them more bargaining power over hospitals for determining reimbursements. In response, hospitals began merging into giant hospital systems, capable of getting higher reimbursements from insurers. The result was a ratcheting up of health care costs, along with fewer choices. In 1992, the average-sized American city had four hospitals; by 2014, it was served by just two.

The consolidation on both sides gave hospitals and insurers together even greater clout. By the time Congress considered the Affordable Care Act, the two groups had enough leverage in Washington to ensure that the legislation would boost the profits of both the big insurers and the giant hospital systems. They made their support of the proposed legislation contingent on a requirement that everyone buy insurance and not get a "public option" to choose Medicare-like public insurance over private insurance. Their winnings have amounted to hundreds of billions of dollars. Directly or indirectly, the rest of us pay.

Why isn't antitrust law as effective at curbing the new monopolists as it was the older forms of monopoly? Partly because antitrust enforcement has lost sight of one of its original goals: preventing large aggregations of economic power from gaining too much political influence.

Markets need rules for determining the degree to which economic power can be concentrated without damaging the system. But there's no obvious "correct" answer. It depends on weighing efficiencies that come from large-scale enterprises against the power of such enterprises to raise prices; balancing innovations enabled by common platforms and standards against their capacity to squelch innovation by others; and determining an appropriate allocation of economic power among various groups.

It also depends on something even more basic: the effects of concentrated economic power on elected officials and on the prosecutors, attorneys general, and judges they appoint or confirm and on how these people, in turn, affect the above-mentioned decisions about the rules of the market.

We do not talk about this any longer but the political influence of concentrated economic power was a central concern in the late nineteenth century when Congress enacted the nation's first antitrust law. As I have noted, the field of economics was then called "political economy," and inordinate power could undermine both. This was the era of the robber barons—including Andrew Carnegie, John D. Rockefeller, and Cornelius Vanderbilt—whose steel mills, oil rigs and refineries, and railroads laid the foundations of America's industrial might. They also squeezed out rivals who threatened their dominant positions, and they ran roughshod over democracy. They ran their own slates for office and brazenly bribed public officials, even sending lackeys with sacks of money to be placed on the desks of pliant legislators. "What do I care about the law?" Vanderbilt infamously growled. "Hain't I got the power?" Forty-eight of the seventy-three men who held cabinet posts between 1868 and 1896 either lobbied for railroads, served railroad clients, sat on railroad boards, or had relatives who were connected to the railroads.

The public grew deeply concerned about the economic and political power of their combinations, then called "trusts." "The enterprises of the country are aggregating vast corporate combinations of unexampled capital, boldly marching, not for economic conquests only, but for political power," Edward G. Ryan, the chief justice of Wisconsin's Supreme Court, warned the graduating class of the state university in 1873. "The question will arise, and arise in your day, though perhaps not fully in mine, 'Which shall rule—wealth or man; which shall lead—money or intellect; who shall fill public stations—educated and patriotic free men, or the feudal serfs of corporate capital?'"

The twin dangers of unchecked economic and political power were clearly connected in the public's mind. Wall Street supplied the glue. Populist reformer Mary Lease, speaking in 1890 on behalf of the Farmers' Alliance, charged, "Wall Street owns the country. It is no longer a government of the people, by the people and for the people, but a government of Wall Street, by Wall Street and for Wall Street." Antitrust was envisioned as a means of breaking the diabolical links between the economic and political power of the new combinations. "Liberty produces wealth, and wealth destroys liberty," wrote Henry Demarest Lloyd in his acclaimed *Wealth Against Commonwealth* (1894). "The flames of the new economic evolution run around us, and we turn to find that competition has killed competition, that corporations are grown greater than the State . . . and that the naked issue of our time is with property becoming master, instead of servant."

Republican senator John Sherman of Ohio did not distinguish between economic and political power when, in 1890, he urged his congressional colleagues to act against the centralized industrial powers that threatened America. Each form of power was viewed as indistinguishable from the other. "If we will not endure a king as a political power," Sherman thundered, "we should not endure a king over the production, transportation, and sale of any of the necessaries of life."

With Americans demanding action, Sherman's Antitrust Act passed the Senate 52 to 1, moved quickly through the House without dissent, and was signed into law by President Benjamin Harrison on July 2, 1890. Perversely, however, in its early years the act was used as a weapon against organized labor; conservative prosecutors and jurists interpreted the Sherman Act to bar unions, as I will show. But by the Progressive Era, commencing in 1901, presidents were willing to use the Sherman Act as Congress had intended, to break the connection between economic and political power. President Teddy Roosevelt—castigating the "malefactors of great wealth," who were "equally careless of the working men, whom they oppress, and of the State, whose existence they imperil"—used the act against E. H. Harriman's giant Northern Securities Company, which had been cobbled together to dominate transportation in the Northwest. As Roosevelt later recounted, the lawsuit "served notice on everybody that it was going to be the Government, and not the Harrimans, who governed these United States." Antitrust lawsuits were also brought against DuPont and the American Tobacco Company. President William Howard Taft broke up Rockefeller's sprawling Standard Oil empire in 1911. President Woodrow Wilson explained the dangerous connection between excessive economic and political power in similar terms, in his 1913 book, *The New Freedom:* "I do not expect to see monopoly restrain itself. If there are men in this country big enough to own the government of the United States, they are going to own it."

In subsequent years, however, antitrust lost its central concern with political power. Republican presidents of the 1920s were not especially worried about economic combinations large enough to own the government of the United States, because they depended on the beneficence of America's largest corporations. After the Great Crash of 1929, even Franklin D. Roosevelt encouraged businesses to cooperate rather than compete (until 1938, when he put Thurman Arnold in charge of the antitrust division of the Justice Department and Arnold let loose with a buzz saw of antitrust suits). After World War II, antitrust focused almost exclusively on consumer welfare—that is, preventing large companies or combinations from gaining the market power to raise prices excessively. The giant AT&T Bell System monopoly was broken up in 1984, not because of its formidable political and legal clout but because it was thought to undermine competition and keep prices too high.

We are now in a new gilded age of wealth and power similar to the first Gilded Age, when the nation's antitrust laws were enacted. The political effects of concentrated economic power are no less important now than they were then, and the failure of modern antitrust to address them is surely related to the exercise of that power itself. In this new gilded age, we should remind ourselves of a central guiding purpose of America's original antitrust law and use it no less boldly.

6

The New Contracts

Contracts are a third building block of capitalism. They are agreements between buyers and sellers to do or provide something in exchange for something else. If property and market power lie at the heart of capitalism, contracts are its lifeblood—the means by which trades are made and enforced. But as with property and market power, contracts do not just happen. Although reputations for trustworthiness are important, promises are not kept automatically, and contracts are not self-enforcing. Any system of exchange requires rules about what can be bought and sold, what circumstances constitute fraud or coercion, and what happens when parties cannot fulfill what they have promised. In a democracy, these rules emerge from legislatures, agencies, and courts.

Here again, the debate over the "free market" versus government disguises how these rules are made and who has the most influence over making them. The age-old debate thereby prevents us from seeing and debating two central issues: whom the current rules actually serve, and what the rules ought to be in order to serve the rest of us. The underlying rule-making process is especially difficult to see today because so many of the things that are bought and sold are intangible, such as a television series streamed over the Internet or shares in a bond fund. New technologies have also created services that entail vexing moral questions, such as the renting out of a womb for surrogate pregnancy. And the technologies also connect buyers and sellers on different sides of the planet who will never meet one another. These changes have, in turn, created a host of new questions about what should be traded. The complexity and abundance of information also, paradoxically, makes it harder to define fraud or coercion or to determine who is at fault when a contract is breached and fairly allocate the losses. This has opened the way for political influence over all aspects of the new contracts.

Social norms play some role. For example, advances in medicine, online communication, and transportation have made it easier to buy and sell human organs, blood, surrogate pregnancies, and sex. That doesn't mean such sales are legal, however. Sales of organs are banned in the United States. (The ban dates back to 1984, when Virginia physician Dr. H. Barry Jacobs announced a plan to purchase kidneys, mainly from poor people eager to sell one of their own, and market them to whoever could afford to buy them. The American public was so horrified that Congress stopped Dr. Jacobs in his tracks. Several other nations have similar bans.) On the other hand, you can sell your blood in the United States, as well as in Mexico, Thailand, Ukraine, and India. But you can't in Canada and Britain. You can rent out your womb for money in most American states (in 2014, the going rate for gestational surrogacy was $20,000 to $30,000), but not in most of Europe (Britain allows surrogates to be paid expenses, but no more).

In 1999, Sweden decided that selling sex was no longer illegal and stopped treating prostitutes as criminals. But the country made it illegal to pay for sex. Swedish police found that the number of women trafficked into Sweden thereafter dropped sharply, as compared with the many thousands trafficked into neighboring Denmark, where paying for sex remained legal.

Where trades in body parts, blood, wombs, or sex are banned, it is often due to concerns that poor people will otherwise be exploited by the wealthier in ways that are degrading and dangerous. Rich people rarely sell their kidneys or blood, and affluent women usually don't rent out their wombs or become prostitutes. Studies find that most prostitutes come from poor families and are pushed into the trade in their early teens by adult men. Vulnerability also figures in. Even when it comes to legal drugs, America worries about sales to buyers who might not be able to make informed decisions about them. In 2012, the pharmaceutical giant GlaxoSmithKline settled with the Justice Department by paying a $3 billion fine and agreeing to stop promoting to children under eighteen an antidepressant approved only for adults; pushing two other antidepressants for unapproved purposes, including remedying sexual dysfunction; and, to further boost sales of prescription drugs, showering doctors with gifts, consulting contracts, speaking fees, even tickets to sporting events.

Buried within the rules about what can be traded and what cannot are also assumptions reflecting the status and power of different groups in society. Powder cocaine, for example, is the drug of choice for many in the elite, while crack cocaine is used by the poor. They are two forms of the same prohibited drug, but before 2010, those who sold or purchased crack cocaine faced sentences one hundred times longer than those caught using the powdered form. This was part of the reason African Americans served as much time in prison for nonviolent drug offenses as whites did for violent offenses. In 2010, Congress enacted the Fair Sentencing Act, reducing the sentencing disparity between crack and powder cocaine to eighteen to one.

Harm to society as a whole is another consideration. Although you cannot easily buy or sell guns in Canada or most of Europe, America's National Rifle Association has gone to great lengths to ensure Americans the "right" to buy even rapid-fire machine guns. (It has stopped short of surface-to-air missiles or atomic bombs, however.)

Similarly, you are not allowed to buy and sell votes in the United States, although anyone even vaguely familiar with how political campaigns are financed might harbor some doubts about the nation's commitment to this principle. Before the twentieth century, contracts to lobby government officials were not enforceable on the grounds that lobbying was contrary to public policy. In the 1874 case *Trist v. Child*, for example, Trist, a former diplomat, had hired Child to lobby Congress to authorize payment of money Trist claimed the government owed him and then refused to pay Child when Congress finally came through. Child sued. The Supreme Court declined to enforce the contract between Trist and Child, reasoning that such contracts could lead to corruption. "If any of the great corporations of the country were to hire adventurers who make market of themselves in this way, to procure the passage of a general law with a view to the promotion of their private interests," the court argued, "the moral sense of every right-minded man would instinctively denounce the employer and the employed as steeped in corruption, and the employment as infamous." That logic obviously failed to impress the Supreme Court eighty-six years later when it decided that corporations are people under the First Amendment, entitled to hire as many lobbyist adventurers as they can possibly afford.

It is true that if a society bans certain agreements between willing parties, they might still occur in black markets. Prohibition of alcohol was a notorious failure in the 1920s, just as bans on the purchase and sale of marijuana are today. Black markets are inherently risky and dangerous since illegal contracts can only be enforced through violence or the threat of violence (which is an argument for regulating sales of things that attract eager buyers but pose minimal harm to the public, rather than trying to prevent them altogether).

Meanwhile, technology is continuously creating opportunities for new products and services, raising additional questions about what can be sold. Indentured servitude is banned, but what about students seeking to sell shares of their future earnings in exchange for money up front to pay for their college tuitions? Price gouging is also prohibited, but what about Uber drivers who, during bad storms, charge up to eight times the normal fare? High-frequency stock trading now accounts for more than half the trading volume on public exchanges, but is it fair for such traders to profit from receiving data on stock trades a fraction of a second before everyone else receives it, by devising ultrafast communications systems unavailable to most investors?

Increasingly, political power is determining what can be traded and how. For example, a practice presumably banned in the Securities Exchange Act of 1934 is the buying and selling of stocks based on insider information available to people who receive data likely to affect share price before other investors get the same data. (The act didn't specifically ban the practice but has been interpreted by the courts as if it did.) That's because trading on confidential information gives the insiders an advantage and rigs the stock market to the benefit of anyone they tip off, a fraud perpetrated on other investors. Over the years, commissioners at the SEC, federal prosecutors, and judges have defined illegal insider traders to include any investor who knows the information he or she relies on was obtained from someone who violated a duty to keep the information confidential in return for a personal benefit. But in a world where information spreads almost instantaneously, and in which large amounts of money can be made getting such information a fraction of a second before everyone else, insider trading is difficult to police, let alone define. In 2014, after hedge fund Level Global Investors made $54 million by shorting Dell Computer stock based on insider information from a Dell employee, Global Investors' co-founder Anthony Chiasson claimed he didn't know where the tip came from or whether the leaker benefitted from the leak, and that few traders on Wall Street ever know *where* the inside tips they use come from because confidential information is, according to Chiasson's lawyer, the "coin of the realm in securities markets." Chiasson was convicted nonetheless. But in December 2014, the court of appeals overturned

Chiasson's conviction, ruling that Chiasson was so far removed from the leak that he could not possibly have known the source of the information or whether the tipper received a "substantial benefit" in return. The court thereby made official what had been the unofficial law on the Street: It's all about who you know. If, for example, the CEO of a company gives his golfing buddy a confidential tip about what the company is about to do, and the buddy tells a hedge-fund manager who then makes a fortune off that confidential information, the winnings are perfectly legal.

Because confidential information is the "coin of the realm" on Wall Street, it's likely that a significant portion of what is earned on the Street is based on information unavailable to average investors. Insiders fix the market for their own benefit. What's the chance that Congress will change the law to rein in insider trading? Almost zero as long as the Street continues to provide a significant share of the campaign contributions that members of Congress and the president rely on to get elected. In Europe, by contrast, trading on confidential information is illegal. If a trader knows or has reason to know that specific information is not yet public, he may not use it.

If the only goal were economic efficiency, it would make little sense to ban insider trading and no sense to define it as strictly as it is defined in Europe. The faster financial markets adjust to all available information, confidential or not, the more efficient markets become. So-called high-frequency trading, which lets certain traders know a fraction of a second before everyone else where money is going, makes the market even more efficient, although it gives these fast traders a large advantage over everyone else. If insider trading were defined broadly to prohibit all trades on information not equally available to all traders, such efficiencies would be lost. Yet systemic inequalities like these strike many people as unfair, as if the dice were loaded, and they undermine the confidence of small investors in the integrity of financial markets, which is why many people might be uncomfortable to learn that inside information is the "coin of the realm" on Wall Street.

Small traders aren't the only ones disadvantaged when insiders trade on confidential information. Employees who invest part of their paychecks into the stock market through corporate-sponsored pension funds are also harmed when, for example, the funds charge them higher than normal fees and then rebate the excess to the corporation in the form of discounts on other financial services. The information the corporation does not share with its employees amounts to a conflict of interest, tantamount to fraud. But this practice has been found to be perfectly legal. Here again, the underlying issue is not whether the free market is superior to government but how government officials decide how the market is to be organized and which outside groups have the most influence over such decisions. And once more, the pattern in recent decades has been for large corporations, Wall Street banks, and wealthy individuals to have ever-greater clout.

To take another example, the law has long held that a contract will not be enforced if a party has been coerced into making an agreement. This is also a moral principle: Parties to an agreement should not be forced into making promises against their will. No one should be obligated to keep, and the law will not enforce, a contract entered into at gunpoint.

But how is "coercion" defined? Buyers and sellers have no real alternatives when a large corporation has locked up a market through its intellectual property, control over standards or network platforms, and armies of lawyers and lobbyists. Under such circumstances, contracts are inherently coercive, or so it might seem. And contracts today are often filled with conditions (likely in small print) that deny employees, borrowers, and customers any meaningful choice. Nonetheless, large corporations possess the political and legal clout to make sure they're enforced.

One contractual provision that has become common in recent years is the requirement to take any grievances or claims of being denied basic rights to an arbitrator, often picked by the company, and accept the arbitrator's verdict without appealing it to a court. This provision obviously fixes the game in favor of large corporations that insert such clauses into their standard contracts. According to a recent study, employees complaining of job discrimination got relief only 21 percent of the time when their complaints went to arbitration but 50 to 60 percent of the time when they went to court.

Similarly, many popular Internet sites require users to agree to terms of service that prohibit them from suing (individually or within class actions) the owners of the site if something goes awry. On some sites, users click on an icon that confirms they accept such terms and conditions, which they almost never read and about which they have no choice anyway. Other sites provide only a link to the terms, with which visitors are presumed to agree merely by using the site. In consequence, many users subsequently discover they have given up legal rights they assume they had. For example, when consumers sued several hotels and online travel agencies for allegedly conspiring to fix hotel room prices, lawyers for Travelocity, one popular site, successfully defended the company in court by arguing that consumers who used its site could not participate because they had "agreed" not to sue.

Such clauses can even prevent small businesses from alleging that large businesses with whom they've contracted have monopolized an industry, thereby giving the small businesses little or no choice but to accept the contract. When the owner of a small restaurant, Italian Colors, located in Oakland, California, accused American Express of abusing its monopoly power by imposing unreasonable rates on the restaurant, American Express responded that such a claim was prohibited by the mandatory arbitration clause in the contract Italian Colors had signed with it. The case went to the Supreme Court, and in 2013 a majority of the court (including all of the court's Republican appointees) agreed with American Express. But as Justice Elena Kagan argued in dissent, the court's decision puts small businesses in an impossible bind and gives large monopolists an easy out. "The monopolist gets to use its monopoly power to insist on a contract effectively depriving its victims of all legal recourse."

Purchasers who check "I accept" might even relinquish their privacy rights. If you want Apple to store personal data on its iCloud, you must first agree to its terms of service, which stipulate:

> You are solely responsible for maintaining the confidentiality and security of your Account and for all activities that occur on or through your Account. . . . Provided we have exercised reasonable skill and due care, Apple shall not be responsible for any losses arising out of the unauthorized use of your Account resulting from you not following these rules.

In other words, if a hacker grabs compromising photos of you off iCloud and distributes them around the world, that's too bad. Apple isn't responsible. Technically, you had a choice because you didn't have to agree to Apple's terms of service. As a practical matter, you didn't have a choice because every other service has the same terms.

The new contracts do not result from negotiations between two parties with roughly equal bargaining power. They are faits accomplis, emanating from giant corporations that have the power to demand acceptance. Mortgage applicants are required to sign a small mountain of bank conditions to qualify for a loan, even though they may thereby forfeit their right to go to court alleging predatory lending practices. Lower-income borrowers must agree to double-digit fees and interest rates if they fail to pay on time, even though they rarely know they're accepting those terms. Students seeking college loans have no choice but to waive certain claims. Small-business franchisees must sign agreements setting forth their obligations in such detail that parent corporations can close them down for minor violations in order to resell the franchises at high prices to new owners.

State and federal lawmakers once sought to protect vulnerable consumers, employees, and borrowers by setting limits on certain contractual terms large corporations and finance companies can demand. But in recent years, those limits have been whittled back under political pressure from corporations and banks. For example, lawmakers in several states have increased interest rates lenders can charge on personal loans utilized by millions of low-income borrowers, resulting in installment loans now carrying rates of up to 36 percent. It's not unusual for borrowers who want a $100 to $500 advance on an upcoming paycheck to agree to repay within a few weeks—at an annualized interest rate of 300 percent or more. Citigroup's OneMain Financial unit, one of the leading lenders making these types of loans, has been hugely profitable as a result, which explains why Citigroup and similar lenders have been pouring money into state legislative races. "There was simply no need to change the law," Rick Glazier, a North Carolina legislator who opposed raising interest-rate limits there, told *The New York Times.* "It was one of the most brazen efforts by a special interest group to increase its own profits that I have ever seen."

Meanwhile, employees of large corporations often have to sign noncompete clauses prohibiting them from working for rival companies, thereby reducing the employees' future job prospects. (California and North Dakota bar such clauses except in limited circumstances.) Their job prospects are further reduced when their employers make antipoaching agreements with competitors. In 2014, for example, a federal judge found that Silicon Valley's tech companies engaged in "an overarching conspiracy" against their own employees by agreeing not to poach one another's engineers. Court papers showed that in 2005, when Google sought to hire a group of Apple engineers, Steve Jobs, Apple's CEO, threatened, "If you hire a single one of these people, that means war." Not only did Google back down, but Jobs even got Google to fire one of its recruiters for attempting to hire from Apple. Apologists for noncompete clauses and nonpoaching agreements say employees have the same bargaining power as employers. That is rarely the case.

When large corporations have disproportionate power—not only over what's sold, but also over the rules for deciding what contracts are permissible and enforceable by law—those who are relatively powerless have no choice. The "free market" is not, in this sense, free. It offers no practical alternative.

7

The New Bankruptcy

On the day Trump Plaza opened in Atlantic City in 1984, Donald Trump stood in a dark topcoat on the casino floor celebrating his new investment as the finest building in the city and possibly the nation. Thirty years later, the Trump Plaza folded, leaving some one thousand employees without jobs. Trump, meanwhile, was on Twitter claiming he had "nothing to do with Atlantic City" and praising himself for his "great timing" in getting out of the investment.

In America, people with lots of money can easily avoid the consequences of bad bets and big losses by cashing out at the first sign of trouble. The laws protect them through limited liability and bankruptcy. But workers who move to a place like Atlantic City for a job, invest in a home there, and build their skills have no such protection. Jobs vanish, home values plummet, and skills are suddenly irrelevant. They're stuck with the mess. Bankruptcy was designed so people could start over. But these days, the only ones starting over with ease are big corporations, wealthy moguls, and Wall Street, who have had enough political clout to shape bankruptcy law to their needs.

Bankruptcy is the fourth basic building block of the market. It reflects a trade-off between competing goals, as do the other market rules. Contracts depend on a mechanism for dealing with failures to pay what's due. If purchasers, debtors, and borrowers are too easily let off the hook, they may be just as careless about future obligations they enter into—and that carelessness may be infectious. (Such moral hazard can even affect big Wall Street banks.) Yet if those who can't pay their debts are locked away in prison or otherwise punished (as was typically the case in the mid-nineteenth century), they may have no way of earning back the money needed to repay what they owe.

This can be true of entire nations: Those with crippling debt obligations may sink further into the hole, plunging their entire societies into deeper economic and social crisis (many historians argue that German reparations after World War I facilitated the rise of Nazism). In the late nineteenth century, when America's giant railroad companies had gotten so deep in hock that they couldn't repay their debts, creditors threatened to tear up the railroads' tracks and sell them as scrap metal. Cunning businessmen figured that the creditors would do better if they agreed to reduce the amounts of their claims in order to keep the railroads running, thereby giving the railroad companies revenue to pay off most if not all of what they owed.

Bankruptcy is the system used in most capitalist economies for finding the right balance—allowing debtors to reduce their IOUs to a manageable level while spreading the losses equitably among all creditors, under the watchful eye of a bankruptcy judge. The central idea is shared sacrifice—between debtors and creditors as a whole, and among the creditors. Here again, the mechanism requires decisions about all sorts of issues, and these decisions are often hidden in court decisions, agency directives, and the subclauses of legislation. For example, who gets to use bankruptcy, and for what types of debts? What's an equitable allocation of losses among creditors? And what happens when bankruptcy isn't available? These questions and hundreds of others related to them have to be answered somehow. The "free market" itself doesn't offer solutions. Most often, powerful interests do.

The U.S. Constitution (article I, section 8, clause 4) authorizes Congress to enact "uniform Laws on the subject of Bankruptcies throughout the United States," and Congress has done so repeatedly—in 1800, 1841, 1867, 1874, 1898, 1938, 1978, 1994, and 2005. Wall Street banks and giant credit card companies have played major roles in formulating the most recent iterations, as have major corporations. (The credit card industry spent more than $100 million lobbying the 2005 bill; Wall Street bankers didn't need to spend quite as much because their formidable campaign contributions had already guaranteed them a major seat at the table.)

Over the last two decades, every major U.S. airline has been through bankruptcy at least once, usually in order to renege on previously agreed-upon labor union contracts. Under the bankruptcy code (again, largely crafted by credit card companies and bankers), labor contracts stipulating workers' pay have a relatively low priority when it comes to who gets paid off first. That means even the threat of bankruptcy can be a potent weapon for getting union members to sacrifice wages already agreed to. In 2003, American Airlines CEO Don Carty used such a threat to wring almost $2 billion of concessions from American's major unions. Carty preached the necessity of "shared sacrifice" but failed to disclose that he had secretly established a supplemental executive retirement plan whose assets, locked away in a trust, couldn't be touched in the event of bankruptcy. When Carty resigned he walked off with close to $12 million, courtesy of the secret plan.

Despite employee concessions, American slipped into bankruptcy in 2011. The corporation then promptly rejected what remained of its former labor agreements and froze its employee pension plan. On emerging from bankruptcy in 2013, American's creditors were fully repaid, with interest. Even the company's shareholders came out of bankruptcy richer than they went in. (American's stock rose even further after its merger with US Airways later that year.) To top it off, Tom Horton, the CEO who had ushered the firm through bankruptcy, received a severance award valued at more than $19.9 million. Everyone came out ahead—except for American's employees, who, even they retained their jobs, had lost much of their pay and benefits. So much for "shared sacrifice."

The granddaddy of all failures to repay occurred in 2008, when, as noted, Wall Street nearly melted down. The Street's biggest banks had bought hundreds of billions of dollars' worth of risky products, such as subprime mortgages, collateralized debt obligations, and mortgage-backed securities. Although the banks sold many of these off to unwary investors, they also kept many on their books at full value. When the debt bubble exploded, the banks and many investors found themselves with near worthless IOUs. Some commentators (including yours truly) urged that the banks be forced to grapple with their problems in bankruptcy. That was not to be the case. When Lehman Brothers went into bankruptcy in September 2008—by far the largest bankruptcy in history, with more than $691 billion of assets and far more in liabilities—the event so shook the Street that Henry Paulson, Jr., the outgoing secretary of the Treasury, persuaded Congress to authorize several hundred billion dollars of funding to protect the other big banks. The banks also received an estimated $83 billion of low-interest loans from the Federal Reserve. Paulson and his successor at the helm of the Treasury Department, Tim Geithner, didn't explicitly state that big banks were too big to fail. They were, rather, too big to be reorganized under bankruptcy.

The real burden of Wall Street's near meltdown fell on small investors and homeowners. As home prices plummeted, many homeowners found themselves owing more on their mortgages than their homes were worth and unable to refinance. Yet Chapter 13 of the bankruptcy code (whose drafting was largely the work of the financial industry) prevents homeowners from declaring bankruptcy on mortgage loans for their primary residence. When the financial crisis hit, some members of Congress, led by Illinois senator Dick Durbin, tried to amend the code to allow distressed homeowners to use bankruptcy. That would give them a powerful bargaining chip for preventing the banks and others servicing their loans from foreclosing on their homes. If the creditors didn't agree, their cases would go to a bankruptcy judge, who presumably would reduce the amount to be repaid rather than automatically force people out of their homes.

The bill passed the House, but when in late April 2009 Durbin offered his amendment in the Senate, the financial industry flexed its muscles to prevent its passage, arguing that it would greatly increase the cost of home loans. (No convincing evidence showed this to be the case.) The bill garnered only forty-five Senate votes, even though Democrats were in the majority. Partly as a result, distressed homeowners had no bargaining power. More than five million of them lost their homes, and by 2014 another two million were near foreclosure. So much, again, for shared sacrifice.

Another group of debtors who cannot use bankruptcy to renegotiate their loans are former students laden with student debt. In the disappointing jobs recovery following the Great Recession, many with college degrees found themselves unable to find work but burdened with high levels of student debt. By 2014, according to the Federal Reserve Bank of New York, student loans constituted 10 percent of all debt in the United States, second only to mortgages and higher than auto loans (8 percent) and credit card debt (6 percent). But the bankruptcy code does not allow student loan debts to be worked out under its protection. If debtors cannot meet their payments, therefore, lenders can garnish their paychecks. (If people are still behind on their student loan payments by the time they retire, lenders can even garnish their Social Security checks.) The only way graduates can reduce their student debt burden, according to a 1998 law enacted at the behest of the student loan industry, is to prove in a separate lawsuit that repayment would impose an "undue hardship" on them and their dependents. This is a stricter standard than bankruptcy courts apply to gamblers seeking to reduce their gambling debts.

Congress and its banking patrons are understandably worried that college graduates might declare bankruptcy without ever trying to repay their student loans. But a better alternative—more consistent with the ideal of shared sacrifice—would be to allow former students to use bankruptcy in cases where the terms of the loans are obviously unreasonable (such as double-digit interest rates) or when loans were made to attend schools whose students have low rates of employment after graduation.

Although not, strictly speaking, a part of the "free market," cities that enter bankruptcy can have significant effects on how the market is organized to allocate losses. In 2013, Detroit was the largest city ever to seek bankruptcy protection, looking to shed $7 billion of its debt and restore $1.7 billion of city services. Its bankruptcy was seen as a model for other American cities teetering on the edge. Among creditors from whom Detroit sought sacrifices were its own former employees, who depended on pensions and health care benefits the city had years before agreed to pay, and investors who had bought certificates the city issued in 2005. In the fall of 2014, at a trial to confirm or reject a plan for allocating the sacrifices and thereby allowing Detroit to emerge from bankruptcy, both groups claimed they were unfairly burdened. In the end, the investors holding 2005 certificates lost big, but many retirees had their pensions trimmed considerably, along with costly reductions in their health care benefits.

Yet one very large and prosperous group was left untouched. The mostly white citizens of neighboring Oakland County, far richer than those in mostly black Detroit, were not called upon to share the pain. Oakland County was one of the wealthiest counties in the United States, among counties with a million or more residents. In fact, Greater Detroit, which includes the Oakland County suburbs, ranked among the nation's top financial centers and its top four centers of high-technology employment, and it was the second-largest source of engineering and architectural talent. The median household in the region earned close to $50,000 a year. The median household in Birmingham, Michigan, just across Detroit's city limits, earned more than $99,000 in recent years; in nearby Bloomfield Hills, still within the Detroit metropolitan area, the median was nearly $148,000. Detroit's upscale suburbs had excellent schools, rapid-response security, and resplendent parks.

Forty years earlier, Detroit had a mixture of wealthy, middle class, and poor. But between 2000 and 2010, Detroit lost a quarter of its population as middle-class and white residents fled to the suburbs. By the time of the bankruptcy, Detroit had become almost entirely poor. Its median household income was about $26,000. More than half of its children were impoverished. That left it with depressed property values, abandoned neighborhoods, empty buildings, and dilapidated schools. Forty percent of its streetlights didn't work. Two-thirds of its parks had closed within the previous five years. In 2014, monthly water bills in Detroit were running 50 percent higher than the national average, and officials had begun shutting off the water to 150,000 households whose occupants couldn't pay them.

If the official boundaries had encompassed both Oakland County and Detroit, Oakland's more affluent citizens (as well as their banks and creditors) would have had some responsibility to address Detroit's problems, and Detroit would likely have had enough money to pay all its bills and provide its residents with adequate public services. But requiring that the poor inner city take care of its compounded problems by itself got the whiter and more affluent suburbs, and the banks that served them, off the hook. In fact, the mere whiff of suggestion that they might have some responsibility invited righteous indignation. "Now, all of a sudden, they're having problems and they want to give part of the responsibility to the suburbs?" scoffed L. Brooks Patterson, the Oakland County executive. "They're not gonna talk me into being the good guy. 'Pick up your share?' Ha ha."

Buried within the staid laws of bankruptcy are fundamental political and moral questions. Who are "we" and what are our obligations to one another? Is American Airlines just its shareholders and executives, or its employees as well? Is a financial crisis that brings down both big banks and homeowners a common problem or two distinct problems? When graduates cannot repay their student debts, do lenders have any responsibilities? Does society, which enjoys many of the benefits of a well-educated workforce? Are Detroit, its public employees, retirees, and poor residents the only ones who should make sacrifices when "Detroit" can't pay its bills, or does the relevant sphere of responsibility include Detroit's affluent suburbs, to which many of the city's wealthier residents fled as the city declined, as well as the banks?

Bankruptcy and contracts conveniently mask such questions. It is far easier to assume that one party to an agreement is simply unable to fulfill its obligation to another party, and the only pertinent question therefore is how to make amends. The "free market" requires nothing more—while the underlying mechanism remains unexamined.

8

The Enforcement Mechanism

The fifth building block of the market is enforcement. Property must be protected. Excessive market power must be constrained. Contractual agreements must be enforced (or banned). Losses from bankruptcy must be allocated. All are essential if there is to be a market. On this there is broad consensus. But decisions differ on the details—what "property" merits protection, what market power is excessive, what contracts should be prohibited or enforced, and what to do when a party to an agreement is unable to pay. The answers that emerge from legislatures, administrative agencies, and courts are not necessarily permanent; in fact, they are reconsidered repeatedly through legislative amendment, court cases overturning or ignoring precedent, and changes in administrative laws and rules.

Every juncture in this process offers opportunities for vested interests to exert influence. And they do, continuously. They also exert influence on how all of this is enforced. In many respects, the enforcement mechanism is the most hidden from view because decisions about what *not* to enforce are not publicized; priorities for how to use limited enforcement resources are hard to gauge; and the sufficiency of penalties imposed are difficult to assess. Moreover, wealthy individuals and corporations that can afford vast numbers of experienced litigators have a permanent, systemic advantage over average individuals and small businesses that cannot.

Begin with the issue of liability—who's responsible when something goes wrong. Entire industries with notable political clout have gained immunity from prosecution. In 1988, for example, the pharmaceutical industry persuaded Congress to establish the National Vaccine Injury Compensation Program, effectively shielding vaccine manufacturers and doctors from liability for vaccines that have harmful side effects. Gun manufacturers are also shielded from liability for any mayhem the use of their products creates. In 2004, after a court awarded the relatives of eight people shot by a sniper near Washington, D.C., $2.5 million from the maker and seller of the rifle used in the shootings, the National Rifle Association went into action. In 2005, Congress enacted the Protection of Lawful Commerce in Arms Act, which sharply limited the liability of gun manufacturers, distributors, and dealers for any harm caused by the guns they sold.

Not all industries have been as successful. Decades ago, the automobile industry dubbed cars safe and seat belts unnecessary, and the tobacco industry promoted the alleged health benefits of cigarettes. After tens of thousands of deaths and hundreds of millions of dollars in damage awards to victims, both industries began changing their tunes. Today, cars are safer, and fewer Americans smoke.

Individual companies with deep pockets can still avoid responsibility by persuading friendly congressional patrons and regulators to go easy on them. Long before Japan's Fukushima Daiichi plant contaminated a large swath of the Pacific Ocean with radioactive material in 2011, for example, General Electric marketed the Mark 1 boiling water reactor used in the plant (as well as in sixteen American nuclear plants), a cheaper alternative to competing reactors because it used a smaller and less expensive containment structure. Yet the dangers associated with the Mark 1 reactor were well known. In the mid-1980s, Harold Denton, an official with the Nuclear Regulatory Commission, warned that Mark 1 reactors had a 90 percent probability of bursting if their fuel rods overheated and melted in an accident. A follow-up report from a study group convened by the commission found that "Mark 1 failure within the first few hours following core melt would appear rather likely."

Why hasn't the commission required General Electric to improve the safety of its Mark 1 reactors? One factor may be General Electric's formidable political and legal clout. In the presidential election year of 2012, for example, its executives and PACs contributed almost $4 million to political campaigns (putting it sixty-third out of 20,766 companies), and it spent almost $19 million lobbying (the fifth-highest lobbying tab of 4,372 companies). Moreover, 104 of its 144 lobbyists had previously held government posts.

Similarly, the national commission appointed to investigate the giant oil spill in the Gulf of Mexico in 2010 found that BP failed to adequately supervise Halliburton Company's installation of the deep-water oil well—even though BP knew Halliburton lacked experience in testing cement to prevent blowouts and hadn't performed adequately before on a similar job. In short, neither company had bothered to spend enough to ensure adequate testing of the cement. Meanwhile, the Minerals Management Service of the Department of the Interior (now renamed the Bureau of Ocean Energy Management, Regulation, and Enforcement) had not adequately overseen the oil and oil-service companies under its watch because it had developed cozy relationships with them. The revolving door between the regulator and the companies it was responsible for overseeing was well oiled. Similarly, the National Highway Traffic Safety Administration has shown itself more eager to satisfy the needs of the automobile industry than to protect drivers and passengers. For decades the industry's powerful allies in Congress, led by Michigan congressman John Dingell, ensured that would be the case.

Or consider the New York branch of the Federal Reserve Board, which has lead responsibility to monitor Wall Street banks. Even after the Street's near meltdown, the banks' legal prowess and political clout reduced the ardor of examiners from the New York Federal Reserve Bank. Senior Fed officials instructed lower-level regulators to go easy on the big banks and not pry too deeply. In one meeting that came to light in 2014, a banker at Goldman Sachs allegedly told Fed regulators that "once clients are wealthy enough certain consumer laws don't apply to them." Afterward, when one of the regulators who attended the meeting shared with a more senior colleague her concern about the comment, the senior colleague told her, "You didn't hear that."

Another technique used by moneyed interests to squelch a law they dislike is to ensure Congress does not appropriate enough funds to enforce it. For example, the West, Texas, chemical and fertilizer plant that exploded in April 2013, killing fourteen and injuring more than two hundred, had not been fully inspected for almost three decades. The Occupational Safety and Health Administration (OSHA) and its state partners had only 2,200 inspectors charged with protecting the safety of 130 million workers in more than eight million workplaces. That came to about one inspector for every 59,000 workers. Over the years, congressional appropriations to OSHA had dropped. The agency had been systematically hollowed out. So, too, with the National Highway Traffic Safety Administration, charged with automobile safety. Its $134 million budget for 2013, supposedly enough to address the nation's yearly toll of some 34,000 traffic fatalities, was less than what was spent protecting the U.S. embassy in Iraq for three months of that year.

The Internal Revenue Service (IRS) has also been hollowed out. Despite an increasing number of wealthy individuals and big corporations using every tax dodge imaginable—laundering money through phantom corporations and tax havens and shifting profits abroad to where they'd be taxed least—the IRS budget by 2014 was 7 percent lower than it had been as recently as 2010.

During the same period, the IRS lost more than ten thousand staff—an 11 percent reduction in personnel. This budget stinginess didn't save the government money. To the contrary, less IRS enforcement means less revenue. For every dollar that goes into IRS enforcement, an estimated $200 is recovered of taxes that have gone unpaid. Less enforcement does, however, reduce the likelihood that wealthy individuals and big corporations would be audited.

In a similar vein, after passage of the Dodd-Frank financial reform law, Wall Street made sure that government agencies charged with implementing it did not have the funds to do the job. As a result, fully six years after the near meltdown of Wall Street, some of Dodd-Frank—including much of the so-called Volcker Rule restrictions on the kind of derivatives trading that got the Street into trouble in the first place—was still on the drawing board.

When an industry doesn't want a law enacted but fears a public backlash if it openly opposes the proposed law, it quietly makes sure that there aren't enough funds to enforce it. This was the case when the food industry went along with the Food Safety Modernization Act, which became law in 2011, after thousands of people were sickened by tainted food. Subsequently, the industry successfully lobbied Congress to appropriate so little to enforce it that it has been barely implemented.

Defanging laws by hollowing out the agencies charged with implementing them works because the public doesn't know it's happening. The enactment of a law attracts attention. There might even be a signing ceremony at the White House. News outlets duly record the event. But the defunding of the agencies supposed to put the law into effect draws no attention, even though it's the practical equivalent of repealing it.

An even quieter means of rescinding laws is to riddle them with so many loopholes and exceptions that they become almost impossible to enforce. Typically, such holes are drilled when agencies attempt, through rule making, to define what the laws mean or prohibit. Consider, for example, the portion of the Dodd-Frank law designed to limit bets on the future values of commodities. For years Wall Street has profitably speculated in futures markets— food, oil, copper, other commodities. The speculation has caused prices to fluctuate wildly. The Street makes bundles from these gyrations by betting, usually correctly, which way prices will go, but they have raised costs for consumers—another hidden redistribution from the middle class and poor to the wealthy. Dodd-Frank instructed the Commodity Futures Trading Commission (CFTC) to come up with a detailed rule reducing such betting. The commission thereafter considered fifteen thousand comments, largely generated by and from the Street. The agency also undertook numerous economic and policy analyses, carefully weighing the benefits to the public of any such regulation against its costs to the Street.

After several years, the commission issued its proposed rule, including some of the loopholes and exceptions the Street sought. But Wall Street still wasn't satisfied. So the commission agreed to delay enforcement of the new rule for at least a year, allowing the Street more time to voice its objections. Even this wasn't enough for the big banks. Its lawyers then filed a lawsuit in the federal courts, seeking to overturn the rule—arguing that the commission's cost-benefit analysis wasn't adequate. It was a clever ploy, since costs and benefits are difficult to measure. And putting the question into the laps of federal judges gave the Street a significant tactical advantage because the banks had almost infinite funds to hire so-called experts (many of them academics who'd say just about anything for the right price) using elaborate methodologies to show the CFTC had exaggerated the benefits and underestimated the costs.

It was not the first time the big banks had used this ploy. In 2010, when the Securities and Exchange Commission tried to implement a Dodd-Frank requirement making it easier for shareholders to nominate company directors, Wall Street sued the SEC. It alleged that the commission's cost-benefit analysis for the new rule was inadequate. A federal appeals court—inundated by the banks' lawyers and hired "experts"—agreed. That put an end to Congress's effort to give shareholders more power in nominating company directors, at least temporarily.

Obviously, government should weigh the costs and benefits of every significant action it takes. But big corporations and large banks have an inherent advantage in the weighing: They can afford to pay for experts and consultants whose studies will invariably measure costs and benefits in the way big corporations and large banks want them to be measured. Few, if any, other parties to regulatory proceedings have pockets remotely as deep to pay for studies nearly as comprehensive to back up their own points of view.

In addition, when it comes to regulating Wall Street, one overriding cost does not make it into any individual weighing: the public's mounting distrust of the entire economic system, a distrust generated in part by the Street's repeated abuses. Wall Street's shenanigans have convinced a large portion of America that the economic game is rigged.

Capitalism, alas, depends on trust. Without trust, people avoid even sensible economic risks. They also begin thinking that if the big guys can get away with cheating in big ways, small guys like them should be able to get away with cheating in small ways— causing even more people to distrust the economic system. Moreover, people who believe the game is rigged are easy prey for political demagogues with fast tongues and dumb ideas.

Tally up these costs and it's a whopper. Wall Street has blanketed America in a miasma of cynicism. Most Americans still believe, with some justification, that the Street got its taxpayer-funded bailout without strings in the first place because of its political clout, which was why the banks were not required to renegotiate the mortgages of Americans who, because of the collapse brought on by the Street's excesses, remained underwater for years. It's why taxpayers did not get equity stakes in the banks they bailed out nearly as large, in proportion, as Warren Buffett got when he helped bail out Goldman Sachs. When the banks became profitable again, taxpayers did not reap many of the upside gains. We basically just padded their downside risks.

The Street's political clout is not unrelated to the fact that top bank executives who took great risks or overlooked excessive risk taking retained their jobs, evaded prosecution, avoided jail, and continued to rake in vast fortunes. And why the Dodd-Frank Act, intended to avoid another financial crisis, was watered down and the rules to implement it were filled with loopholes big enough for Wall Street executives to drive their Ferraris through. The costs of such cynicism have leached deep into America, contributing to the suspicion and anger that have subsequently consumed American politics.

Just as such litigation over agency rules waters them down, so too do fines that are so small, and settlements so mild, as to have the practical effect of repealing inconvenient laws. Consider JPMorgan Chase, the largest bank on the Street with the deepest pockets to dabble in politics and protect its interests with a squadron of high-priced legal talent. In 2012, the bank lost $6.2 billion by betting on credit default swaps tied to corporate debt and then lied publicly about the losses. It later came out that the bank paid illegal bribes to get the business in the first place. That same year, the bank was accused of committing fraud in collecting credit card debt; using false and misleading means of foreclosing on mortgages; hiring the children of Chinese officials to help win business, in violation of the Foreign Corrupt Practices Act; and much else. All this caused the Justice Department and the Securities and Exchange Commission to launch multiple investigations.

JPMorgan's financial report for the fourth quarter of 2012 listed its legal imbroglios in nine pages of small print and estimated that resolving all of them might cost as much as $6.8 billion. Yet $6.8 billion was a pittance for a company with total assets of $2.4 trillion and shareholder equity of $209 billion. Which is precisely the point: The expected fines did not deter JPMorgan Chase from ignoring the laws to begin with. No big bank or corporation will avoid the opportunity to make a tidy profit unless the probability of getting caught and prosecuted, multiplied by the amount of any potential penalty, exceeds the potential gains. A fine that's small compared to potential winnings becomes just another cost of doing business.

Not even JPMorgan's $13 billion settlement with the Justice Department in 2013, for fraudulent sales of troubled mortgages occurring before the financial meltdown, had any observable effect on its stock price. Nor, for that matter, did Citigroup's $7 billion settlement in 2014, over the same sorts of fraud. Nor even Bank of America's record-shattering $16.65 billion settlement in 2014. In fact, in the days leading up to the Bank of America settlement, when news of it was already well known on the Street, the price of Bank of America's stock rose considerably. That was because many of these payments were tax deductible. (The test for deductibility is whether payments go to parties who have been harmed. At least $7 billion of Bank of America's $16.65 billion settlement, for example, was for relief to homeowners and blighted neighborhoods, which clearly would be deducted by the bank from taxable income.) Moreover, the size of the settlement paled in comparison to the bank's earnings. Bank of America's pretax income was $17 billion in 2013 alone, up from $4 billion in 2012.

In 2014, Attorney General Eric Holder announced the guilty plea of giant bank Credit Suisse to criminal charges of helping rich Americans to avoid paying taxes. "This case shows that no financial institution, no matter its size or global reach, is above the law," Holder crowed. But financial markets shrugged off the $2.8 billion fine. In fact, the bank's shares rose the day the plea was announced. It was the only large financial institution to show gains that day. Its CEO even sounded upbeat in a news briefing immediately following the announcement: "Our discussions with clients have been very reassuring and we haven't seen very many issues at all," he said. That may have been, in part, because the

Justice Department hadn't even required the bank to turn over its list of tax-avoiding clients.

When maximum penalties are included in a law, they are often quite low. This is another political tactic used by industries that do not want to look as if they're opposing a law but want it defanged. In 2014, for example, General Motors was publicly berated for its failure to deal with defective ignition switches, which had led to at least thirteen fatalities. For decades, GM had received complaints about the ignition switch but had chosen to do nothing. Finally, the government took action. "What GM did was break the law. . . . They failed to meet their public safety obligations," scolded Secretary of Transportation Anthony Foxx, after imposing on the automaker the largest possible penalty the National Traffic and Motor Vehicle Safety Act allows: $35 million. Thirty-five million dollars was, of course, peanuts to a hundred-billion-dollar corporation. The law does not even include criminal penalties for willful violations of safety standards that result in death.

In 2013, Halliburton pleaded guilty to a criminal charge in which it admitted destroying evidence in the *Deepwater Horizon* oil spill disaster. The criminal plea made headlines. But the fine it paid was a mere $200,000, the maximum allowed under the law for such a misdemeanor. (The firm also agreed to make a $55 million tax-deductible "voluntary contribution" to the National Fish and Wildlife Foundation.) Halliburton's revenues in 2013 totaled $29.4 billion, so the $200,000 fine amounted to little more than a rounding error. And no Halliburton official went to jail.

Government officials like to appear before TV cameras sounding indignant and announcing what appear to be tough penalties against corporate lawbreakers. But the indignation is for the public, and the penalties are often tiny relative to corporate earnings. The penalties emerge from settlements, not trials. In those settlements, corporations do not concede they've done anything wrong, and they agree, at most, to vague or paltry statements of fact. That way, they avoid possible lawsuits from shareholders or other private litigants who have been harmed and would otherwise use a conviction against them.

The government, for its part, likes to settle cases because doing so avoids long, drawn-out trials that government agencies charged with enforcing the law can't possibly afford on their skimpy budgets. In addition, because the lawyers in such agencies are paid a fraction of what partners in law firms hired by Wall Street banks and big corporations are paid, they are generally much younger and without the same experience and don't have nearly the same number of paralegals and other staff to collect documents and depositions in preparation for a trial; a settlement avoids the risk of an embarrassing defeat in court. Such settlements therefore seem to be win-wins—both for the corporations and the government. But they undermine the enforcement mechanism.

Corporate executives who ordered or turned a blind eye to the wrongdoing, meanwhile, get off scot-free. After several settlements and guilty pleas in which Pfizer, the pharmaceutical giant, promised to behave better, it again pleaded guilty in 2009 to bribing doctors to prescribe an off-label painkiller, and paid a criminal fine of $1.2 billion. But no senior Pfizer executive was ever charged with or convicted of a crime. Similarly, six years after Wall Street's near meltdown, not a single executive on the Street had been convicted or even indicted for crimes that wiped out the savings of countless Americans. It was well established, for example, that Lehman Brothers' Repo 105 program—which temporarily moved billions of dollars of liability off the bank's books at the end of each quarter and replaced them a few days later at the start of the next quarter—was intentionally designed to hide the firm's financial weaknesses. This was a carefully crafted fraud, detailed by a court-appointed Lehman examiner. But no former Lehman executive ever faced criminal prosecution for it. Contrast this with the fact that a teenager who sells an ounce of marijuana can be put away for years.

.　　.　　.

Mention should also be made of the large number of state judges and attorneys general who are elected to their positions, providing another channel for big money to influence how market rules are interpreted and enforced.

Thirty-two states hold elections for judges of state supreme courts, appellate courts, and trial courts. Nationwide, 87 percent of all state court judges face elections. This is in sharp contrast to other nations, where judges are typically appointed with the advice and consent of legislative bodies. As former Supreme Court justice Sandra Day O'Connor said, "No other nation in the world does that, because they realize you're not going to get fair and impartial judges that way."

Until the 1980s, judicial elections were relatively low-profile affairs. But beginning in the early 1990s, campaigns became far more costly and contentious. After the Supreme Court's *Citizens United* decision in 2010 opened the floodgates to corporate campaign donations, spending on judicial elections by outside groups skyrocketed. In the 2012 election cycle, independent spending was $24.1 million, compared with about $2.7 million spent in the 2001–02 election cycle, a ninefold increase. A 2013 study by Professor Joanna Shepherd of Emory University School of Law showed that the more donations justices receive from businesses, the more likely they are to rule in favor of business litigants. A Center for American Progress report also found corporate spending on judicial elections paying off for corporations. "In the span of a few short years, big business succeeded in transforming courts such as the Texas and Ohio supreme courts into forums where individuals face steep hurdles to holding corporations accountable," wrote the author, showing, for example, that the insurance industry in Ohio donated money to judges who then voted to overturn recent decisions the industry disliked, and energy companies in Texas funded the campaigns of judges who then interpreted laws to favor them.

State attorneys general, in charge of enforcing the rules by bringing lawsuits, are also subject to election and re-election, and they, too, are receiving increasing amounts of corporate money for their campaigns. An investigation by *The New York Times* in late 2014 found that major law firms were funneling corporate campaign contributions to attorneys general in order to gain their cooperation in dropping investigations of their corporate clients, negotiating settlements favorable to their clients, and pressuring federal regulators not to sue. The attorney general of Utah, for example, dismissed a case pending against Bank of America, over the objections of his staff, after secretly meeting with a Bank of America lobbyist who also happened to be a former attorney general. Pfizer, the pharmaceutical giant, donated hundreds of thousands of dollars to state attorneys general between 2009 and 2014, to encourage favorable settlements of a case brought against the company by at least twenty states for allegedly marketing its drugs for unapproved uses. AT&T was a major contributor to state attorneys general who opted to go easy on the corporation after a multistate investigation into the firm's billing practices.

Enforcement of market rules doesn't depend solely on government prosecutors. Individuals, companies, and groups who feel they have been wronged may also sue—for patent infringement, monopolization, breach of contract, fraud, and other alleged violations of the rules. But such litigation is expensive. Many small businesses and most typical Americans cannot afford it—unless the litigation is over an injury serious enough to attract a trial lawyer who anticipates a large damage award in which he will share.

This gives the biggest corporations and wealthiest individuals, able to hire lawyers to sue on their behalf or to defend against lawsuits, an inherent advantage. Monsanto, Comcast, Google, Apple, GE, Citigroup, Goldman Sachs, and other corporations with deep pockets use litigation strategically, often as a barrier to entry against upstarts without anything near the same legal resources. Suits, or the mere threat of such lawsuits, can deter the most ardent small-business owner or entrepreneur. Wealthy individuals also deploy squadrons of lawyers, often defending themselves from all potential claims and threatening to sue at the slightest provocation. Predatory litigation is another way economic dominance leads to legal and political power, which further entrenches and enlarges economic dominance.

Until recently, small businesses and average individuals had been able to join together in class actions, but these suits have become harder to mount. As we have seen, mandatory arbitration clauses in many contracts effectively bar them. In addition, the Republican majority members of the Supreme Court, whose sensitivity to corporate interests that backed their appointments has never been in doubt, have been busily closing the door to class actions. In 2011, in *AT&T Mobility v. Concepcion,* they ruled that companies could legally bar class actions within consumer contracts. The following year, according to a survey by Carlton Fields Jorden Burt, the number of large companies that included class-action bans in their contracts more than doubled. Subsequently, in their 2013 decision *Comcast v. Behrend,* the five Republican members of the court threw out $875 million in damages Philadelphia-area subscribers had won from Comcast for allegedly eliminating competition and overcharging them. Justice Antonin Scalia, writing for the court, said the Comcast subscribers had failed to show that Comcast's wrongdoing was common to the entire group and that damages were therefore an appropriate remedy for all of them rather than for individuals.

The effect of these rulings has been to reduce the ability of groups of consumers—or, for that matter, employees or small businesses—to band together to enforce the law. The power of giant corporations like AT&T and Comcast to suppress the voices of individual consumers and employees cannot be overestimated.

9

Summary: The Market Mechanism
as a Whole

A summary is in order. Markets are made by human beings—
just as nations, governments, laws, corporations, and baseball are
the products of human beings. And as with these other systems,
there are many alternative ways markets can be organized. However organized, the rules of a market create incentives for people.
Ideally, they motivate people to work and collaborate, to be productive and inventive; they help people to achieve the lives they
seek. The rules will also reflect their moral values and judgments
about what is good and worthy and what is fair. The rules are not
static; they change over time, we hope in ways that most participants consider to be better and fairer. But this is not always the
case. They can also change because certain people have gained
the power to change them for their own benefit. Such has been
the case in America and many other nations in recent decades.

Private property, constraints on monopoly, contract, bankruptcy or other means for coping with default, and enforcement
of such rules are essential building blocks of any market. Capitalism and free enterprise require them. But each of them can
be tilted to the benefit of a few rather than the many. As noted,
every one of these five building blocks depends on a large range of
decisions by lawmakers, agency heads, and judges. They amend

or modify such decisions as circumstances change, technologies evolve, new issues and problems rear up, and old solutions become outmoded. This critical mechanism has nothing whatever to do with the size or "intrusiveness" of government. It has no bearing on how much the government taxes or the amount it spends. The market simply cannot function without these decisions. Legislatures, agencies, and courts must make them regardless of whether government is relatively large or small.

What guides such decisions? Abstract notions of the public good are unhelpful because there's often no consensus about what's good for the public. "Improved efficiency" provides little practical guidance because of the difficulty of measuring the benefits and costs of many proposed measures. Moreover, even if a decision makes some people better off without imposing a hardship on anyone else, such a measure may worsen inequality if its beneficiaries are already among the best off. Ideally, such decisions reflect the best judgments of people authorized by a democratic system to make them, in response to the values and wishes of a majority of its citizens.

In recent decades, however, the real decisions are more often hashed out behind closed doors, in negotiations influenced disproportionately by giant corporations, big banks, and wealthy individuals with enough resources to be heard. Their money buys lobbyists, campaign contributions, public relations campaigns, squadrons of experts and studies, armies of lawyers, and quiet promises of future jobs.

As I've shown, the effect on legislators is often direct and immediate, as is the effect on elected judges and elected attorneys general. The effect on appointed officials who implement and enforce the law is less direct but no less potent. (While historically some Supreme Court justices have veered far away from the views of the presidents who appointed them, justices appointed in more recent years are more predictably partisan.)

The mechanism thereby creates and perpetuates a vicious cycle: Economic dominance feeds political power, and political power further enlarges economic dominance. To an ever-growing extent, large corporations and the wealthy influence the political institutions whose decisions organize the market, and they benefit most from those decisions. This enhances their wealth and thereby their capacity to exert more influence over such decisions in the future.

What I have described is not the same as corruption. Few if any public officials in the United States solicit or receive direct bribes. The seduction is more subtle. It is simply easier for officials to choose a path that's been carefully laid out for them by lobbyists, paid experts, and smart and experienced lawyers than to strike out on their own through territory often regarded by the establishment as menacing. The lures of campaign contributions and well-paying jobs after government service only make the preferred path more enticing.

Widening inequality of wealth and income, then, is not due solely to globalization and technological changes that reward the very well educated and well connected while punishing those without these advantages. Nor is it due mainly to successful lobbying by corporate and wealthy elites for lower taxes, wider loopholes, and more generous government subsidies. As I have noted, government taxes and subsidies constitute a small part of the overall picture. Rather, widening inequality has become baked into the building blocks of the "free market" itself. Even without globalization and technological change, and even absent the tax breaks and subsidies, the share of total national income going to corporations and to the executives and investors whose incomes largely depend on corporate profits would still be rising relative to the share going to labor. The vicious cycle would achieve this on its own.

In 2014, corporate profits before taxes reached their highest share of the total economy in at least eighty-five years, tying the previous record set in 1942 when World War II pushed up profits (only to have most then taxed away). Between 2000 and 2014, quarterly corporate after-tax profits rose from $529 billion to

$1.6 trillion. This rise didn't reflect increasing returns to capital; it reflected increasing economic power. As I will show, this pushed the stock market to unprecedented heights, thereby enriching investors—most of whom are already in the upper ranks of the nation's wealthy. Meanwhile, labor's share of the economy has dropped. In 2000, labor's share of nonfarm business income was 63 percent. In 2013, it was 57 percent, representing a shift from labor to capital of about $750 billion annually. Importantly, much of the increase in income inequality has occurred *within* labor's share, as the paychecks of high earners have diverged from those of low earners (see figures 2 and 3).

The process I have described helps explain a puzzle in economist Thomas Piketty's powerful thesis in his book *Capital in the Twenty-First Century*, about the tendency of capitalism to move toward widening inequality. Piketty posits that capital's share of an economy will continue to grow as long as the return to capital is greater than the rate of economic growth over the long term. But he fails to explain why the returns to capital don't decline over time. Normally, the more wealth that has been accumulated, the more difficult it is to earn good returns on it. Nor does his thesis account for the fact that, at least in the United States, most of the super-rich in recent decades have derived their wealth from work rather than inheritance. The likely explanation is that those who control an increasing share of the wealth also have gained growing influence over the rules by which the market itself functions.

This vicious cycle is neither inevitable nor irreversible. Equally possible is a virtuous cycle in which widely shared prosperity generates more inclusive political institutions, which in turn organize the market in ways that further broaden the gains from growth and expand opportunity. The United States and several other societies experienced something very much like this in the first three decades after World War II. In Part III of this book I will explore how we might achieve this once again.

The idea of a "free market" separate and distinct from government has functioned as a useful cover for those who do not want

FIGURE 2. CORPORATE PROFITS AFTER TAX, AS A PERCENTAGE OF GDP

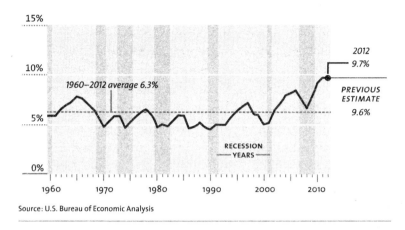

Source: U.S. Bureau of Economic Analysis

FIGURE 3. PERSONAL WAGE AND SALARY INCOME, AS A PERCENTAGE OF GDP

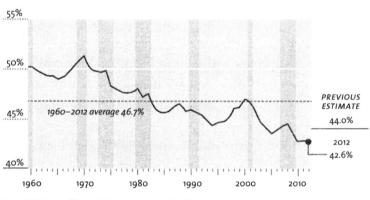

Source: U.S. Bureau of Economic Analysis, via Haver Analytic
Graphs courtesy of Floyd Norris, *The New York Times*

the market mechanism fully exposed. They have had the most influence over it and would rather keep it that way. The mythology is useful precisely because it hides their power. The first step in reversing the vicious cycle, therefore, is to see the market mechanism for what it is. That was the objective of Part I.

The next step, which I will now take, is to see the consequences of the market mechnanism for who gets what—and the distance separating those consequences from what we might consider to be necessary and fair. Are the current incentives operating on the richest members of society required in order to get them to do the work they do? Do these incentives fairly reflect the value of their work relative to the value of the work that others do? Are the current incentives operating on the middle class adequate to provide most people the standard of living they desire, as well as sufficient hope that through hard work they and their children can do even better? Are the current incentives for the poor large enough to get them to do what society expects of them, while providing them some measure of dignity? As I will show, the answer to all these questions is no.

PART II

Work and Worth

10

The Meritocratic Myth

A few years ago I was invited to speak to a group of employees at a power plant who were considering whether to form a union. One young man who intended to vote against it told me he was worth no more than the fourteen dollars an hour he was then paid. "I say for these people making their millions, that's fantastic. I could have done the same thing if I went to school and had the brains for it. I do not, so I'm a laborer."*

The man apparently had no knowledge of the 1950s, when more than 30 percent of the nation's private-sector workforce was unionized. That gave the nation's blue-collar laborers enough bargaining power to summon the equivalent (on average, and in today's dollars) of thirty dollars an hour—even though many hadn't finished high school. It wasn't their brains that accomplished this. It was their bargaining clout. But the power of trade unions to negotiate good wages for hourly workers has declined markedly since then. That's why the young man I met was "worth" no more than fourteen dollars an hour.

Yet the notion that you're paid what you're "worth" is by now

---

* This conversation was filmed and appears in *Inequality for All*, the Sundance Film Festival award-winning documentary directed by Jacob Kornbluth.

so deeply ingrained in the public consciousness that many who earn very little assume it's their own fault. They feel ashamed of what they see as a personal failure—a lack of brains or a deficiency of character. The same notion allows those who earn vast sums to believe they must be extraordinarily clever, daring, and superior; otherwise, they wouldn't be doing so well. This reassuring conviction seemingly justifies not only their great wealth but also their high status in society. They would prefer not to view their money as winnings in an economic contest over whose rules they and others like them have disproportionate influence. Presumably they would prefer the public not to see it that way, either.

In 2013, the hedge-fund manager Steven A. Cohen earned $2.3 billion. During his twenty years at the helm of SAC Capital Advisors, he had amassed a fortune estimated to be around $11 billion. Was he really worth it? In the trivial, tautological sense he must have been, because that is what he earned. "Private hedge fund people only make money because others voluntarily decide that it's worth it to invest their money with them," noted Dan Mitchell of the Washington-based Cato Institute, in response to my public questioning of Cohen's pay.

But there may be a reason people decided to invest their money with Steven A. Cohen that raises a deeper question about his "worth." According to a criminal complaint filed by the Justice Department in 2013, insider trading at SAC Capital under Cohen's leadership was "substantial, pervasive, and on a scale without known precedent in the hedge fund industry." Nine of Cohen's present or former employees pleaded guilty to using insider information. The firm itself entered a guilty plea and paid a $1.8 billion fine. For years, investors had put their money into SAC Capital presumably because the firm's trades on inside information generated huge returns. Had the firm's insider trading been discovered and prosecuted earlier, those returns would not have been nearly as high, investors would not have put their money there, and Cohen's wealth would never have amounted to $11 billion (minus the $1.8 billion fine).

In other words, if unions were as strong today as they were six decades ago, the laborer I spoke with might well have earned thirty dollars an hour instead of fourteen. And if the ban on insider trading had been stronger and fully enforced, Steven A. Cohen would not have accumulated $11 billion, and his clients would not have "voluntarily" decided it was "worth it" to invest their money with him.

People are "worth" what they're paid in the market in the trivial sense that if the market rewards them a certain amount of money they must be. Some confuse this tautology for a moral claim that people deserve what they are paid. One of the most broadly held assumptions about the economy is that individuals are rewarded in direct proportion to their efforts and abilities—that our society is a meritocracy.* But a moment's thought reveals many factors other than individual merit that play a role in determining earnings—financial inheritance, personal connections, discrimination in favor of or against someone because of how they look, luck, marriage, and, perhaps most significantly, the society one inhabits. "If we are very generous with ourselves," economist Herbert Simon once said, "I suppose we might claim that we 'earned' as much as one fifth of [our income]. The rest is the patrimony associated with being a member of an enormously productive social system."

This "enormously productive social system" now distributes a very large portion of the income it generates to those at its uppermost rungs—a higher portion to the one-tenth of 1 percent than in more than eighty years. This lopsidedness, in turn, is largely the consequence of how power has been allocated and utilized.

---

* The term "meritocracy" was coined by British sociologist Michael Young in his 1958 satirical essay, *The Rise of the Meritocracy*, to depict a society so wedded to standard measures of intelligence that it ignored many gifted and talented people while overlooking character flaws in those who tested well. Since then, however, the term's meaning has changed to become a positive description of a society in which anyone can make it based on individual merit—through qualities such as natural intelligence, hard work, ambition, and courage—and in which financial rewards are directly proportional to individual effort and ability. See Stephen J. McNamee and Robert K. Miller, Jr., *The Meritocracy Myth* (Lanham, MD: Rowman & Littlefield, 2009).

Unless one assumes that the allocation of power is just, it does not follow that people deserve what they are paid in any moral sense.

As I noted earlier, starting in the early 1980s, large corporations and their top executives, major actors on Wall Street, and other wealthy individuals have exercised disproportionate and increasing influence over how the market is organized. The basic building blocks of capitalism thereby give an advantage to the owners of capital (corporations, their shareholders, and their executives; Wall Street traders, hedge-fund managers, and private-equity managers) and handicap average workers. This helps explain why, as I have pointed out, share prices have risen while the median wage has dropped.

Higher share prices have added substantially to the incomes and the wealth of those at the top.* In the bull market that sent stocks soaring from 1994 to 2014 (the downturn from 2008 to 2011 notwithstanding), America's rich hit the jackpot. By 2010, the richest 1 percent of Americans owned 35 percent of the value of American-owned shares, both directly and indirectly through their pension plans. The richest 10 percent owned more than 80 percent. Yet most Americans did not benefit from the bull market because they were not able to save enough to invest much, if anything, in stocks. The bottom 90 percent owned just 19.2 percent, directly or indirectly. In 2014, more than two-thirds of Americans were living from paycheck to paycheck.

If the rules governing how the market is organized took full account of the benefits to society of various roles and occupations, moreover, some people would be paid far more. Social work, teaching, nursing, and caring for the elderly or for children are among the lowest-paid professions, yet evidence suggests that talented and dedicated people in these positions generate societal

---

* "Income" is usually measured as a yearly flow of earnings. "Wealth" is the pool into which yearly flows of unspent income accumulate. It is usually held in the form of stocks, bonds, real estate, and other assets. Wealth also generates its own income: interest and dividends from savings and investments and rental income from real estate.

benefits far out of proportion to their pay. One such study found that good teachers increase the average present value of their students' lifetime income by $250,000 per classroom, for example. Presumably, if teaching jobs paid better they would attract many more such teachers.

On the other hand, the worth to society of many CEOs, hedge-fund managers, investment bankers, "high-frequency" traders, lobbyists, and high-end corporate lawyers may be less than they command in the market. Much of what they do entails taking money out of one set of pockets and putting it into another, in escalating zero-sum activity. High-frequency traders, for example, profit by getting information a fraction of a second earlier than other traders, necessitating ever-greater investments in electronic systems that give them that tiny edge. Similarly, squadrons of corporate lawyers are paid substantial sums by their clients because squadrons of corporate lawyers on the other side are paid vast sums to attack them and defend their own clients.

People in these professions do not generate discoveries that transform society or create works of art that enrich and deepen human consciousness. Their innovations are financial and tactical—finding new ways to squeeze more money out of a given set of assets, including employees, or to expropriate the assets and incomes of others. Such contests also use up the time and energies of some of the nation's most educated young people, whose talents could, one supposes, be put to more socially beneficial uses.

Just before the financial crisis, almost half of Harvard's graduating class took jobs on Wall Street. That portion dropped during the financial crisis but began rising again after 2009. According to research by sociologist Lauren Rivera, around 70 percent of Harvard's senior class routinely submit résumés to Wall Street and corporate consulting firms. The percentages are similar at other Ivy League colleges. At Princeton, close to 36 percent of 2010 graduates went into finance, down from the pre–financial crisis high of 46 percent in 2006. Add in corporate management consulting, and it was more than 60 percent.

The hefty endowments of such elite institutions are swollen with the tax-subsidized donations of wealthy alumni, many of whom seek to increase the odds that their own kids will be admitted so they too can become enormously wealthy financiers, management consultants, and corporate executives. Personally, I could think of a better way for taxpayers to subsidize occupations with more social merit: Forgive the student debts of graduates who choose social work, child care, elder care, nursing, legal aid, and teaching.

The prevailing assumption that individuals are paid what they're "worth" is a tautology that overlooks the legal and political institutions defining the market. Most fundamentally, it ignores power. As such, it lures the unsuspecting into thinking nothing can or should be done to alter what people are paid because the market has decreed it.

According to this logic, the minimum wage should not be raised because workers at today's minimum are worth no more than they are already paid. If they were worth more, they would be paid more. Any attempt to force employers to pay them more will cause employers to lay off workers. By the same logic, the median wage of the bottom 90 percent has stagnated for thirty years and dropped since 2000 because middle-income workers are worth less than they were before new software technologies and globalization made many of their old jobs redundant. The only way they can get better pay is by getting better skills, so they are worth more.

CEOs of big companies, by this reasoning, are worth every penny of their compensation packages, which fifty years ago averaged twenty times that of the typical worker but now average almost three hundred times. CEOs must be worth these sums or they wouldn't receive them. Any reduction or limitation on their pay would deter them from working as hard and as well as they do, to the detriment of all who depend on them. By the same logic, the denizens of Wall Street must be worth the tens or hundreds of millions they are paid every year because people are willing to pay them that much. Limiting their pay would reduce their incentives, distort the market, and cause the financial system to become vastly and perhaps terminally inefficient.

This fabricated logic is a substitute for clear thought. As I have shown, large corporations have increased their profits and stock prices through their influence over the basic rules of the "free market"—property, market power, contract, bankruptcy, and enforcement. A growing portion of the compensation of top corporate executives and Wall Street bankers, hedge-fund managers, and private-equity managers—who together constitute the majority of the top one-tenth of 1 percent of earners—turn on these rising profits and stock prices. To this must be added the political influence of corporate executives and Wall Street traders and managers over specific rules pertaining to fraud, conflicts of interest, insider trading, and limited liability, which also affect their compensation. An analysis of their after-tax incomes would reveal their growing influence over the effective tax rates they pay as well, but my focus here is on their more consequential and less understood roles in shaping the basic rules of the game. As I hope I make clear, the current incentives operating on the richest members of society are not at all necessary in order to get them to do the work they do, and those incentives do not in any meaningful way reflect the social value of their work relative to the value of the work that others do.

I will also show that increasing political and economic power at the top is related to decreasing political and economic power in the middle class. Further, I will show that the current incentives operating on the middle class are inadequate to provide most people the standard of living they desire and do not provide them sufficient hope that through hard work they and their children can do even better.

Finally, we will look at the rise of two groups whose existence is antithetical to the meritocratic justifications often given for why some Americans are poor and others are wealthy: the working poor and the non-working rich. As I will show, the current incentives for the working poor are not nearly large enough to get them to do what society expects of them, while providing them some measure of dignity. Meanwhile, the financial incentives for the non-working rich are far greater than can be justified by any measure of their contribution to society.

11

The Hidden Mechanism
of CEO Pay

Anyone who still believes people are paid what they're worth is obliged to explain the soaring compensation of CEOs in America's large corporations over the last three decades, relative to the pay of average workers—from a ratio of 20 to 1 in 1965, to 30 to 1 in 1978, 123 to 1 in 1995, 296 to 1 in 2013, and over 300 to 1 today. Overall, CEO pay climbed 937 percent between 1978 and 2013, while the pay of the typical worker rose just 10.2 percent.

Starting in the mid-1990s, CEOs of big companies became especially comfortable. Consider that in 1992, the average total compensation of America's five hundred highest-paid corporate executives was $8.9 million (in 2012 dollars). Most of that came from realized gains on stock options and awards, which I'll explain in a moment. Twenty years later, the average had exploded to $30.3 million, again including such realized gains. Even in 2009, when the economy hit the bottom of the worst downturn since the Great Depression, average CEO pay, adjusted for inflation, was almost twice its level in 1992.

Not only did CEO pay explode; the pay of top corporate executives just below them soared as well. Consider Comcast, whose formidable economic and political prowess I examined earlier. In 2012, Comcast CEO Brian L. Roberts's total compensation was

$29.1 million, according to the corporation's 2013 proxy statement, ranking him tenth among the nation's highest-paid CEOs. Roberts was hardly alone at Comcast. Steve Burke, the president and CEO of NBCUniversal, a Comcast subsidiary, received $26.3 million that year. Comcast's chief financial officer, Michael Angelakis, received $23.2 million. Neil Smit, president and CEO of Comcast Cable Communications, got $18.3 million, and David Cohen, a Comcast executive vice president, $15.9 million.

The share of corporate income devoted to compensating the five highest-paid executives of large public firms went from an average of 5 percent in 1993 to more than 15 percent in 2013. Not incidentally, this was money corporations could have invested in research and development, additional jobs, or higher wages for average workers. In addition, almost all of it was deducted from corporate income taxes, which means the rest of us paid more taxes proportionally in order to make up the shortfall.

One justification is that CEOs and top executives are worth their soaring pay because the stock market has also soared during these years, and the job of CEOs and top executives is to maximize shareholder returns. Ergo, they have accomplished their mission. As Harvard economist N. Gregory Mankiw argues, for example, "The most natural explanation of high CEO pay is that the value of a good CEO is extraordinarily high." But even assuming maximizing shareholder returns should be their goal (I'll get back to this later), it hardly follows that CEOs are worth so much more than they used to be. The entire stock market boomed over this period. Even had a CEO locked himself in his office and played online solitaire for these three decades, his company would still have become far more valuable. Unless the company did better than the stock market as a whole, there is no reason to suppose the CEO did anything in particular to justify his escalating pay.

Besides, as noted, the stock market surge has had a great deal to do with changes in the rules that have favored big companies and major banks—stronger and more extensive property rights, especially for intellectual property; increasing market power in large firms, particularly in the form of control over standard platforms and networks (and declining market power for average workers, who no longer have strong unions negotiating on their behalf); coercive contracts that bind employees, borrowers, customers, and franchisees to one-sided terms favoring big corporations, along with insider trading, to the detriment of small investors; bankruptcy rules favoring big banks and corporations over employees and small borrowers; and enforcement mechanisms benefitting the biggest corporations and Wall Street banks. It is true that some CEOs may have contributed to such favorable outcomes through their lobbying and other political activities— making and bundling generous political contributions and offering jobs to pliant government officials—but these are not the sort of activities normally used to justify mammoth CEO pay.

So why, exactly, did CEO pay skyrocket, even though these top executives may have made no direct economic contribution to the growing values of their companies? One theory is that CEOs play large roles in appointing their corporations' directors, for whom a reliable tendency toward agreeing with the CEO has become a prerequisite. Directors are amply paid for the three or four times a year they meet and naturally want to remain in the good graces of their top executives. Being a board director is the best part-time job in America. In 2012, the average compensation for a board member at an S&P 500 company was $251,000. In addition, boards consist of other CEOs who have considerable interest in ensuring their compatriots are paid generously. To advise on executive pay, boards typically hire people euphemistically called "compensation consultants," whose actual roles are more akin to that of the oldest profession in the world. Such consultants typically establish benchmarks based on the pay of other CEOs, whose boards typically hire them for the same purpose. Since all boards want to demonstrate to their CEO as well as to analysts on Wall Street their willingness to pay generously for the very best, pay packages ratchet upward annually in this faux competition, conducted and directed by CEOs for CEOs, in the interest of CEOs.

Corporate law in the United States gives shareholders at most an advisory role on CEO pay. "Say on pay" votes are required under the 2010 Dodd-Frank financial legislation, but the votes are not binding on a corporation. Billionaire Larry Ellison, the CEO of Oracle, received a pay package in 2013 valued at $78.4 million, a sum so stunning that Oracle shareholders rejected it. That made no difference, because Ellison controlled the board. In Australia, by contrast, shareholders have the right to force an entire corporate board to stand for re-election if 25 percent or more of a company's shareholders vote against a CEO pay plan two years in a row. That rule has contributed to the far more modest pay raises Australian CEOs have been granted in recent years relative to their American counterparts, in 2013 averaging only seventy times the pay of the typical Australian worker.

Such cronyism in American boardrooms has been common for decades. Although it explains why CEOs are paid a great deal, it fails to explain why CEO pay has surged in recent years. To answer this you need to understand that since the mid-1990s, a steadily larger portion of CEO pay has come in the form of shares of corporate stock, which boards have eagerly doled out to CEOs and other top executives in the form of stock options (the chance to buy shares at a given price) and stock awards (activated when share prices reach a certain level). When share prices dip, boards readily provide additional options and awards to make up for losses, so that when share prices rise again—even if the rise is temporary—CEOs can realize the gains by copiously cashing out.

This form of pay gives CEOs a significant incentive to pump up the value of their firms' shares in the short run, even if the pumping takes a toll over the longer term. Professor William Lazonick of the University of Massachusetts Lowell has documented that a major means by which corporations accomplish such pumping is to use their earnings, or to borrow additional money, to buy back shares of stock. This maneuver pumps up share prices by reducing the number of shares owned by the public. A smaller supply effortlessly increases the price of each remaining share. In recent years, such buybacks have become a major corporate expenditure. Between 2001 and 2013, they accounted for a whopping $3.6 trillion in outlays of companies in the Standard & Poor's 500 index.

Corporations must disclose publicly when boards have approved buybacks and the overall amounts, but they do not have to announce when they are actually entering the stock market to buy back shares of stock. Buybacks are executed anonymously through the company's broker. So share prices can rise without investors having any idea buybacks are the cause. (If they knew of the artifice, they might be less willing to buy or hold the shares of stock.) Yet CEOs can use their own inside knowledge of when the buybacks will occur and how large they'll be in order to time their own stock sales and exercise their own stock options. Presumably, they'll time them to coincide with the rise in share prices, which all too often is temporary.

If this sounds a lot like insider trading, or a conflict of interest with the CEO's fiduciary duty to shareholders, it is no coincidence. Between 1934 and 1982, the Securities and Exchange Commission regarded stock buybacks as potential vehicles for stock manipulation and fraud. It required companies to disclose the volume of their buybacks and prohibited companies from repurchasing more than 15 percent of the value of their stock on any given day. But in 1982, John Shad, the new chairman of the SEC, appointed by Ronald Reagan, removed these restrictions. Henceforth, CEOs could use buybacks to manipulate the prices of their companies' shares.

Adding to the allure of stock options was a subsequent decision by the SEC, in 1991, to permit top executives, even though technically company insiders with knowledge of the timing of their company's stock buybacks, to quietly cash in their stock options without public disclosure. Then, in 1993, the Clinton administration decided to allow companies to deduct from their taxable income executive pay in excess of $1 million if that pay was linked to corporate performance—that is, if it came in the form of stock options and awards linked to share prices. Not surprisingly, stock options thereafter boomed.

Corporate buybacks thereafter soared because they became a ready means for top executives to pump up stock prices and cash in their stock options. Between 2003 and 2012, the chief executives of the ten companies that repurchased the most stock (totaling $859 billion) received 68 percent of their total pay in stock options or stock awards. In 2013 alone, companies in the Standard & Poor's 500 index repurchased $500 billion of their own shares, thereby disposing of a third of their cash flow. That was close to the record level of buybacks reached in the bubble year of 2007.

Not only do stock buybacks enrich CEOs and other top executives at the expense of smaller investors who do not know about the timing or amounts of buybacks, they also drain away money the corporation might otherwise spend on research and development, long-term expansion, worker retraining, and higher wages. Every dollar CEOs "realize" from their sale of shares whose price has been pumped up by buybacks requires that many more corporate dollars be dedicated to making the repurchases. The perverse effect on corporate priorities is unmistakable. In the first three decades after World War II, major American corporations typically retained and reinvested their earnings. But beginning in the 1980s, a steadily increasing portion of corporate earnings went to share buybacks.

Between 2003 and 2012, S&P 500 companies put most of their net earnings into stock buybacks that boosted share prices—and, not incidentally, also boosted CEO pay. IBM, for example, once prided itself on giving its workers lifelong employment and making long-term investments in technologies of the future. But in the 1990s IBM shifted priorities—laying off employees, scrimping on research, borrowing heavily, and using the money to buy back its shares of stock. Between 2000 and 2013, it spent $108 billion buying back its own shares, thereby pumping up share prices even though revenues remained flat. By 2014, IBM showed signs of reaching the end of the game. As its stock price finally began to sink, *The New York Times* said that "all these 'shareholder friendly' maneuvers have been masking an ugly truth: IBM's success in recent years has been tied more to financial engineering than actual performance." Nevertheless, the strategy had paid off for IBM's CEOs, whose cumulative pay between 2003 and 2012 was $247 million, mostly in stock options and stock awards.

Hewlett-Packard followed a similar formula. It, too, had a lifelong employment policy, but by the late 1990s was firing employees and from 2004 to 2011 spent $61.4 billion on buybacks—more than its entire income—followed by a $12.7 billion loss in 2012. Between 2003 and 2012, Hewlett-Packard's CEOs received a total of $210 million, more than a third of it in options and awards. In 2013, Apple borrowed $17 billion and used most of it to buy back its shares of stock. Not incidentally, Apple CEO Tim Cook received $73.8 million in compensation in 2013, almost all in stock options that he'd presumably cash in when the buybacks had maximum effect.

Stock options and restricted stock grants have become by far the largest portion of CEO pay. Time Warner chief executive Jeff Bewkes was paid $15.9 million in stock awards and options in 2013, along with a base salary of a modest $2 million. His contract with Time Warner extended through 2017 and included a generous exit package. But Facebook's Mark Zuckerberg takes the prize. In 2013 he cashed in $3.3 billion worth of stock options. His base salary that year was $1.

CEOs are "worth" their pay, then, in the perversely narrow sense that the prices of their companies' shares typically rise before CEOs cash in their stocks, as they did in 2007, just before the stock market crash of 2008. Stock prices also rose to nosebleeding heights before the Great Crash of 1929. The more pertinent question is the relationship, if any, between CEO pay and the longer-term profitability of the companies they run.

One recent study provides an answer. Professors Michael J. Cooper of the University of Utah, Huseyin Gulen of Purdue University, and P. Raghavendra Rau of the University of Cambridge studied 1,500 large companies and how they performed, in three-year periods, from 1994 to 2011. They then compared these companies' performance to other companies in their same fields. They discovered that the 150 companies with the highest-paid CEOs returned about 10 percent *less* to their shareholders than did their industry peers. In fact, the more these CEOs were paid, the worse their companies did. Companies that were the most generous to their CEOs—and whose high-paid CEOs received more of that compensation as stock options—did 15 percent worse than their peer companies, on average. "The returns are almost three times lower for the high-paying firms than the low-paying firms," said Cooper. "This wasteful spending destroys shareholder value." Even worse, the researchers found that the longer a highly paid CEO was in office, the more the firm underperformed. "The performance worsens significantly over time," they concluded.

In theory, companies that do badly over the longer term could claw back the stock options and awards their CEOs cashed in when the company's stock prices were riding high. This is not unheard of. In 2013, following a disappointing fiscal year, Sony CEO Kazuo Hirai and his top executives returned roughly $10 million in bonuses. But it seems doubtful this practice will become the norm. Twenty-first-century America already has a rich tradition of moving in the opposite direction—CEOs raking in millions after screwing up royally. On the list: Martin Sullivan, who got $47 million when he left AIG, even though the company's share price dropped by 98 percent on his watch and American taxpayers had to pony up $180 billion just to keep the firm alive; Thomas E. Freston, who lasted just nine months as CEO of Viacom before being fired, and departed with a severance payment of $101 million; Michael Jeffries, CEO of Abercrombie & Fitch, whose company's stock price dropped more than 70 percent in 2007, but who received $71.8 million in 2008, including a $6 million retention bonus; William D. McGuire, who in 2006 was forced to resign as CEO of UnitedHealth over a stock-options scandal, and for his troubles got a pay package worth $286 million; Hank A. McKinnell, Jr., whose five-year tenure as CEO of Pfizer was marked by a $140 billion drop in Pfizer's stock market value but who left with a payout of nearly $200 million, free lifetime medical coverage, and an annual pension of $6.5 million (at Pfizer's 2006 annual meeting a plane flew overhead towing a banner reading "Give it back, Hank!"); Douglas Ivester of Coca-Cola, who stepped down as CEO in 2000 after a period of stagnant growth and declining earnings, with an exit package worth $120 million; and, as I have noted, Donald Carty, former CEO of American Airlines, who established a secret trust fund to protect his and other executive bonuses even as the firm was sliding into bankruptcy in 2003 and seeking wage concessions from the airline's employees. If anything, pay for failure appears to be on the rise. In September 2011, Leo Apotheker was shown the door at Hewlett-Packard, with an exit package worth $12 million. The list of shameless CEOs continues to lengthen.

Meanwhile, you and I, and other taxpayers, are subsidizing all this. That's because corporations deduct CEO pay from their income taxes, requiring the rest of us to pay more proportionally in taxes to make up the difference. To take but one example, Howard Schultz, CEO of Starbucks, received $1.5 million in salary for 2013, along with a whopping $150 million in stock options and awards. That saved Starbucks $82 million in taxes. The 1993 provision allowing corporations to deduct from their tax bills executive compensation in excess of $1 million if tied to company "performance" soon became a sham. Even Senator Charles Grassley, the Republican chairman of the Senate Finance Committee in 2006, saw through it: "It was well-intentioned," he said. "But it really hasn't worked at all. Companies have found it easy to get around the law. It has more holes than Swiss cheese. And it seems to have encouraged the options industry. These sophisticated folks are working with Swiss-watch-like devices to game this Swiss-cheese-like rule."

One such game has been to hand out stock "performance

awards" on the basis of nothing more than an upward drift in the value of the stock market as a whole, over which CEOs presumably played no role other than watch as their company's stock price rose along with that of almost every other company. The Economic Policy Institute estimated that between 2007 and 2010, a total of $121.5 billion in executive compensation was deducted from corporate earnings. Roughly 55 percent of this total was for such effortless "performance-based" compensation.

As if all this weren't enough, the tax system is biased toward the owners of wealth and against people whose income comes from wages. Capital gains are taxed at a lower rate than ordinary income. Among the biggest winners are CEOs whose options and bonuses are tied to the stock market, which can therefore be treated as capital gains when cashed in. The bull market of 2010 to 2014 gave them all fabulous after-tax windfalls.

If shareholders have a property right in a publicly held corporation—if they in fact own it (an issue to which I will return)—presumably shareholders are the ones who should decide on CEO pay. In addition, CEOs presumably would have to disclose to shareholders how much shareholder money they spend on political activities. If the notion of "pay for performance" has any practical meaning as a contract between a CEO and shareholders, presumably a CEO should also be responsible for the company's long-term performance and required to return to the company any pay reflecting mere temporary increases in share prices. If bankruptcy were on a level playing field, CEOs would not be permitted to sock away generous executive pay out of the reach of a bankruptcy judge. If enforcement of these building blocks were not tilted toward CEOs, presumably the Securities and Exchange Commission would bar CEOs from pumping up share prices through buybacks and then cashing in their options, as the SEC once did. Moreover, CEO pay in excess of $1 million would not be deductible, even if linked to performance. If all the building blocks were not tilted toward large corporations, these companies would not be earning the substantial profits that have allowed their top executives to earn princely sums to begin with.

But none of this is in the cards because CEOs of big corporations have sufficient political power to stop any such initiatives. The campaign contributions of CEOs constitute a substantial share of all contributions. Many are also major bundlers of contributions coming from other top executives in their firms. Taken together, their campaign contributions, bundled contributions, influence over their corporate political action committees, lobbyists, and implicit promises of future employment to certain government officials give them substantial say over the rules of the game.

So are CEOs worth their pay in any sense other than the senseless tautology equating the compensation packages they receive with their worth? Any objective assessment would conclude they are not.

12

The Subterfuge of
Wall Street Pay

If you still believe those at the top are paid what they're worth, take a closer look at Wall Street, whose inhabitants typically earn even more than top corporate executives. Are Wall Street bankers "worth" it? Not if you figure in the hidden subsidy flowing to the big Wall Street banks that since the bailout of 2008 have been considered too big to fail. Recall that their near meltdown was brought on by excessive risk taking. During the ensuing financial crisis, the biggest banks then received significantly more help from the government than other banks, in order to keep them from going under. In important ways, that subsidy continues to this day, because the biggest banks are still too big to fail.

Here's how the hidden subsidy works. People who park their savings in these banks accept a lower interest rate on deposits or loans than they require from America's smaller banks. That's because smaller banks are riskier places to park money than the big banks, which will almost certainly be bailed out if they get into trouble. This gives Wall Street's biggest banks a competitive advantage over the nation's smaller banks. In consequence, the biggest banks make even more money. And as their profits grow, the big banks grow even larger. If they were too big to fail before, they're absolutely too big to fail now. As I've noted, by 2014, Wall Street's five largest banks held about 45 percent of America's banking assets, up from 25 percent in 2000. They are far too big to fail or jail or curtail.

How large is the hidden subsidy? Two researchers, Kenichi Ueda of the International Monetary Fund and Beatrice Weder di Mauro of the University of Mainz, have calculated it to be about eight-tenths of a percentage point. This may not sound like much, but multiply it by the total amount of money parked in the ten biggest Wall Street banks and you get a very large sum. In 2013, this hidden subsidy came to $83 billion. This estimate, by the way, is consistent with estimates of other researchers from the International Monetary Fund and the Government Accountability Office. Economists from New York University, Virginia Tech, and Syracuse University, comparing the interest rates offered by small banks on money-market accounts over the FDIC guarantee with rates offered by the large banks, found the big banks had an advantage of more than a percentage point, which would make the actual subsidy far higher.

You do not have to be a rocket scientist or even a Wall Street banker to calculate that the hidden subsidy the Wall Street banks enjoy because they are too big to fail totaled about three times Wall Street's 2013 bonus payments of $26.7 billion. Without the subsidy there would have been no bonus pool at all. The lion's share of that subsidy, $64 billion, went to the top five banks—JPMorgan, Bank of America, Citigroup, Wells Fargo, and Goldman Sachs. Sixty-four billion dollars just about equals these banks' typical annual profits. In other words, take away the subsidy and not only does the bonus pool disappear, so do all the profits.

The reason Wall Street bankers got $26.7 billion in bonuses in 2013 was not because they worked so much harder or were so much more clever or insightful than most other Americans. They received those bonuses because they happen to work in institutions that hold a privileged place in the American political economy. The subsidy going to the big banks comes from you and me and other taxpayers because we paid for the last bailout, and it is assumed we will pay for the next one.

Under the Dodd-Frank financial reform act, each of the biggest Wall Street banks was required to create a "living will," to go into effect if it was ever again unable to pay its bills. Essentially, these living wills were supposed to be blueprints for unwinding the banks' operations without harming the rest of the financial system. But don't bank on it. After reviewing these wills, investigators from the Federal Reserve Board and the Federal Deposit Insurance Corporation concluded in August 2014 that they were "unrealistic." Thomas Hoenig, vice chairman of the FDIC, called each of the plans "deficient" because each "fails to convincingly demonstrate how, in failure, any one of these firms could overcome obstacles to entering bankruptcy without precipitating a financial crisis." If you have followed my argument, you will understand why the biggest banks would rather that their living wills remain unrealistic. Realistic plans for avoiding another bailout would cause the hidden subsidies—and the competitive advantage they produce, along with the bonuses that embody that competitive advantage—to vanish.

The Federal Reserve has made moves toward increasing the capital requirements of big banks, which may trim their sails slightly. But it seems doubtful Congress or administrators will force them to come up with realistic living wills, or limit their size, or break them up, or impose a special tax on them equal to the amount of the hidden subsidy. As I have pointed out, the reason these institutions continue to hold such a privileged place in the American political economy is that Wall Street accounts for such a large proportion of campaign donations to major candidates for Congress and the presidency of both parties and maintains a lucrative revolving door connecting it to Washington. The executives of small banks, let alone most Americans, do not have these unique capacities. They cannot afford to make major contributions or offer lucrative jobs to former public officials. This helps explain why most small bankers don't earn large bonuses, and neither do most other Americans.

Not incidentally, the $26.7 billion distributed to Wall Street bankers in 2013 bonuses would have been enough to more than double the pay of every one of America's 1,007,000 full-time minimum-wage workers that year. The remainder of the $83 billion hidden subsidy going to the biggest banks on the Street was $20 billion more than what the government provided that year to twenty-eight million low-wage workers and their families in the form of wage subsidies under the Earned Income Tax Credit.

This hidden subsidy does not completely account for the sums commanded by others on the Street, such as Steven A. Cohen's $2.3 billion in 2013. That year the top twenty-five hedge-fund managers took home, on average, almost $1 billion each. Even run-of-the-mill portfolio managers at large hedge funds averaged $2.2 million each. Some economists have suggested the reason they command these sums (typically in the form of a 2 percent annual fee plus 20 percent of returns over a given benchmark) is that investors want to reduce the temptation of hedge-fund and portfolio managers to pocket some of the vast amounts of money they manage. The theory is that the managers will not rake off any for themselves illegally for fear of losing the generous incomes they receive legally. As economist Eric Falkenstein explains, "The portfolio managers know the best price, outsiders don't, that's why they get paid a lot. In the context of a moving market, and illiquid securities (such as mortgages), you don't really know how much money you are leaving on the table, but look at the incentives at the individual level, and expect people to act in their self interest."

By this logic, which might apply equally well to many of the Street's investment bankers and traders, the earnings of hedge-fund managers are best understood as bribes paid by investors so that the managers don't rob them blind. The more money hedge-fund managers oversee, the higher the bribes need to be.

The problem with this logic is that the bribes still provide no guarantee that hedge-fund and portfolio managers will not skim off some investor money in side deals and kickbacks. In fact, that is exactly what the portfolio managers at Cohen's SAC Capital were caught doing. It is a fair supposition that other managers and traders on Wall Street do the same but are not caught. As I have noted, Congress banned insider trading in 1934 but gave wide latitude to the members of the Securities and Exchange Commission, federal prosecutors, and judges to determine its precise meaning. Cohen's moneymaking methods had been well known on the Street for many years. SAC Capital managed so much money that it typically accounted for as much as 3 percent of the average daily trading on the New York Stock Exchange and 1 percent of NASDAQ's. It thereby handed over more than $150 million annually in commissions to bankers on the Street, who possessed a great deal of information of potential value to Cohen and his associates at SAC Capital. This generated possibilities for lucrative deals. In fact, according to a *Bloomberg Businessweek* story from 2003, a decade before the prosecutions, the commissions that SAC routinely gave the bankers "grease the superpowerful information machine that Cohen has built" and "[win] Cohen the clout that often makes him privy to trading and analyst information ahead of rivals." One analyst is quoted as saying, "I call Stevie personally when I have any insight or news tidbit on a company. I know he'll put the info to use and actually trade off it." The firm's credo, according to one of its former traders, was always to "try to get the information before anyone else."

But even though nine of Cohen's portfolio managers were convicted of insider trading, Cohen himself got off rather lightly. His firm was fined $1.8 billion, but the rest of his accumulated gains were left untouched in the settlement with federal prosecutors. Nor was he sent to jail. Perhaps Cohen was spared because the battalion of high-priced lawyers he hired to represent him showed federal prosecutors how long and difficult any legal confrontation would be. (In this sense, his lawyers were worth what they were paid.) But Cohen's treatment may also have had something to do with the fact that during the years he earned much of his fortune, between 2000 and 2008, Republican appointees headed the Justice Department and the Securities and Exchange Commission, and that Cohen had been one of the Republican Party's major contributors, and that in the 2008 election, SAC and Cohen became big supporters of Obama.

If confidential information is indeed "the coin of the realm" on the Street, as the lawyer for Anthony Chiasson (an alumnus of Cohen's SAC Capital) claimed in 2014 when Chiasson was charged with insider trading—a view with which the court of appeals seemed to agree when it reversed his conviction—SAC Capital is not that unusual. Given the huge flows of money under the hedge-fund industry's supervision, the ready availability of confidential information, and the large amounts that can be earned on trades that utilize such information, it would not be unreasonable to conclude that much if not all of the business is premised on confidential information. Hedge-fund managers are well positioned to receive such coins of the realm and to cash them in royally. In consequence, their vast compensation packages likely reflect two different sources of largesse: legal bribes from investors who don't want to be ripped off, and illegal (or at best legally questionable) kickbacks from investors with whom they trade confidential information. It is a win-win, at least for them. If they devote even a small portion of these winnings to political candidates, lobbyists, and platoons of lawyers, they can minimize the risk and the costs of getting caught and prosecuted for insider trading. Consider Steven A. Cohen, for example.

They can also continue to get a tax loophole available to them but to few others, allowing hedge-fund and private-equity managers to treat their incomes as capital gains, subject to a lower tax rate than ordinary income. No logical argument can be summoned for this loophole. Such managers do not even risk their own capital; they invest other people's money. When, in 2007, Michigan congressman Sander M. Levin proposed treating such carried interest, as it is called, as ordinary income, annual political spending by the hedge-fund industry increased dramatically. Not surprisingly, such legislation has gone nowhere since then.

. . .

Are those on Wall Street "worth" the vast amounts of money they receive? Apart from the platitude that everyone is, by definition, worth what he or she earns in the market, the specific mechanism by which they earn their incomes—including the hidden too-big-to-fail subsidy as well as the utilization of insider information—suggests that much of what they receive is involuntarily transferred to them from taxpayers and small investors. They have enough wealth to influence the rules of the game, but they are not "worth" their pay in any meaningful sense of the term.

13

The Declining Bargaining Power
of the Middle

When I was a boy, my father sold dresses and blouses to the wives of factory workers, as I said earlier. As the wages of those workers rose in the late 1940s and through the 1950s, my father earned enough to expand his business to a second shop in another town not far away. We were by no means rich, but he earned enough to make us solidly middle class.

For three decades after World War II, the average hourly compensation of American workers rose in lockstep with productivity gains. It was a virtuous cycle, from which our family and tens of millions of others benefitted: As the economy grew, the middle class expanded, and as its purchasing power rose, the economy grew faster, spawning new investments and innovations that further enriched and enlarged the middle class.

But then, beginning in the late 1970s, the virtuous cycle came to a halt. While productivity gains continued much as before and the economy continued to grow, wages began to flatten (see figure 4). Starting in the early 1980s, the median household's income stopped growing altogether, when adjusted for inflation. In 2013, the typical middle-class household earned $51,939, nearly $4,500 below what it earned before the start of the Great Recession in 2007. By 2013, the median household was earning less than it did in 1989, nearly a quarter of a century before. Job security also declined, as did the percentage of working-age Americans with jobs. In short, much of the American middle class has become poorer. (My father, not incidentally, had to close his shops.)

In 2013, an American household smack in the middle of the earnings scale received less than the equivalent household did fifteen years before, in 1998, when pay is adjusted for inflation. Median household earnings were 8 percent below what they were in 2007. It was much the same story for individual workers paid an hourly wage. Their average pay was $20.67 in September 2014. After adjusting for inflation, this was almost the same purchas-

FIGURE 4. THE ROOT OF AMERICAN INEQUALITY: WAGES DETACHING FROM PRODUCTIVITY

Net productivity and real hourly compensation of production/nonsupervisory workers, 1948–2012

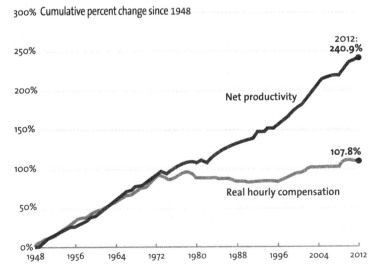

Note: Data are for compensation of production/nonsupervisory workers in the private sector (in 2012 dollars); net productivity is for the total economy and is equal to the growth of output of goods and services minus depreciation per hour worked.
Source: Economic Policy Institute analysis of unpublished total economy productivity data from Bureau of Labor Statistics (BLS) Labor Productivity and Costs program, BLS Current Employment Statistics, and Bureau of Economic Analysis National Income and Product Accounts
This chart originally appeared at go.epi.org/2013-productivity-wages.

ing power such workers had in 1979 and even less than they had in January 1973 (which would have been $22.41 in 2014 dollars).

The standard explanation attributes this U-turn to "market forces," especially globalization and technological improvements that have rendered many working Americans less competitive. Their jobs could be outsourced to workers in Mexico and then Asia who were eager to do them far more cheaply, or done at home more cheaply by automated equipment, computerized machine tools, and robots. Either way, it is commonly argued, American workers who had once earned good paychecks had priced themselves out of the labor market. If they want jobs, they have to settle for lower wages and less security. If they want better jobs, they need better skills. So hath the market decreed.

Yet, while surely relevant, the standard explanation cannot account for much of what has happened. It does not explain why the transformation occurred so suddenly, over a relatively brief number of years, nor why other advanced economies facing similar forces did not succumb to them as readily. (By 2011, the median income in Germany, for example, was rising faster than it was in the United States, and Germany's richest 1 percent took home about 11 percent of total income, before taxes, while America's richest 1 percent took home more than 17 percent.) And the standard explanation doesn't tell us why the average incomes of the bottom 90 percent actually dropped during the first six years of recovery from the Great Recession.

Nor, finally, does the standard explanation account for the striking fact that the median wages of younger college graduates also stopped growing, adjusted for inflation. While recent college graduates continued to earn higher wages than young people without college degrees, their wages no longer rose. In fact, between 2000 and 2013, the real average hourly wages of young college graduates declined (see figure 5). By 2014, according to the Federal Reserve Bank of New York, the share of recent college graduates working in jobs that typically do not require a college degree was 46 percent, versus 35 percent for college gradu-

FIGURE 5. REAL AVERAGE HOURLY WAGES OF YOUNG COLLEGE GRADUATES, BY GENDER, 2000–2014*

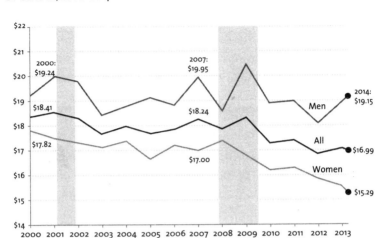

*Data for 2014 represent twelve-month average from April 2013 to March 2014.
Note: Data are for college graduates age 21–24 who do not have an advanced degree and are not enrolled in further schooling. Shaded areas denote recessions.
Source: Economic Policy Institute analysis of Current Population Survey Outgoing Rotation Group microdata (http://stateofworkingamerica.org/chart/swa-wages-table-4-18-hourly-wages-entry/)

ates overall. *The New York Times* called this group "Generation Limbo"—highly educated young adults "whose careers are stuck in neutral, coping with dead-end jobs and listless prospects."

A fuller understanding of what has happened to the middle class requires an examination of changes in the organization of the market that increased the profitability of large corporations and Wall Street while reducing the middle class's bargaining power and political clout. This transformation has amounted to a redistribution upward, but not as "redistribution" is normally defined. The government did not tax the middle class and poor and transfer a portion of their incomes to the rich. The government—and those with the most influence over it—undertook the upward redistribution less directly, by altering the rules of the game.

First consider the fundamental change that occurred over property rights in corporations. Before the 1980s, as I have noted, large corporations were in effect owned by all their stakeholders, who were assumed to have legitimate claims on them. As early as 1914, the popular columnist and public philosopher Walter Lippmann called on America's corporate executives to be stewards of America. "The men connected with [the large corporation] cannot escape the fact that they are expected to act increasingly like public officials. . . . Big businessmen who are at all intelligent recognize this. They are talking more and more about their 'responsibilities,' and their 'stewardship.'"

Subsequently, in 1932, Adolf A. Berle and Gardiner C. Means, a lawyer and an economics professor, respectively, published *The Modern Corporation and Private Property*, a highly influential study showing that top executives of America's giant companies were not even accountable to their own shareholders but operated the companies "in their own interest, and . . . divert[ed] a portion of the asset fund to their own uses." The solution, Berle and Means concluded, was to enlarge the power of all groups within the nation who were affected by the large corporation, including employees and consumers. They envisioned the corporate executive of the future as a professional administrator who dispassionately weighed the claims of investors, employees, consumers, and citizens and allocated benefits accordingly. "It seems almost essential," Berle and Means wrote, "if the corporate system is to survive—that the 'control' of the great corporations should develop into a purely neutral technocracy, balancing a variety of claims by various groups in the community and assigning each a portion of the income stream on the basis of public policy rather than private cupidity."

This vision of corporate governance came to be widely accepted by the end of World War II. "The job of management," proclaimed Frank Abrams, chairman of Standard Oil of New Jersey, in a 1951 address that typified what other chief executives were saying at the time, "is to maintain an equitable and working balance among the claims of the various directly affected interest groups . . . stockholders, employees, customers, and the public at large. Business managers are gaining professional status partly because they see in their work the basic responsibilities [to the public] that other professional men have long recognized as theirs."

In the early 1950s, *Fortune* magazine urged CEOs to become "industrial statesmen," which in many respects they did—helping to pilot an economy generating broad-based prosperity. In November 1956, *Time* magazine noted that business leaders were willing to "judge their actions, not only from the standpoint of profit and loss" in their financial results "but of profit and loss to the community." General Electric, noted the magazine, famously sought to serve the "balanced best interests" of all its stakeholders. Pulp and paper executive J. D. Zellerbach told *Time* that "the majority of Americans support private enterprise, not as a God-given right but as the best practical means of conducting business in a free society. . . . They regard business management as a stewardship, and they expect it to operate the economy as a public trust for the benefit of all the people."

But a radically different vision of corporate ownership erupted in the late 1970s and early 1980s. It came with corporate raiders who mounted hostile takeovers, wielding high-yield junk bonds to tempt shareholders to sell their shares. They used leveraged buyouts and undertook proxy fights against the industrial statesmen who, in their view, were depriving shareholders of the wealth that properly belonged to them. The raiders assumed that shareholders were the only legitimate owners of the corporation and that the only valid purpose of the corporation was to maximize shareholder returns.

This transformation did not happen by accident. It was a product of changes in the legal and institutional organization of corporations and of financial markets—changes that were promoted by corporate interests and Wall Street. In 1974, at the urging of pension funds, insurance companies, and the Street, Congress enacted the Employee Retirement Income Security Act. Before then, pension funds and insurance companies could only invest in high-grade corporate and government bonds—a fiduciary obligation under their contracts with beneficiaries of pensions and insurance policies. The 1974 act changed that, allowing pension funds and insurance companies to invest their portfolios in the stock market and thereby making a huge pool of capital available to Wall Street. In 1982, another large pool of capital became available when Congress gave savings and loan banks, the bedrocks of local home mortgage markets, permission to invest their deposits in a wide range of financial products, including junk bonds and other risky ventures promising high returns. The convenient fact that the government insured savings and loan deposits against losses made these investments all the more tempting (and ultimately cost taxpayers some $124 billion when many of the banks went bust). Meanwhile, the Reagan administration loosened other banking and financial regulations and simultaneously cut the enforcement staff at the Securities and Exchange Commission.

All this made it possible for corporate raiders to get the capital and the regulatory approvals necessary to mount unfriendly takeovers. During the whole of the 1970s there had been only 13 hostile takeovers of companies valued at $1 billion or more. During the 1980s, there were 150. Between 1979 and 1989, financial entrepreneurs mounted more than 2,000 leveraged buyouts, each over $250 million. (The party was temporarily halted only when raider Ivan Boesky agreed to be a government informer as part of his plea bargain on charges of insider trading and market manipulation. Boesky implicated Michael Milken and Milken's junk bond powerhouse, Drexel Burnham Lambert, in a scheme to manipulate stock prices and defraud clients. Drexel pleaded guilty. Milken was indicted on ninety-eight counts, including insider trading and racketeering, and went to jail.)

Even where raids did not occur, CEOs nonetheless felt pressured to maximize shareholder returns for fear their firms might otherwise be targeted. Hence, they began to see their primary role as driving up share prices. Roberto Goizueta, CEO of Coca-Cola, articulated the new philosophy, which was in sharp contrast to that of the corporate statesmen of the earlier decades: "We have one job: to generate a fair return for our owners," he said. Everyone understood that by "fair return" he meant the maximum possible.

The easiest and most direct way for CEOs to accomplish this feat was to cut costs—especially payrolls, which constitute most firms' largest single expense. Accordingly, the corporate statesmen of the 1950s and 1960s were replaced by the corporate butchers of the 1980s and 1990s, whose nearly exclusive focus was—in the meat-ax parlance of that era—to "cut out the fat" and "cut to the bone." When Jack Welch took the helm of GE in 1981, the company was valued by the stock market at less than $14 billion. When he retired in 2001, it was worth about $400 billion. Welch accomplished this largely by cutting payrolls. Before his tenure, most GE employees had spent their entire careers with the company. But between 1981 and 1985, a quarter of them—one hundred thousand in all—lost their jobs, earning Welch the moniker "Neutron Jack." Even when times were good, Welch encouraged his senior managers to replace 10 percent of their subordinates every year in order to keep GE competitive.

Other CEOs tried to outdo even Welch. As CEO of Scott Paper, "Chainsaw" Al Dunlap laid off eleven thousand workers, including 71 percent of headquarters staff. Wall Street was impressed, and the company's stock rose 225 percent. When Dunlap moved to Sunbeam in 1996, he promptly laid off half of Sunbeam's twelve thousand employees. (Unfortunately for him, though, he was caught cooking Sunbeam's books; the SEC sued him for fraud and he settled for $500,000, agreeing never again to serve as an officer or director of any publicly held company.) I have already made mention of IBM and Hewlett-Packard, both of which, before the transformation, had been known for their policies of lifetime employment and high wages. Afterward, both wielded the ax.

In consequence, share prices soared, as did the compensation packages of CEOs, as I have noted (see figure 6).

FIGURE 6. THE DOW JONES INDUSTRIAL AVERAGE

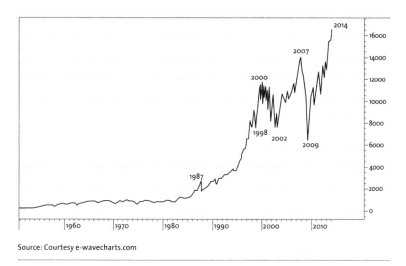

Source: Courtesy e-wavecharts.com

The results have been touted as efficient because resources theoretically have been shifted to higher and better uses. But the human costs of this transformation have been substantial. Ordinary workers have lost jobs and wages, and many communities have been abandoned. Nor have the efficiency benefits been widely shared. As corporations have steadily weakened their workers' bargaining power, the link between productivity and workers' income has been severed. Since 1979, the nation's productivity has risen 65 percent, but workers' median compensation has increased by just 8 percent. Almost all the gains from growth have gone to the top. As noted, the average worker today is no better off than his equivalent was thirty years ago, adjusted for inflation. Most are less economically secure. Not incidentally, few own any shares of stock.

Wages have also been kept down by workers so worried about keeping their jobs that they have willingly accepted lower pay (and its equivalent in the form of paychecks that do not keep up with inflation). Here again, political decisions have played a significant role. Some of the prevailing job insecurity has been the direct consequence of trade agreements that have invited American companies to outsource jobs abroad. As I noted previously, the conventional view equating "free trade" with the "free market," in contrast to government "protectionism," is misguided. Since all nations' markets reflect political decisions about how they should be organized, as a practical matter "free trade" agreements entail complex negotiations about how different market systems are to be integrated. The most important aspects of such negotiations concern items such as intellectual property, finance, and labor. Within these negotiations, the interests of large corporations and Wall Street—to fully protect the value of their intellectual property and financial assets—time and again trump the interests of average working Americans to protect the value of their labor. (A personal confession: When I was secretary of labor in the Clinton administration, I argued against the North American Free Trade Agreement within the confines of the administration but did not air my concerns publicly, believing I could do more good remaining inside than resigning in protest over this and related White House decisions I disagreed with, such as bringing China into the World Trade Organization. In subsequent years I have often wondered whether I made the right choice.)

High levels of unemployment have also contributed to the willingness of workers to settle for lower wages. And here, too, government policies play a significant role. When the Federal Reserve raises interest rates and Congress opts for austerity— more interested in reducing budget deficits than stimulating the economy and reducing unemployment—the resulting joblessness undermines the bargaining power of average workers and translates into lower wages. When the Federal Reserve and Congress do the opposite, the result is more jobs and higher wages. During the Clinton administration the rate of unemployment became so low that hourly workers gained enough bargaining power to get higher wages—the first and only period of sustained wage growth among hourly workers since the late 1970s.

But corporate executives and the denizens of Wall Street prefer most workers to have low wages, in order to generate higher corporate profits, which translate into higher returns for shareholders and, directly and indirectly, for themselves. This is not a winning strategy over the long term because higher returns ultimately depend on more sales, which requires that the vast middle class have enough purchasing power to buy what can be produced. But from the limited viewpoint of the CEO of a single large firm, or of an investment banker or fund manager on Wall Street, all operating globally and more concerned about the next quarter's returns than about profits over the long term, low wages appear advantageous. Low wages are also thought to reduce the risk of inflation, which can erode the value of their assets.

Reducing the bargaining power of the middle class has also entailed shifting the risks of economic change to them. Public policies that emerged during the New Deal and World War II had placed most of the risks squarely on large corporations by means of strong employment contracts, along with Social Security, worker's compensation, forty-hour workweeks with time and a half for overtime, and employer-provided health benefits (wartime price controls encouraged such tax-free benefits as substitutes for wage increases). A majority of the employees of large companies remained with the companies for life, and their paychecks rose steadily with seniority, productivity, the cost of living, and corporate profits. By the 1950s this employment relationship was so commonplace that it was not an exaggeration to say that employees possessed, in effect, property rights in their jobs and their companies.

But after the junk bond and takeover mania of the 1980s, that relationship broke down. Even full-time workers who have put in decades with a company can now find themselves without a job overnight—with no severance pay, no help finding another job, and no health insurance. Nearly one out of every five working Americans is in a part-time job. A growing number are temporary workers, freelancers, independent contractors, or consultants, whose incomes and work schedules vary from week to week or even day to day. By 2014, 66 percent of American workers were living paycheck to paycheck.

The risk of getting old with no pension is also rising. In 1980, more than 80 percent of large and medium-sized firms gave their workers defined-benefit pensions that guaranteed them a fixed amount of money every month after they retired. Now, the share is below one-third. Instead, they offer defined-contribution plans, where the risk has been shifted to the workers. When the stock market tanks, as it did in 2008, their 401(k) plans tank along with it. Today, a third of all workers with matching defined-benefit plans contribute nothing because they don't have the cash, which means their employers do not provide any matching funds. Among workers earning less than $50,000, the share that contributes to a defined-benefit plan is even lower. Overall, the portion of workers with any pension connected to their job has fallen from just over half in 1979 to under 35 percent today. In MetLife's 2014 survey of employees, 40 percent anticipated that their employers would reduce benefits even further.

Meanwhile, the risk of a sudden loss of income also continues to rise. Even before the crash of 2008, the Panel Study of Income Dynamics at the University of Michigan found that over any given two-year stretch, about half of all families experienced some decline in income. And those downturns were becoming progressively larger. In the 1970s, the typical drop was about 25 percent. By the late 1990s, it was 40 percent. By the mid-2000s, family incomes rose and fell twice as much as they did in the mid-1970s, on average.

Workers who are economically insecure are not in a position to demand higher wages. They are driven more by fear than by opportunity. This is another central reality of American capitalism as organized by those with the political power to make it so.

A third driving force behind the declining power of the middle class has been the demise of unions. Fifty years ago, when General Motors was the largest employer in America, the typical GM worker earned $35.00 an hour in today's dollars. By 2014, America's largest employer was Walmart, and the average hourly wage of Walmart workers was $11.22. (Walmart will raise the pay of its lowest-paid workers to $10.00 dollars an hour, starting in February 2016.) This does not mean the typical GM employee a half century ago was "worth" more than three times what the typical Walmart employee in 2014 was worth. The GM worker was not better educated or more motivated than the Walmart worker. The real difference was that GM workers a half century ago had a strong union behind them that summoned the collective bargaining power of all autoworkers to get a substantial share of company revenues for its members. And because more than a third of workers across America belonged to a labor union, the bargains those unions struck with employers raised the wages and benefits of nonunionized workers as well. Nonunion firms knew they would be unionized if they did not come close to matching the union contracts.

Today's Walmart workers do not have a union to negotiate a better deal. They are on their own. And because fewer than 7 percent of today's private-sector workers are unionized, most employers across America do not have to match union contracts. This puts unionized firms at a competitive disadvantage. The result has been a race to the bottom.

Some argue that the decline of American unions is simply the result of "market forces." But other nations, such as Germany, have been subject to many of the same "market forces" and yet continue to have strong unions. And these unions continue to provide their middle classes sufficient bargaining power to command a significant share of economic growth—a much larger share than that received by the middle class in the United States. In contrast to decades of nearly stagnant wage growth for most Americans, real average hourly pay in Germany has risen by almost 30 percent since 1985. And as I said earlier, while the percentage of total income going to the top 1 percent in the United States grew from 10 percent in the 1960s to well over 20 percent by 2013, the richest 1 percent of German households continues to receive about 11 percent of total income there. That percentage has remained roughly the same for four decades.

Why the difference? Look to politics and the allocation of power, especially when it comes to unions. Here it is useful to consider the building block of capitalism I refer to as market power, and the role of government in establishing its limits. In the first few decades that the Sherman Antitrust Act was in place, unions were among the primary targets. When railroad workers went on strike in 1894, the federal courts ruled the strike an "illegal restraint of trade" under the act. President Grover Cleveland dispatched two thousand troops to break it up, resulting in the death of a dozen strikers and the demise of the incipient American Railway Union. The union movement was thought by many business leaders to pose a fundamental threat to the nation, and its objectives to run counter to the principles of economics. The president of the National Association of Manufacturers warned in 1903 that "organized labor knows but one law and that is the law of physical force—the law of the Huns and the Vandals, the law of the savage. . . . Composed as it is of the men of muscle rather than the men of intelligence, and commanded by leaders who are at heart disciples of revolution, it is not strange that organized labor stands for principles that are in direct conflict with the natural laws of economics."

But as average working Americans gained political power, they were able to legitimize unions and establish them as a critical part of the economy. In the Progressive Era, Congress passed the Clayton Antitrust Act of 1914, which appeared to exempt unions from the antitrust laws by enunciating the principle that "the labor of a human being is not a commodity or article of commerce." After the Supreme Court in 1921 somewhat recalcitrantly interpreted the Clayton Antitrust Act to outlaw unions (with Justices Holmes, Brandeis, and Clarke dissenting), Congress finally and forever legalized them in the Norris-LaGuardia Act of 1932. The National Labor Relations Act of 1935 went further, guaranteeing workers the right to organize into unions and imposing on employers the legal responsibility to bargain with them.

As unions gained economic power in the late 1930s and 1940s, they gained further political power and wielded it to further enlarge the bargaining clout of American workers. After the legendary Treaty of Detroit in 1950, when Big Business and Big Labor agreed to share productivity gains in exchange for labor peace, the rate of unionization increased dramatically, as did wages and benefits. Which is why, by the mid-1950s, almost a third of all employees in the private sector of the economy belonged to a union, and why the median wage increased in tandem with productivity growth.

Starting in the late 1970s, the process went into reverse. Union membership began to decline, as did the economic and political power of unions, along with the bargaining clout of most workers. The reasons for the decline involved the changes I've already noted—globalization combined with labor-replacing technologies, as well as the shift in corporate mission toward maximizing shareholder returns. But it was also the consequence of political and legal decisions that diminished the economic clout of unions and, in consequence, the political power of unions to avoid further erosion. Ronald Reagan's notorious firing of the nation's air traffic controllers for going on strike—something he had every right to do because they had no right to strike—also signaled to the nation's large employers that America had embarked on a different era of labor relations. CEOs whose corporations had high percentages of unionized workers insisted on wage concessions as a condition for maintaining their jobs. Many moved, or threatened to move, their facilities to "right-to-work" states, which had laws permitting employees to forgo union dues and membership as a condition of employment.

As I have noted, the strategic use of bankruptcy to eliminate union contracts, utilized by American Airlines in 2013, was another practice begun in the 1980s. In what would become a repeating nightmare for unionized airline workers, Frank Lorenzo, who was CEO of Continental Airlines in 1983, took the cash-strapped carrier into bankruptcy, ripped up its labor contracts, laid off thousands of workers, and hired replacements for striking pilots and flight attendants. He then paid his new employees half what they had been paid under the former contracts and demanded they work longer hours. In 1993, Northwest Airlines threatened bankruptcy and insisted on wage concessions from flight attendants and mechanics. A decade later, when more than four thousand Northwest mechanics went on strike, the airline outsourced most of their jobs. In 2002, United Airlines entered bankruptcy—forcing its pilots and flight attendants to accept pay cuts ranging from 9.5 percent to 11.8 percent—and then emerged from bankruptcy in 2006, more profitable than ever.

When the Taft-Hartley Act of 1947 allowed right-to-work laws, the practical consequence was to let workers who did not pay dues get a free ride off of those who did, thereby undermining the incentive for anyone to join a union in the first place. Yet until the 1980s, such laws had minimal effect because they were enacted in southern and western states, while most industries remained in the North and Midwest. But as corporations came under increasing pressure to show high returns and cut labor costs, many CEOs found right-to-work states more alluring. In 2012, even the old heartland industrial states of Indiana and Michigan enacted right-to-work laws. In 2015, Wisconsin joined in.

Workers who inhabited the local service economy—retail, restaurants, custodial, hotels, elder and child care, hospitals, transportation—faced a different challenge from their counterparts in big industry. Their jobs were in less danger of disappearing because they couldn't be outsourced abroad and most would not be automated. In fact, the number of local service jobs in America has continued to grow. The real problem is that these jobs have tended to pay very low wages, rarely include any benefits, and provide little chance of advancement. Significantly, most of them are not unionized. If they were, these workers would have more bargaining power with their employers.

Walmart and major fast-food chains have been aggressively anti-union. Facing the possibility that their workers might seek to be unionized, the firms have erected procedural roadblocks to union votes, used delaying tactics to retaliate against workers who try to organize, and intimidated others into rejecting the union. Many of these tactics were illegal under the National Labor Relations Act, but in the 1980s, as noted, Congress cut appropriations for enforcing the act. As a result, the National Labor Relations Board, charged with protecting workers' rights to form unions and bargain collectively, developed long backlogs of cases. Even when employers were found to have violated the law by firing workers illegally, the board imposed minuscule penalties on them, such as merely requiring them to pay the wrongly fired workers the wages lost since they were dismissed from their jobs. A succession of Democratic presidents promised legislation streamlining the process for forming unions and increasing penalties on employers who violated the law, but nothing came of these promises.

The result has been a steady decline in the percentage of private-sector workers who are unionized. Not incidentally, that decline parallels the decline in the share of total income going to the middle class (see figure 7).

The underlying problem, then, is not that average working Americans are "worth" less in the market than they had been, or that they have been living beyond their means. The problem is that they have steadily lost the bargaining power needed to receive as large a portion of the economy's gains as they commanded in the first three decades after World War II, and their means have not kept up with what the economy could otherwise provide them.

FIGURE 7. AS UNION MEMBERSHIP DECLINES, THE SHARE OF INCOME GOING TO THE MIDDLE CLASS SHRINKS

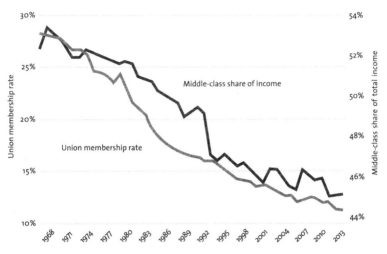

Source: Center for American Progress Action Fund analysis based on union membership rates from updated Barry T. Hirsch, David A. MacPherson, and Wayne G. Vroman, "Estimates of Union Density by State," *Monthly Labor Review* 124, no. 7 (2001):51–55, available at http://unionstats.gsu.edu/MonthlyLaborReviewArticle.htm. Middle-class share of total income is from Bureau of the Census, Table H-2: *Share of Aggregate Income Received by Each Fifth and Top 5 Percent of Households* (2013), available at http://www.census.gov/hhes/www/income/data/historical/household.

To attribute this to the impersonal workings of the "free market" is to ignore how the market has been reorganized since the 1980s, and by whom. It is to disregard the power of moneyed interests who have received a steadily larger share of economic gains as a result of that power. It is not to acknowledge that as their gains have continued to accumulate, so has their power to accumulate even more. And it is to overlook the marked decline of *counter-vailing* power in our political-economic system.

14

The Rise of the Working Poor

The standard assumption that work determines worth—and validates one's personal virtue and social responsibility—is further confounded by a substantial increase in the number of people working full-time who are still poor, and a simultaneous surge in the comparatively smaller ranks of people who do not work at all but are rich. It is difficult to hold firm to the belief that people are "worth" what they earn when more and more people who are working full-time do not earn enough to lift themselves and their families out of poverty, while another group of people at the opposite end of the income spectrum have so much wealth—much of it inherited—that they can live comfortably off the income it generates without ever breaking a sweat.

Until quite recently, poverty was largely confined to those who did not work—widows and children, the elderly, the disabled and seriously ill, and those who had lost their jobs. Public safety nets and private charities were created to help them. It was rare for a full-time worker to be in poverty because, for the reasons I have noted, the economy generated a plethora of middle-class jobs that paid reasonably well and were inherently secure. This is no longer the case. Some politicians cling to the view, as expressed, for example, by Speaker of the House John Boehner in 2014, when he said the poor have "this idea" that "I really don't have to work. I don't really want to do this. I think I'd rather just sit around." The reality is that America's poor work diligently, often more than forty hours a week, sometimes in two or more jobs. Yet they and their families remain poor.

There are several reasons for the growth of America's working poor. First, wages at the bottom have continued to drop, adjusted for inflation. By 2013, the ranks of the working poor had swelled to forty-seven million people in the United States, one out of every seven Americans. One-fourth of all American workers were in jobs paying below what a full-time, full-year worker needed in order to support a family of four above the federally defined poverty line. The downward trend of low wages continued even in the so-called recovery following the Great Recession. Between 2010 and 2013, average incomes for the bottom fifth dropped 8 percent, and their average wealth declined 21 percent. According to a study by Oxfam America, more than half of America's forty-six million users of food pantries and other charitable food programs in 2013 had jobs or were members of working families.

It is doubtful that all these working people came to be "worth" that much less, except in the tautological sense that their pay dropped. In reality, the decline has had a great deal to do with their lack of economic and political power. CEOs seeking profits in a lackluster economy have continued to slash labor costs, often by outsourcing the work, substituting automated machines, or forcing workers to accept lower wages. This process has pushed many previously middle-class workers into local service jobs that pay less than the jobs they once had. Low-paying industries such as retail and fast food accounted for 22 percent of the jobs lost in the Great Recession. But they generated 44 percent of the jobs added between the end of the recession and 2013, according to a report from the National Employment Law Project. Employers in these industries tend to be virulently anti-union and have fought successfully against any efforts to organize their workers.

·　　·　　·

Meanwhile, the real value of the federal minimum wage has been steadily eroded by inflation. Congress (to be more precise, Republicans in Congress) has chosen not to raise it to compensate for this decline. The National Restaurant Association and the National Retail Federation, along with the largest fast-food chains and retailers that support them, have lobbied against any increase in the federal minimum wage, which is tantamount to allowing it to erode even further. By 2014, its real value ($7.25 an hour) was below the level to which it had been raised in 1996, when, as secretary of labor, I had led the political fight to raise it. Had the minimum wage retained the value it had in 1968, it would be $10.86 an hour. And, of course, by 2014 the nation's economy was far larger than it was then, and far more productive.

Some have claimed, nonetheless, that any attempt to restore the real value of the minimum wage will cause employers to fire workers at the lowest rungs, because such workers would no longer be "worth" the cost. In June 2014, at a conference for the Republicans' largest donors hosted by Charles and David Koch at the luxurious St. Regis Monarch Beach Resort in Dana Point, California, Richard Fink, the Kochs' in-house economist, sounded off against the minimum wage. "The big danger of minimum wage isn't the fact that some people are being paid more than their value-added," he said. "It's the five hundred thousand people that will not have a job because of minimum wage." Fink warned that such a large group of disillusioned and unemployed people would become "the main recruiting ground for totalitarianism, for fascism." The conference-goers presumably nodded in sober agreement before getting back to their foie gras.

The mythology that a minimum-wage increase (or, in real terms, restoring it to its 1968 level) would cause employers to reduce employment is a common trope. A corollary is that getting rid of the minimum wage altogether and allowing employers to pay what employees are "worth" will reduce or even eliminate unemployment. As former congresswoman Michele Bachmann once put it, if the minimum wage were repealed "we could potentially virtually wipe out unemployment completely because we would be able to offer jobs at whatever level." Theoretically, Bachmann is correct. But her point is irrelevant. It is no great feat for an economy to create a large number of very-low-wage jobs. Slavery, after all, was a full-employment system.

In fact, evidence suggests that few if any jobs would be lost if the minimum wage were to be increased at least to its 1968 level, adjusted for inflation. Unlike industrial jobs, minimum-wage retail service jobs cannot be outsourced abroad. Nor are these workers likely to be replaced by automated machinery and computers, because the service they provide is personal and direct: Someone has to be on hand to help customers or dole out the food. In addition, and significantly, the gains from a higher minimum wage extend well beyond those who receive it directly. More money in the pockets of low-wage workers means more sales in the places where they live, which in turn creates faster growth and more jobs. Research by Arindrajit Dube, T. William Lester, and Michael Reich confirms this. They examined employment in several hundred pairs of adjacent counties lying on opposite sides of state borders, each with different minimum wages (one at the federal minimum, the other at a higher minimum enacted by a state) and found no statistically significant increase in unemployment in the higher-minimum-wage counties, even after four years. (Other researchers who found contrary results failed to control for counties where unemployment was already growing before the minimum wage had been increased.) Dube, Lester, and Reich also found that employee turnover was lower where the minimum wage was higher, presumably saving employers money on recruiting and training new workers.

Most workers earning the minimum wage are no longer teenagers seeking additional spending money. According to the Bureau of Labor Statistics, the median age of fast-food workers in 2014 was twenty-eight, and the median age of women in those jobs, who constituted two-thirds of such workers, was thirty-two. The median age of workers in big-box retail establishments was over thirty. More than a quarter of them have children. These workers are typically major breadwinners for their families, accounting for at least half their family's earnings.

Needless to say, a higher minimum wage would also reduce the necessity for other taxpayers to pay for the Medicaid, food stamps, and additional assistance these workers and their families need in order to cope with poverty. A study by my colleagues at the University of California, Berkeley and researchers at the University of Illinois at Urbana-Champaign found that in 2012, 52 percent of fast-food workers were dependent on some form of public assistance, and they received almost $7 billion in support from federal and state governments. That sum is in effect a subsidy the rest of American taxpayers pay the fast-food industry for the industry's failure to pay its workers enough to live on.

Whatever wage gains these workers receive are rarely passed on to consumers in the form of higher prices. That is because big-box retailers and fast-food chains compete intensely for customers and have no choice but to keep their prices low. It is notable, for example, that in Denmark, where McDonald's workers over the age of eighteen earn the equivalent of twenty dollars an hour, Big Macs cost only thirty-five cents more than they do in the United States. Any wage gains low-paid workers receive will more than likely come out of profits—which, in turn, will slightly reduce returns to shareholders and the compensation packages of top executives. I do not find this especially troubling. According to the National Employment Law Project, most low-wage workers are employed by large corporations that, by 2013, were enjoying healthy profits. Three-quarters of these employers (the fifty biggest employers of low-wage workers) were generating higher profits than they did before the recession. Between 2000 and 2013, the compensation of the CEOs of fast-food companies quadrupled, in constant dollars, to an average of $24 million a year. Walmart, too, pays its executives handsomely. In 2012, Walmart's CEO received $20.7 million. Not incidentally, the wealth of the Walton family—which still owns the lion's share of Walmart stock—by then exceeded the wealth of the bottom 40 percent of American families combined, according to an analysis by the Economic Policy Institute.

Another reason for the rise in the number of working poor is a basic shift in the criteria used by the government to determine eligibility for government assistance. As I noted, assistance used to be targeted to the nonemployed. Now, those who are out of work receive very little. By 2014, only 26 percent of jobless Americans were receiving any kind of jobless benefit. Typically, recipients of public assistance must be working in order to qualify. Bill Clinton's welfare reform of 1996 pushed the poor off welfare and into work, but the work available to them has provided low wages and offered few ladders into the middle class. The Earned Income Tax Credit, a wage subsidy, has been expanded. But here, too, having a job is a prerequisite. Although it's not necessary to have a job in order to get food stamps, it turns out that a large and growing share of food stamp recipients are employed as well. (The share of recipients with earnings has risen from 19 percent in 1980 to 31 percent in 2012. And since about a third of food stamp recipients cannot work because they're elderly or disabled, far more than 31 percent of those able to work are employed.)

Overall, the new work requirements have not reduced the number or percentage of Americans in poverty. The poverty rate in 2013 was 14.5 percent, well above its levels of 11.3 percent in 2000 and 12.5 percent in 2007. In effect, the new work requirements have merely reduced the number of poor people who are jobless, while increasing the number of poor people who have jobs.

An additional and perhaps more fundamental explanation for the increasing numbers of working poor is found in what has happened to the rest of America. Some would rather deny such a connection and assume the shrinking middle class and redistribution of income and wealth to the top have no bearing on what has happened to those at the bottom. The question we ought to be asking, according to Harvard economist Greg Mankiw, is "How do we help people at the bottom, rather than thwart people at the top?"

Yet the issues are inseparable. As more of the gains have gone to the top, the middle class has lost the purchasing power necessary for ensuring that the economy grows as quickly as it did as recently as the early 2000s. Once the middle class exhausted all its methods for maintaining spending in the face of flat or declining wages—with wives and mothers surging into paid work in the 1970s and 1980s, everyone putting in longer hours in the 1990s, and households falling ever deeper into debt before 2008—the middle class as a whole was unable to spend more. The inevitable consequence has been fewer jobs and slower growth. Both have hit the poor especially hard. Those at the bottom are the first to be fired, last to be hired, and most likely to bear the brunt of declining wages and benefits.

As the income ladder has lengthened and many of its middle rungs have disappeared, moreover, the challenge of moving upward has become more daunting. A smaller middle class yields fewer opportunities for joining it. Shortly after World War II, a child born into poverty had a somewhat better than fifty-fifty chance of becoming middle class by the time he or she was an adult. Today, 43 percent of children born into poverty in the United States will remain in poverty for their entire lives.

Some continue to believe that the poor remain poor because they lack ambition. But what they really lack is opportunity and the political power to get the resources needed to realize that opportunity. It begins with inadequate child care and extends through primary and secondary schools, which helps explain the growing achievement gap between lower- and higher-income children. Thirty years ago, the average gap on SAT-type tests between children of families in the richest 10 percent and bottom 10 percent was about 90 points on an 800-point scale. By 2014 it was 125 points. The gap in the mathematical abilities of American kids, by income, is one of the widest among the sixty-five countries participating in the Program for International Student Assessment. On their reading skills, children from high-income families score 110 points higher, on average, than those from poor families.

The achievement gap between poor kids and wealthy kids isn't mainly about race. In fact, the racial achievement gap has been narrowing. It's a reflection of the nation's widening gulf between poor and wealthy families, of how schools in poor and rich communities are financed, and of the nation's increasing residential segregation by income. According to the Pew Research Center's analysis of the 2010 census tract and household income data, residential segregation by income has grown over the past three decades across the United States.

This matters, because a large portion of the money to support public schools comes from local property taxes. The federal government provides only about 10 percent of all funding, and the states provide 45 percent, on average. The rest is raised locally. Most states do try to give more money to poor districts, but most also cut way back on their spending during the recession and haven't nearly made up for the cutbacks. Meanwhile, real estate markets in lower-income communities remain weak, so local tax revenues are down. As we segregate by income into different communities, schools in lower-income areas have fewer resources than ever. The result is widening disparities in funding per pupil, to the direct disadvantage of poor kids.

The wealthiest, highest-spending districts are now providing about twice as much funding per student as are the lowest-spending districts, according to a federal advisory commission report. In some states, such as California, the ratio is greater than three to one. What are called "public schools" in many of America's wealthy communities aren't really public at all. In effect, they're private schools, whose tuition is hidden away in the purchase price of upscale homes there, and in the corresponding property taxes.

Even where courts have required richer school districts to subsidize poorer ones, large inequalities remain. Rather than pay extra taxes that would go to poorer districts, many parents in upscale communities have quietly shifted their financial support to tax-deductible parents' foundations designed to enhance their own schools. About 12 percent of the more than fourteen thousand school districts across America are funded in part by such foundations. They're paying for everything from a new school auditorium (Bowie, Maryland) to a high-tech weather station and language arts program (Newton, Massachusetts). "Parents' foundations," observed *The Wall Street Journal*, "are visible evidence of parents' efforts to reconnect their money to their kids"—and not, it should have been noted, to kids in another community, who are likely to be poorer.

As a result of all this, the United States is one of only three out of thirty-four advanced nations surveyed by the Organization for Economic Cooperation and Development (OECD) whose schools serving higher-income children have more funding per pupil and lower student-teacher ratios than do schools serving poor students (the two others are Turkey and Israel). Other advanced nations do it differently. Their national governments provide 54 percent of funding, on average, and local taxes account for less than half the portion they do in America. And they target a disproportionate share of national funding to poorer communities. As Andreas Schleicher, who runs the OECD's international education assessments, told *The New York Times*, "The vast majority of OECD countries either invest equally into every student or disproportionately more into disadvantaged students. The U.S. is one of the few countries doing the opposite."

Money isn't everything, obviously. But how can we pretend it doesn't count? Money buys the most experienced teachers, less-crowded classrooms, high-quality teaching materials, and after-school programs. Yet we seem to be doing everything except getting more money to the schools that most need it. We're requiring all schools to meet high standards, requiring students to take more and more tests, and judging teachers by their students' test scores. But until we recognize that we're systematically hobbling schools serving disadvantaged kids, we're unlikely to make much headway.

In all these ways, poverty among those who work and their political powerlessness are intimately connected.

15

The Rise of the Non-working Rich

As the ranks of the working poor have swelled, so too have those of the non-working rich. Although constituting a far smaller group, their incomes have soared in recent years. They do not need to work because they have ample earnings from income-producing assets such as stocks, bonds, and real estate. Are they "worth" it? To be sure, some of the non-working rich have accumulated their assets through their own savings, based on work that has been "worth" it to the extent we have already examined. When these assets increase in value, though, their current owners are rarely responsible. Assets appreciate for many reasons, such as population growth, limits on the supply of a valued commodity, or, as we have observed with share prices, changes in the incentives and bargaining relationships underlying a corporation. Politics and policy can play significant roles here, as well. For example, the value of a house or apartment building may rise dramatically because people are drawn to a neighborhood by virtue of improved schools and better public transportation or, alternatively, because buyers have more money due to the relaxation of lending standards.

A growing portion of the non-working rich have never worked, however. They have inherited their wealth. Their good fortune lies in being born into families that not only give them every advantage when they are young but also bequeath to them sufficient wealth that they continue to have every advantage regardless of what they do or fail to do for the rest of their lives.

The "self-made" man or woman, the symbol of American meritocracy, is disappearing. Six of today's ten wealthiest Americans are heirs to prominent fortunes. As I've noted, the Walmart heirs have more wealth than the bottom 40 percent of Americans combined.

And this is just the beginning. America is on the cusp of the largest intergenerational transfer of wealth in history. A study from the Boston College Center on Wealth and Philanthropy projects that $36 trillion could be passed down to heirs in the half century leading up to 2061. A U.S. Trust bank poll in 2013 of Americans with more than $3 million of investable assets shows a significant generational divide: Nearly three-quarters of those over age sixty-nine and a majority of boomers just below them are the first in their generation to accumulate significant wealth. For the rich under the age of thirty-five, however, inherited wealth is more common. This is the dynastic form of wealth that, as French economist Thomas Piketty reminds us, has provided the major source of income for European aristocracy for centuries. It is about to become the major source for a new American aristocracy.

The reason for the rise of the non-working rich should by now be apparent. As income from work has become more concentrated, a relatively small number of very wealthy Americans have invested their income in capital assets. They have also invested some of it in politics—either directly, through their own contributions and connections, or indirectly, through their corporations, trade associations, and the managers of their financial portfolios. In consequence, the rules of the game have favored their accumulation of wealth. By 2014, the compounded result of these capital investments and corresponding political investments was to concentrate wealth even faster than to concentrate income.

Consider that in 1978, the richest 1 percent of households accounted for 20 percent of business income. By 2007 they accounted for 49 percent. They were also taking in 75 percent of all capital gains. By 2014, the value of the stock market was significantly higher than it was before the crash of 2008. Accordingly, the top was earning substantially more from their investments and acquiring even more of all capital gains.

Both political parties have been complicit in this great wealth transfer, but Republicans have encouraged it more ardently than Democrats. For example, family trusts used to be limited to about ninety years. Legal changes implemented under the Reagan administration led many states to extend them in perpetuity. So-called dynasty trusts now allow super-rich families to pass on to their heirs money and property largely free from taxes, and to do so for generations. George W. Bush's largest tax reductions, in 2001 and 2003, helped high earners but provided even more help to people living off their accumulated wealth. While the top tax rate on income from work dropped from 39.6 percent to 35 percent, the top rate on dividends went from 39.6 percent (taxed as ordinary income) to 15 percent, and the estate tax was completely eliminated.

Barack Obama rolled back some of these cuts, but many remained. Before George W. Bush was president, the estate tax applied to assets in excess of $2 million per couple, at a rate of 55 percent. By 2014, it applied only to assets in excess of $10 million per couple, at a 40 percent rate. House Republicans sought to go even further. Representative Paul Ryan's so-called road map eliminated all taxes on interest, dividends, capital gains, and estates. By 2013, only 1.4 out of every 1,000 estates owed any estate tax, and the effective rate they paid was only 17 percent.

Meanwhile, the tax rate paid by America's wealthy on their capital gains—the major source of income for the non-working rich—dropped from 33 percent in the late 1980s to 23.8 percent in 2014, putting it substantially lower than the tax rate on ordinary income. Another large and well-hidden benefit enjoyed by heirs to large fortunes is found in a tax law providing that if the owner of a capital asset whose worth increases over his lifetime holds on to it until he dies, his heirs do not have to pay any capital gains taxes on that asset's appreciated value. These so-called unrealized gains have become a major source of dynastic wealth in America, generating ever-greater value as they pass from generation to generation, without incurring any capital gains taxes. They now account for more than half the value of assets held by estates worth more than $100 million.

Yet the specter of an entire generation that does nothing for its money other than speed-dial its wealth management advisors is not particularly attractive. Nor is it good for our economy and society. It puts more and more of the responsibility for investing a substantial portion of the nation's assets into the hands of a small number of people who have never had to work for their incomes and have no idea how average people live and what they need. It is also increasingly dangerous to our democracy, as dynastic wealth inevitably and invariably accumulates even more political influence and power.

These growing accumulations of wealth by people who do not work for a living are sometimes justified by their philanthropic generosity. Undoubtedly, super-rich family foundations, such as the Bill & Melinda Gates Foundation, are doing a great deal of good. Wealthy philanthropic giving is on the rise, paralleling the rise in super-rich giving that characterized the late nineteenth century, when magnates (the aforementioned robber barons) such as Andrew Carnegie and John D. Rockefeller established philanthropic institutions that survive today. We are living through what Professor Rob Reich of Stanford University (no relation) calls "the second golden age of American philanthropy."

It is their business how they donate their money, of course.

But not entirely. Donors can deduct such donations from their taxable incomes, and the charitable foundations or endowments that receive them do not have to pay taxes on the income they generate. In economic terms, these deductions and tax-free earnings are the equivalent of government subsidies. In 2011, the last year for which good data are available, they totaled an estimated $54 billion. As Reich has pointed out, these public subsidies are doled out typically under the watchful eyes of the wealthy people who made the donations, without any accountability to the public. If you do not approve of how the wealthy are allocating their charitable dollars, you are out of luck. To put this into some perspective, $50 billion is more than the federal government spent in 2011 on the Temporary Assistance for Needy Families program (what's left of welfare), school lunches for poor kids, and Head Start put together.

In addition, although it is called a "charitable deduction," very little of this public subsidy ends up with the poor. A 2005 analysis by Indiana University's Center on Philanthropy showed that even under the most generous assumptions only about a third of "charitable" giving is targeted to helping poor people. A large portion is allocated to operas, art museums, symphonies, and theaters—all worthy enterprises, to be sure, but not "charities" as we normally use the term. A while ago, New York's Lincoln Center held a fund-raising gala supported by the charitable contributions of hedge-fund industry leaders, several of whom take home $1 billion a year. Poor New Yorkers rarely attend concerts at Lincoln Center.

Another portion goes to the elite prep schools and universities that benefactors once attended or want their children to attend. (Such institutions typically give preference in admissions to applicants and legacies whose parents have been notably generous, a kind of affirmative action for the wealthy.) Harvard, Yale, Princeton, and the rest of the Ivy League are important institutions, but they do not educate large numbers of poor young people. (The University of California, Berkeley, where I teach, has almost as many poor students eligible for Pell Grants as the entire Ivy League put together.) Moreover, as I have noted earlier, these elite universities are far less likely to graduate aspiring social workers and legal aid attorneys than aspiring investment bankers and corporate consultants.

Private university endowments in 2014 totaled around $550 billion, centered in a handful of prestigious institutions. Harvard's endowment is more than $32 billion, followed by Yale at $20.8 billion, Stanford at $18.7 billion, and Princeton at $18.2 billion. (In 2013 Harvard launched a capital campaign for another $6.5 billion.) Because of the charitable tax deduction, the amount of government subsidy to these institutions in the form of tax deductions is about one out of every three dollars contributed. A few years back, Meg Whitman, now CEO of Hewlett-Packard, contributed $30 million to Princeton. In return she received a tax break estimated to be around $10 million. In effect, Princeton received $20 million from Whitman and $10 million from the U.S. Treasury—that is, from you and me and other taxpayers who made up the difference. Add in these endowments' exemptions from taxes on capital gains and on income they earn, and the total government expenditure is even larger. Divide by the relatively small number of students attending these institutions, and the amount of subsidy per student is huge. The annual government subsidy to Princeton University, for example, is about $54,000 per student, according to an estimate by economist Richard Vedder. Other elite private universities aren't far behind.

Dean Henry Brady of the Goldman School of Public Policy at Berkeley has pointed out the stark contrast with public universities, responsible for educating more than 70 percent of students pursuing higher education. Public universities have little or no endowment income. Instead, they get almost all their funding from state governments. But these subsidies have been shrinking. State and local financing for public higher education came to about $76 billion in 2013, nearly 10 percent less than a decade before. Since more students attend public universities now than ten years ago, that decline represents a 30 percent drop per student. That means the average annual government subsidy per student at a public university comes to less than $6,000, about one-tenth the per-student government subsidy at Princeton. This is another cause and consequence of the squeeze on the middle class and the poor and the soaring wealth of those at the top.

We are the authors of our own fates. But, as I have made clear, we are not the producers or directors of the larger dramas in which we find ourselves. Other forces are at work in determining not only what we are able to earn but also what we are able to accomplish, as well as the strength of our voices and the efficacy of our ideals. Those who are rich and becoming ever more so are neither smarter nor morally superior to anyone else. They are, however, often luckier, and more privileged and more powerful. As such, their high net worth does not necessarily reflect their worth as human beings.

By the same token, the vast majority who work hard for a living, and struggle against currents that are often pulling them backward and causing them to fear for themselves and their families, are not blameworthy, nor are they alone. Their voices, however, have become muted and many have grown disillusioned or cynical. The laborer who told me that he could have earned more if he "had the brains for it" saw his low pay and lowly status as the product of his own failings rather than of an economic system that has failed him by denying him sufficient bargaining power to do better. Meanwhile, the poor who cannot find their way out of poverty are not losers or failures, either, although that is how many of them view themselves. The far more significant fact is they are utterly powerless in society.

To state it another way, no one should confuse income for virtue, net worth for worthiness. The underlying reality is that capitalism is not working as it should or as it can. The mythology that one is paid what one is worth must be seen for what it is.

I am not accusing the wealthy of doing anything nefarious or intentionally harmful. There is no reason to suppose that top corporate executives, the successes of Wall Street, and other "high-worth" individuals have conspired to hijack the American economy for themselves. Each has merely behaved rationally in pursuit of his or her private interests. As their wealth has increased, so has their political power, and they have quite naturally used that power to enlarge and entrench their wealth. We can criticize them for being selfish and greedy, but they are no more selfish or greedy than are most other people. And some have been enormously generous with their wealth.

But when our system is viewed as a whole—as a political-economic arrangement for allocating rewards for the work people do—there is reason for concern. The meritocratic ideal with which our form of capitalism has been justified does not match the reality in which most of us live and work. The playing field is tilted toward those who have had the resources and power to tilt it in their direction. And as they gain steadily more resources and power, it tilts further.

Globalization and technological changes are real, and they have shaken the economy to its roots—dividing the workforce between a relatively small group that has been able to use these changes to its advantage and a larger number that has not. But that is only a part of the story. The nation could have responded and still can respond to these changes in ways that nonetheless spread prosperity, enlarge the middle class, and provide avenues of upward mobility for the poor. The fact that we have not—that we have instead allowed a relative few at the top to organize the market in ways that have had the opposite effect—is partly our own doing. Reversing this state of affairs is our own responsibility, the topic to which I now turn.

PART III

Countervailing Power

16

Reprise

A summary once again is in order. For what seems like an interminable period of time, the central political debate in American politics (as well as in much of the rest of the capitalist world) has been over the seeming choice between the "free market" and "government." Those on the political right have argued for more market and less government, which normally means lower taxes and less public spending. Those on the political left have wanted more government and less market, which typically has meant higher taxes (at least on the wealthy) and more public services. This debate hides a larger reality: the necessary role of government in designing, organizing, and enforcing the market to begin with. It therefore obscures the myriad choices facing legislators, administrators, and judges in carrying out this basic task, a task that never ceases because ongoing changes in market conditions as well as innovations and technological advances continuously require that new choices be made and old ones be reconsidered.

By ignoring these underlying choices, the old debate over "free market" versus "government" diverts attention from how these decisions are made and hides the growing influence of large corporations, Wall Street, and wealthy individuals over them. As those at the top have gained economic power, their political influence over these basic rules of the game has also increased—which in turn has enhanced their economic power still further. Many of those who most loudly and adamantly celebrate the "free market" are among the largest beneficiaries of this hidden process. By removing the central reality of power from public understanding of how the economy functions, they conveniently remove themselves.

In consequence, the only readily observable phenomena are explicit redistributions by government from the rich to the poor through taxes and transfer payments. These have grown in recent decades as the income gap between the top and the bottom has widened. As a result, inequality after taxes and transfer payments is not as wide as it would be without them.

Yet these downward redistributions constitute only a small part of the overall picture. In reality, most redistribution in recent years has been in the other direction—upward from consumers, workers, small businesses, and small investors to top corporate and financial executives, Wall Street traders and portfolio managers, and the major owners of capital assets. But this upward redistribution is invisible. The main conduits for it are hidden within the rules of the market—property, monopolization, contract, bankruptcy, and enforcement—rules that have been shaped by those with substantial wealth and political clout. It is, in this sense, a *pre*distribution upward that occurs inside the market mechanism itself, a small portion of which government later redistributes downward to the poor through taxes and transfer payments.

As the economy has shifted toward ideas and away from tangible products, these underlying rules (and the choices they reflect) have become even more obscure—and therefore even more easily manipulated by those with the resources to do so. The most valuable property is now intellectual property, such as patents and copyrights, which have quietly been enlarged by giant corporations through patent "product hopping"; "pay-for-delay" agreements between pharmaceutical manufacturers and generic drug companies; and changes in copyright laws that now extend ninety-five years.

Similarly, the most important forms of market dominance now occur over networks such as broadband, genetic seed traits, standard digital platforms, and financial systems controlled by a handful of Wall Street banks. And here, too, large corporations and Wall Street have used their political influence to enlarge their market power and avoid economic incursions by small competitors or legal threats from antitrust law.

Likewise, modern contracts are less about things than about data and ideas. This has enabled powerful interests to use insider information against small investors and to require that employees, franchisees, and customers agree to mandatory arbitration or forced waivers of their legal rights. By the same token, bankruptcy laws entail increasingly complex processes that systematically favor large corporations and big banks over workers, homeowners, and those with student debt obligations. Finance has become so opaque that CEOs can time corporate buybacks to coincide with when they cash in their stock options and awards, thereby expropriating value from small shareholders. Meanwhile, workers' negotiating power has eroded through state right-to-work laws, inadequate enforcement of collective bargaining rights, and trade agreements that protect intellectual property and financial assets but not the economic value of jobs.

All of this has been accompanied by enforcement strategies that systematically understaff agencies charged with inspecting and monitoring large corporations and Wall Street, fail to uphold laws or impose inadequate corporate penalties and fines, fail to hold individual executives criminally liable, provide insufficient legal resources relative to corporate and Wall Street lawyers intent on settlements often amounting to mere slaps on the wrist, limit private rights of action, and narrow standing for class actions.

The influence of big corporations, Wall Street, and wealthy individuals over all these market-creating and market-enforcing decisions takes many forms: contributions to political campaigns or to groups that mount advertising campaigns for a candidate or against a politician's opponent; revolving doors between government jobs and lucrative employment in lobbying firms or on Wall

Street, or implicit offers of such jobs after government service; "think tanks" of paid experts and public relations campaigns to convince the public that a particular policy is in their interest; and squadrons of highly paid lobbyists and lawyers that engulf legislatures, administrative hearings, and the courts. Not even prosecutors and judges are immune.

The "free market" serves as a smoke screen for all this. Because of it, the system for distributing economic gains appears to be the natural and inevitable result of neutral forces. The meritocratic ideal presumes that people are paid roughly in proportion to their worth. Those who are paid very little for their work are assumed to be "worth" no more than they receive, and those who are paid a great deal are assumed to be worth no less. It is a small step to view such payments as corresponding to what people deserve in a moral sense. Within this preferred vision of an American meritocracy, the amount of one's income is equated with one's virtue, and net worth with moral worth. Attempts to constrain high incomes with taxes or supplement low incomes through government transfers are thereby seen as intrusions into the market that risk undermining efficiency, distorting incentives, and compromising the moral underpinnings of meritocracy. (Depending on one's political point of view, such a risk may nonetheless be thought necessary in order to achieve fairness.)

But because the organization of the market increasingly reflects political decisions favoring moneyed interests, the system for distributing economic gains through the market does not necessarily correspond to what people are "worth" in any respect other than the tautological. A close examination of why the pay of top executives of large corporations has soared in recent decades and why the compensation of managers and traders on Wall Street has skyrocketed even further has less to do with any supposed surge in the value of their insights or skills than with their increasing power to set market rules that enrich themselves. Likewise, the declining incomes of the typical middle-class household, and the impoverishment of the working poor, are more related to their waning political and economic influence than to their personal shortcomings. Put simply, large corporations, Wall Street, and wealthy individuals have gained substantial power over market rules that generate outcomes favoring them—power that has been compounded as the additional wealth has accorded them even more influence over the rules. Meanwhile, those in the middle and below have lost much of the power they once had—a process that compounds in the opposite direction as their declining economic positions give them less and less influence over the rules.

As I have taken pains to make clear, I do not mean to suggest that those at the top who are shaping the rules are intentionally malevolent. They are acting out of the same self-interest that has been thought to guide the theoretical "free market" toward efficient, and therefore publicly beneficial, outcomes. But rather than a theoretical "free market" they are acting in the real political economy where economic power generates political influence over the rules of the game, which, in turn, serves to enlarge economic power. They are behaving entirely rationally within this system, although the aggregate consequence of their individually rational calculations is neither efficient nor otherwise rational for the system as a whole. To the contrary, it is gradually undermining the system.

As I will show in the following pages, the problem is not their power or influence, per se. It is the comparative lack of power or influence on the other side. There is no longer any significant *countervailing* power, no force to constrain or balance the growing political strength of large corporations, Wall Street, and the very wealthy. The middle class and poor—and the economic interests they encompass—have little or no agency.

We are then left with three questions. First, how will this trend threaten capitalism if countervailing power is not re-established? Second, how can the middle class and the poor regain sufficient countervailing power to reorganize the market in ways that generate broader-based prosperity? And third, what might that reorganization look like?

17

The Threat to Capitalism

America has faced similar questions before. During eras of significant technological change, workers are typically displaced, social systems become destabilized, and the economy goes through rapid cycles of boom and bust. The owners of capital often reap vast rewards, financial elites gain ground, and economic and political power become highly concentrated. Notwithstanding the potential of the new technologies to create broad-based prosperity, the prevailing political and economic systems do not deliver it because those at the top gain increasing control over politics. Large numbers of people understandably feel the game is rigged. These anxieties and frustrations eventually fuel reforms that spread prosperity more broadly.

As I noted at the outset, this pattern characterized the first industrial revolution as it arrived in America and spawned the reforms of the Jacksonian era of the 1830s. President Andrew Jackson and his followers believed elites had accrued unwarranted privileges that had to be removed before average citizens could gain ground. "It is a fixed principle of our political institutions," declared Roger B. Taney, Jackson's attorney general and then Treasury secretary, who would also become the fifth chief justice of the Supreme Court, "to guard against the unnecessary accumulation of power over persons and property in any hands. And no hands are less worthy to be trusted with it than those of a moneyed corporation." The Jacksonians sought to abolish property requirements for voting and allow business firms to incorporate without specific acts of the legislature, and they opposed the Second Bank of the United States, which they believed would be controlled by financial elites. They did not reject capitalism; they rejected aristocracy. They sought a capitalism that would improve the lot of ordinary people rather than merely the elites. (Notably, however, the Jacksonians, including Chief Justice Taney, did not include native Americans or African American slaves among those deserving protection from the nation's elites.)

Similar questions arose during the last decades of the nineteenth century when the second industrial revolution ushered in railroads, steel, oil, and electricity—and at the same time created vast economic combinations (then called "trusts"), concentrated wealth at the top, and fostered urban squalor and political corruption. The lackeys of robber barons literally deposited sacks of money on the desks of pliant legislators, prompting the great jurist Louis Brandeis to note that the nation had a choice: "We can have a democracy or we can have great wealth in the hands of a few," he said, "but we cannot have both."

America made the choice. Public outrage gave birth to the nation's first progressive income tax. President Theodore Roosevelt, railing at the "malefactors of great wealth," used government power to break up the trusts and impose new regulations barring impure food and drugs. He proposed "all contributions by corporations to any political committee or for any political purpose should be forbidden by law," leading Congress to pass the Tillman Act, the first federal law to ban corporate political donations, and, three years later, the Publicity Act, requiring candidates to disclose the identities of all campaign contributors. Meanwhile, several states enacted America's first labor protections, including the forty-hour workweek.

Another era of innovation in the 1920s centered on large-scale enterprise and the mass production of consumer goods—automobiles, telephones, refrigerators, and other durables powered by electricity. Here again, income and wealth became highly concentrated, and Wall Street's riches and influence soared. By the time of the Great Crash of 1929, most Americans could not pay for all the new products and services without going deeply and hopelessly into debt—resulting in a bubble that loudly and inevitably popped. On the heels of this economic crisis came the reforms of the New Deal, giving organized labor the right to bargain collectively with employers, small investors protection from financial fraud, and small businesses protection from large retail chains. In the election of 1936, big business and Wall Street attacked Franklin D. Roosevelt. In a speech at Madison Square Garden he thundered, "Never before in all our history have these forces been so united against one candidate as they stand today. They are unanimous in their hate for me—and I welcome their hatred."

A similar sequence of events began in the late 1970s, when another wave of innovation—including container ships, satellite communications, new materials, computers, digital technologies, and, eventually, the Internet—spawned a new economy, along with great fortunes centering in a relatively few giant companies and individuals, and the effervescent resurgence of Wall Street. As I have noted, however, also beginning in the late 1970s, the real median household income stagnated. The vast American middle class employed several techniques to maintain its purchasing power notwithstanding.* The first was for mothers to move into paid work; the second, for everyone to work longer hours; the third, to use rising home values to extract money through home equity loans or refinancing. By late 2007, debt reached 135 percent of disposable income. But none of these techniques was sustainable. In 2008, the debt bubble burst, just as a similar bubble had burst in 1929. It is not coincidental that 1928 and 2007

---

* For an extended discussion, see my book *Aftershock: The Next Economy and America's Future* (New York: Alfred A. Knopf, 2010).

marked the two peaks of income concentration in America over the last hundred years, in which the richest 1 percent raked in more than 23 percent of total income. The economy cannot function without the purchasing power of a large and growing middle class.

The so-called recovery from the Great Recession has been among the most anemic recoveries in American economic history, especially given how far the economy fell in 2008 and 2009. The ongoing problem is inadequate overall demand, the same impediment that had delivered the economy into the Great Recession in the first place. After the crash of 2008, most Americans did not have the resources to buy enough goods and services to convince businesses to invest, expand, and hire. Hence, unemployment remained unusually high and most households' incomes stagnated or dropped. And because American consumption is a critically important component of demand in the rest of the world, its relative weakness during the recovery was a drag on the global recovery. In consequence, U.S. exports could not make up for the shortfall in domestic demand.

As I write this, at the start of 2015, a recovery of sorts is under way in the United States. Jobs are returning. But most people's wages still are not rising. And wealth and income are still at near record levels of concentration. The richest four hundred Americans have more wealth than the bottom 50 percent of Americans put together; the wealthiest 1 percent own 42 percent of the nation's private assets; and the share of wealth held by the lower half of households has fallen from 3 percent in 1989 to 1 percent today. One way to get your mind around this is to compare a household at the top with the average household. In 1978, the typical household in the wealthiest 0.01 percent was 220 times richer than the average household. By 2012, the household at the top was 1,120 times richer. Since 2000, adjusted for inflation, the weekly earnings of full-time wage and salary workers at the median have dropped, and average hourly wages adjusted for inflation are lower than they were forty years ago.

As Thomas Piketty has shown in *Capital in the Twenty-First Century*, this was the pattern through much of the eighteenth and nineteenth centuries in Europe and, to a lesser extent, in America. And it is coming to be the pattern once again. Piketty is pessimistic that much can be done to reverse it (his sweeping economic data suggest that slow growth will almost automatically concentrate great wealth in relatively few hands). But he disregards the political upheavals and reforms that such wealth concentrations often inspire—such as America's populist revolts of the 1890s followed by the Progressive Era, or even the German socialist movement in the 1870s followed by Otto von Bismarck's creation of the first welfare state.

The phenomenon I have described transcends the business cycle. Figure 8 puts the current era into context by showing what has occurred during every expansion since World War II, and

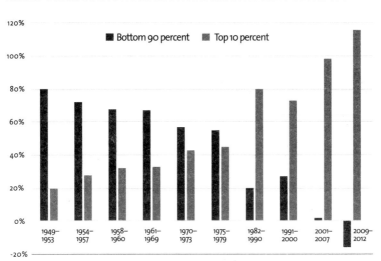

FIGURE 8. DISTRIBUTION OF AVERAGE INCOME GROWTH DURING EXPANSIONS

Source: Pavlina R. Tcherneva, "Reorienting Fiscal Policy: A Bottom-up Approach," *Journal of Post Keynesian Economics* 37, no. 1 (2014): 43–66.

the portion of it going to the wealthiest 10 percent of households and the poorest 90 percent. Three things stand out. First, the bottom 90 percent's share began to drop dramatically between 1982 and 1990. Second, with each upturn, more and more of the benefits have gone to the top. Third, the real incomes of the bottom 90 percent dropped for the first time in the recovery that began in 2009. Never before had median household incomes dropped during an economic recovery. The three-decade pattern suggests the vicious cycle has accelerated: Those with the most economic power have been able to use it to alter the rules of the game to their advantage, thereby adding to their economic power, while most Americans, lacking such power, have seen little or no increase in their real incomes.

This trend is not sustainable, neither economically nor politically. In economic terms, as the middle class and poor receive a declining share of total income, they will lack the purchasing power necessary to keep the economy moving forward. Direct redistributions from the rich sufficient to counter this would be politically infeasible. Meanwhile, as ever-larger numbers of Americans conclude that the game is rigged against them, the social fabric will start to unravel. Confidence in economic institutions is already falling precipitously. In 2001 a Gallup poll found 77 percent of Americans satisfied with opportunities to get ahead by working hard, and only 22 percent were dissatisfied. But since then satisfaction has steadily declined and dissatisfaction increased. By 2014, only 54 percent were satisfied and 45 percent dissatisfied. According to the Pew Research Center, the percentage of Americans who feel that most people who want to get ahead can do so through hard work has dropped by 13 points since 2000.

This pervasive sense of arbitrariness and unfairness undermines economic institutions in several ways. First, it leads to widespread rule breaking. If the game is perceived to be rigged in favor of those at the top, then others are more likely to view cheating as acceptable—stealing and pilfering from employers, rigging time clocks, dissembling about lengths of time away from desk or office, overbilling, skimming off some of the profits, accepting small bribes and kickbacks for awarding a contract or making a deal. But an economy is based on trust. The cumulative effect of even small violations of trust can generate huge costs. Employers feel compelled to tighten rules, giving all employees less discretion; time-consuming screening and security checks are imposed at the end of the workday; additional reviews must be made of all accounts and additional oversight of all transactions; more legal steps and picayune procedures are required so no party will be surprised by opportunist moves of any other. Commercial dealings are hedged about by ever more elaborate contractual provision; creditors demand more burdensome guarantees for additional loans. Across the economy, red tape multiplies with the profusion of finagles it seeks to contain. The only beneficiaries from this economic sclerosis are the lawyers, accountants, auditors, and security staff and screeners whose services are increasingly in demand.

Second, when the game seems rigged and trust deteriorates, loyalty can no longer be assumed. That means less overall willingness to put in extra effort or go the extra mile, to do what is needed but not required, to report unexpected problems or devise novel solutions. Employees or contractors withhold technical information or economic insights that, if shared, could boost joint productivity but could just as easily line the pockets of top executives and reduce the number of jobs. And since investments in such additional knowledge cannot be protected like investments in real estate or machinery or even in intellectual property, generalized distrust reduces the incentives of everyone to make such investments for fear the new knowledge will be expropriated by others.

Third and finally, people who feel subjected to what they consider to be rigged games often choose to subvert the system in ways that cause everyone to lose. Consider, for example, the simulation I do with the students in my Wealth and Poverty class at Berkeley. I have them split up into pairs and ask them to imagine that I'm giving one of the people in each pair $1,000. They can keep some of the money only on the condition that they reach a deal with their partner on how it's to be divided up between them. I explain that they can only make one offer and respond by accepting or declining and can only communicate by the initial recipient writing on a piece of paper how much he'll share with the other, who must then either write "deal" or "no deal" on the paper.

You might think many initial recipients of the imaginary $1,000 would offer $1 or even less to their partner, which their partner would gladly accept. After all, even one dollar is better than ending up with nothing at all. Economic theory tells us such an outcome would be an improvement over the former status quo. But that's not what happens. Most of the $1,000 recipients are far more generous to their partners, offering at least $250. Even more surprising is that most partners decline any offer under $250, even though "no deal" means neither of them will get to keep anything. This game and variations of it have been played by social scientists thousands of times with different groups and pairings, with remarkably similar results.

A far bigger version of the game has been played in recent years on the national stage. But it is for real, as a relative handful of Americans have received ever-larger slices of the total national income while most average Americans, working harder than ever, receive smaller ones. And just as in the simulations, the losers are starting to say "no deal." According to polls, in 2015 most Americans were opposed to the Trans-Pacific Partnership, for example, which was devised by American and Asian trade negotiators to further open trade and commerce between the United States and the nations of the Pacific region. While history and policy point to overall benefits from expanded trade because all of us gain access to cheaper goods and services, in recent years the biggest gains from trade have gone to investors and executives while the burdens have fallen disproportionately on those in the middle and below who have lost good-paying jobs. By 2014, according to polls, most Americans no longer supported trade-opening agreements.

Why would people turn down a deal that makes them better off simply because it makes someone else far, far better off? Some might call this attitude envious or spiteful. But when I ask those of my students who refused to accept anything less than $250 in the distribution game why they did so, they explain that the outcome would otherwise be unfair. Remember, I gave out the $1,000 arbitrarily. The initial recipients didn't have to work for it or be outstanding in any way. In other words, when a game seems rigged, losers are willing to sacrifice some gains in order to prevent winners from walking away with far more—a result that strikes them as unfair. Another explanation I get from students who refused anything less than $250 is they worry that if their partner ends up with more of the money, he'll also end up with far more power, which will rig the game even more. So they're willing to sacrifice some gain in order to avoid a steadily more lopsided and ever more corrupt politics. This suggests that if America's distributional game continues to create a few big winners and many who consider themselves losers by comparison, the losers will try to stop the game—not out of envy but out of a deep-seated sense of unfairness and a fear of unchecked power and privilege.

In summary, when people feel that the system is unfair and arbitrary and that hard work does not pay off, we all end up losing. This is due to several related negative consequences, including widespread cheating or stealing, mounting distrust, and a willingness to forgo joint gains for the sake of preventing those who are well-off from becoming even better off. The gross national product may nonetheless rise due to additional spending on security personnel, accountants, auditors, lawyers, screening devices, monitoring equipment, and so on, but these defensive expenditures do not improve the quality of life of the typical American. The other negative consequence, as we have seen, is chronically inadequate demand for goods and services caused by insufficient purchasing power and economic insecurity. Together, these responses impose incalculable damage on an economic system. They turn an economy and a society into what mathematicians would call a "negative-sum" game. When capitalism ceases to deliver economic gains to the majority, it eventually stops delivering them at all—even to a wealthy minority at the top. It is unfortunate that few of those at the top have yet to come to understand this fundamental truth.

This dynamic threatens not only American capitalism; capitalism is failing elsewhere as well. By 2014, wages were stagnant or falling and economic insecurity rising in much of Europe and in Japan. Consumers in China were gaining ground, but consumption failed to grow as a share of China's increasingly productive economy, while inequality in China soared. China's wealthy elites were emulating the most conspicuous consumption of the rich in the West, and corruption there appeared to be endemic.

If history is any guide, reform is likely to begin in America and inspire reform elsewhere. That's because Americans have always tended to choose pragmatism over ideology. When we have recognized a problem and understood the reason for it, our habit has been to get on with the messy job of solving it. Whenever capitalism has before reached points of crisis, we have not opted for communism or fascism or any other grand scheme. Again and again we have saved capitalism from its own excesses by making necessary corrections. We have counteracted whatever political and economic power has become too concentrated for the system to sustain itself. It is time for us to do so again.

18

The Decline of Countervailing Power

The essential challenge is political rather than economic. It is impossible to reform an economic system whose basic rules are under the control of an economic elite without altering the allocation of political power that lies behind that control.

A study published in the fall of 2014 by Princeton professor Martin Gilens and Professor Benjamin Page of Northwestern University reveals the scale of the challenge. Gilens and Page analyzed 1,799 policy issues in detail, determining the relative influence on them of economic elites, business groups, mass-based interest groups, and average citizens. Their conclusion: "The preferences of the average American appear to have only a minuscule, near-zero, statistically non-significant impact upon public policy." Instead, lawmakers respond to the policy demands of wealthy individuals and moneyed business interests—those with the most lobbying prowess and deepest pockets to bankroll campaigns. It is sobering that Gilens and Page's data come from the period 1981 to 2002, before the Supreme Court opened the floodgates to big money in its *Citizens United* and *McCutcheon* decisions, which we shall get to in a moment. The study also predated the advent of super PACs and "dark money," and even the Wall Street bailout. Presumably their results would be even more skewed toward the moneyed interests if their sample was extended to today.

Some might claim that the average citizen never had much direct political power in America. Walter Lippmann argued in his 1922 book, *Public Opinion,* that the broad public did not know or care about public policy. The public's consent was "manufactured" by an elite that manipulated it. "It is no longer possible . . . to believe in the original dogma of democracy," Lippmann concluded. Nevertheless, in subsequent years American democracy seemed robust compared to other nations that succumbed to communism or totalitarianism.

After World War II, political scientists sought to explain the relative stability and responsiveness of American democracy. They hypothesized that even though the voices of individual Americans counted for little, most people belonged to a variety of interest groups and membership organizations—clubs, associations, political parties, and trade unions—to which politicians were responsive. "Interest-group pluralism," as it was then called, did not conform to the old textbook models of direct or even representative democracy. But it was responsive to the needs and aspirations of most citizens. In the view of these scholars, democratic governance depended on ongoing negotiations among such competing but intertwined groups. "The principal balancing force in the politics of a multi-group society such as the United States," wrote Columbia University political scientist David Truman in *The Governmental Process,* an influential 1951 treatise, consisted of "overlapping membership among organized interest groups." According to Truman, most Americans belonged to several such groups, which in turn conveyed their members' preferences to political leaders. These overlapping groups stabilized democracy while allowing for peaceful change. Yale political scientist Robert A. Dahl, in *A Preface to Democratic Theory,* published in 1956, noted that democracy had succeeded in America while failing elsewhere because it embraced a wide number of such groups, each of which was separately a political minority. Because each of them had to form coalitions with others in order to get anything done, the overall system remained flexible and responsive. The result was neither rule by majority nor by minority but rule by a "majority of minorities."

Research showed that elected leaders paid attention to local elites—small businesses that constituted the local chamber of commerce, for example—and to national organizations whose members were active within local and state chapters, such as the American Legion, the Farm Bureau, and local affiliates of national labor unions. Political parties were likewise layered from the bottom up, based on strong local and state organizations. Communications flowed mainly upward. The American Legion, for example, whose divisions existed in every state, with chapters in every major city, was largely responsible for passage of the GI Bill of 1944, which guaranteed every returning veteran up to four years of postsecondary school education, subsidized home mortgages, and business loans. The Legion was successful precisely because its divisions and chapters mobilized tens of thousands of members to pressure their own senators and representatives.

Even more significant was the federal government's success, beginning with the New Deal and extending through the first decades after World War II, in creating new centers of economic power that offset the power of the giant corporations and Wall Street. As I have noted, unions pushed for and won legislation in 1935 that legitimized collective bargaining, and then, in subsequent decades, built economic and political strength on that foundation. Unorganized workers gained economic power in the form of minimum-wage legislation. Small farmers got federal price supports, as well as a voice in setting agricultural policy. Farm cooperatives, like unions, won exemption from federal antitrust laws. Small retailers obtained protection against retail chains through state "fair trade" laws, requiring wholesalers to charge all retailers the same price and preventing chains from cutting prices. At the same time, the retail chains were allowed to combine into national organizations in order to counter the significant market power of large manufacturers. Small investors gained protection under the Securities Exchange Act against the power of big investors and top corporate executives. Small banks were protected against Wall Street by regulations that barred interstate banking and that separated commercial from investment banking. And so it went, across the economy.

Economist John Kenneth Galbraith approvingly dubbed all this "countervailing power," seeing in these new centers of influence the means by which the benefits of economic growth were widely spread. "In fact, the support of countervailing power has become in the last two decades perhaps the major peacetime function of the federal government," he wrote in 1952. Countervailing power across the economy had created a counterweight to the centralized power of big corporations and Wall Street. "Given the existence of private market power in the economy," Galbraith continued, "the growth of countervailing power strengthens the capacity of the economy for autonomous self-regulation and thereby lessens the amount of over-all government control or planning that is required or sought." These alternative power centers ensured that America's vast middle and working classes received a significant share of the gains from economic growth.

Starting in the 1980s, however, something changed profoundly. It wasn't just that big corporations, Wall Street, and wealthy individuals were becoming more politically potent, as Gilens and Page's research clearly shows. It was also that the centers of countervailing economic power were beginning to wither. Just as the large moneyed interests gained increasing dominance over the rules by which the market runs, these countervailing centers of economic power deteriorated—as did their voices in helping set the rules.

Grassroots membership organizations such as the American Legion shrank, largely because Americans had less time for them. As wages stagnated, most people had to devote more time to work in order to make ends meet. That included the time of wives and mothers who began streaming into the paid workforce in the late 1970s to prop up family incomes threatened by the new fragility of male wages. As sociologist Robert Putnam has documented, Americans stopped being a nation of "joiners." By the 1980s, the vast mosaic of organizations that had given force and meaning to American pluralism was coming apart. By the first decades of the twenty-first century, many of these organizations had all but disappeared, as had their collective voices. They have been replaced by national advocacy organizations, typically headquartered in Washington. "Membership" no longer means active engagement at the local and state levels, with affiliates and chapters communicating their members' preferences upward to national leaders. It means little more than an individual's willingness to send money in response to mass solicitations flowing downward.

At the same time, as I have discussed, union membership began dropping, as corporations starting sending jobs abroad and threatened to send more unless unionized workers agreed to wage and benefit concessions, moved to nonunion "right-to-work" states, and fought attempts of nonunionized workers to form unions. President Ronald Reagan helped legitimize these moves when he fired striking air traffic controllers, but competitive pressures were already pushing CEOs in this direction. Subsequently, as I have shown, the unfriendly takeovers and leveraged buyouts of the 1980s put ever-greater pressure on top executives to cut labor costs by fighting unions. The decline of unions not only reduced the bargaining power of average workers to obtain a share of corporate profits. It also reduced the political power of average working people to negotiate laws and rules that would help maintain their incomes—labor laws that preserved and enlarged upon their contractual rights to bargain collectively, trade agreements that protected their jobs (or adequately compensated them for jobs lost), corporate laws that gave them something of a voice in corporate governance, bankruptcy laws that gave union agreements a high priority.

Unions have continued to lobby and make campaign contributions, but their political and economic clout has waned, especially when compared with that of big corporations, trade associations, Wall Street, and wealthy individuals. In the 2012 elections, for example, the Koch brothers' political network alone spent more than $400 million. This sum was more than twice the political spending of the ten largest labor unions put together. That same year corporations spent fifty-six dollars on lobbying for every dollar spent by labor unions. Democratic candidates no longer rely nearly as much on labor unions to finance their campaigns as they do on wealthy individuals. In 2012, the richest 0.01 percent of households gave Democratic candidates more than four times what unions contributed to their campaigns. The loss of American workers' collective economic power has thereby compounded the loss of their political power, which in turn has accelerated the loss of their economic power.

Other centers of countervailing power—small retail businesses, farm cooperatives, and local and regional banks—have also lost ground. Many small retailers went under due to repeals of state "fair trade" laws and court decisions finding resale price maintenance to violate antitrust laws. The large chains that spearheaded such moves argued that consumers would get better deals as a result. But the moves also opened the way to giant big-box retailers, such as Walmart, which siphoned away so much business from the Main Streets of America that many became ghost towns. The changes also led to the closings of millions of locally owned businesses that had provided their communities with diverse products and services, some produced locally or regionally, and many jobs. Likewise, the deregulation of financial markets—demanded by Wall Street—allowed the Street's biggest banks to become far bigger, taking over markets that state and local banks had previously served and thereby cutting off financing for many small local and regional enterprises.

. . .

Meanwhile, political parties changed their orientation. As income and wealth began concentrating at the top and as the costs of political campaigns escalated, parties that had been centered on state and local organizations that channeled the views of members upward began to morph into giant top-down fundraising machines. The Republican Party was already well attuned to the preferences of large corporations, Wall Street, and other wealthy patrons long before it succumbed to escalating demands for campaign contributions, but in recent years the Democratic Party has become almost as responsive to these same moneyed interests. "Business has to deal with us whether they like it or not, because we're the majority," crowed Democratic representative Tony Coelho, who, as head of the Democratic Congressional Campaign Committee in the 1980s, commenced a shakedown of corporate America. Coelho's Democrats soon achieved a rough parity with Republicans in contributions from corporate and Wall Street campaign coffers, but the presumed dependence of big corporations on the Democratic Congress and the consequential bipartisan generosity of such firms proved a Faustian bargain. Democratic dependence on big corporations became evident when, months before their 1994 trouncing, many congressional Democrats voted against Bill Clinton's health care plan because their corporate sponsors opposed it.

While nonbusiness causes, such as the rights of minorities and women, continue to have better odds of success under Democratic administrations and Democratic Congresses than under Republican ones, business interests have done well under both. For example, in his first two years in office, when Democrats controlled both houses of Congress, Bill Clinton pushed for enactment of the North American Free Trade Agreement, followed by the establishment of the World Trade Organization—two items of central importance to big business. He also committed himself to reducing the federal budget deficit, as Wall Street's bond traders insisted upon. While the Democratic Party of Franklin D. Roosevelt's New Deal had devised financial regulations to constrain

Wall Street, Clinton and his allies in Congress eliminated many of those same restraints. In 1994, Democrats supported the Interstate Banking and Branching Efficiency Act, which eliminated restrictions on interstate banking; in 1999, Clinton pushed for repeal of the 1933 Glass-Steagall Act, which had separated commercial from investment banking; and in 2000, he went along with the Commodity Futures Modernization Act, preventing the Commodity Futures Trading Commission from regulating most over-the-counter derivative contracts, including credit default swaps. Finally, as I have noted, President Clinton moderated his 1992 campaign promise to prevent corporations from deducting executive pay in excess of $1 million and allowed the deduction as long as such pay was linked to "performance" (which came to mean stock options and awards). During the Clinton years, corporate profits exploded, the stock market surged, and CEO compensation went into the stratosphere.

Likewise, Barack Obama—although often criticized by the business community for being anti-business—in fact presided over one of the most pro-business administrations in American history. Obama pumped hundreds of billions of dollars into Wall Street in order to save the Street (and the U.S. economy) from imploding after the crash of 2008, created a stimulus program that avoided another Great Depression, and enacted a broad-based health care law that enriched insurance and pharmaceutical companies. Under Obama's watch the stock market made up for all the losses it suffered in the Great Recession and reached new record highs, and, as I have noted, corporate profits rose to the highest portion of the national economy since 1929.

The career paths of recent Democratic officials before and after holding office confirmed their close ties to business and Wall Street. Bill Clinton's Treasury secretary, Robert Rubin, who chaired Goldman Sachs before going to Washington, upon leaving became chairman of the executive committee of Citigroup. Tim Geithner, Barack Obama's Treasury secretary, who had been handpicked by Rubin to head the New York Fed before arriving in Washington, returned to Wall Street as president of the private-equity firm Warburg Pincus. Jack Lew, who replaced Geithner as Treasury secretary, had been chief operating officer of Citigroup's Alternative Investments division, dedicated to proprietary trading, before joining the Obama administration. Peter Orszag, Obama's director of the Office of Management and Budget, left the administration to become Citigroup's vice chairman of Global Banking and chairman of the Financial Strategy and Solutions division. Perhaps it was not entirely coincidental that the Obama administration never put tough conditions on banks receiving bailout money, never prosecuted a single top Wall Street executive for the excesses that led to the near meltdown, and even refused to support a small tax on financial transactions that would have generated tens of billions of dollars in annual revenues and discouraged program trading.

The pertinent comparison is not between the career paths of Democratic and Republican officials but between people who served in Washington decades before the big money began pouring in and those who served after the deluge began. In the 1970s, for example, only about 3 percent of retiring members of Congress went on to become Washington lobbyists. In recent years, fully half of all retiring senators and 42 percent of retiring representatives have turned to lobbying, regardless of party affiliation. This is not because more recent retirees have had fewer qualms than their predecessors about making money off their contacts and experience gained during government service, but because the financial rewards from corporate lobbying have grown considerably larger.

Wall Street has gained influence among Washington Democrats as well as Republicans as it has poured more money into campaigns. As Connecticut Democratic senator Chris Murphy admitted to an audience at Yale in 2013, when complaining about the necessity of fund-raising, "You spend a lot of time on the phone with people who work in the financial markets. And so you're hearing a lot about problems that bankers have and not a lot of problems that people who work at the mill in Thomaston, Connecticut, have."

Wealthy individuals, meanwhile, have accounted for a growing share of contributions to candidates from both parties. In fact, starting in 1980, the amounts of political contributions by the richest one-hundredth of 1 percent rose even faster than their incomes. In 1980, the top 0.01 percent accounted for 10 percent of total campaign contributions. By 2012, while the richest 0.01 percent of households received about 5 percent of the nation's total income, their campaign donations soared to 40 percent of all contributions to federal elections (see figure 9).

FIGURE 9. CONCENTRATION OF INCOME AND CAMPAIGN CONTRIBUTIONS IN THE TOP 0.01 PERCENT OF HOUSEHOLDS AND VOTING-AGE POPULATION

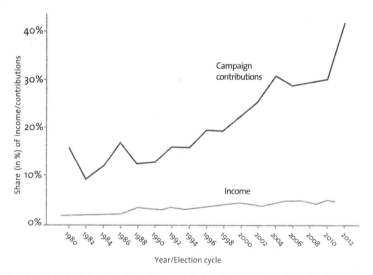

Notes: The dark line tracks the share of campaign contributions in all federal elections donated by the top 0.01 percent of the voting-age population. The number of donors included in the 0.01 percent share of voting-age population grew from 16,444 in 1980 to 24,092 in 2012. During the same period, the minimum amount given to be included in the top 0.01 percent grew in real terms from $5,616 to $25,000 (in 2012 dollars). The shaded line tracks the share of total income (including capital gains) received by the top 0.01 percent of households. The figure includes individual contributions to super PACs and 527 organizations but excludes contributions to nondisclosing 501(c)4 organizations, which are recorded to have spent approximately $143 million in 2010 and $318 million in 2012, much of which was raised from wealthy individuals. Were it possible to include contributions to nondisclosing 501(c)4s, the trend line would likely be 1–2 percentage points higher in 2010 and 2012. Source: A. Bonica, N. McCarty, K. Poole, and H. Rosenthal, "Why Hasn't Democracy Slowed Rising Inequality?" *Journal of Economic Perspectives* 27, no. 3 (Summer 2013): 112; drawn from income data from Piketty and Saez (2013).

In 2012, the two biggest donors were Sheldon and Miriam Adelson, who contributed $56.8 million and $46.6 million, respectively. But the Adelsons were only the tip of a vast iceberg of contributions from the überwealthy. Of the *Forbes* list of four hundred richest Americans that year, fully 388 made political contributions. They accounted for 40 of the 155 contributions of $1 million or more. Out of the 4,493 board members and CEOs of Fortune 500 corporations, more than four out of five contributed (many of the noncontributors were foreign nationals who were prohibited from giving). In the run-up to the 2016 elections, billionaire brothers Charles and David Koch joined forces with their wealthy friends to assemble a war chest of nearly $1 billion—allowing their political organization to operate on the same scale as the Republican and Democratic parties.

The increasing dominance of money from the superwealthy would be less significant if their concerns and attitudes paralleled the concerns and attitudes of most other Americans with the same party affiliations. Under these circumstances, the power of Democratic billionaires presumably would countervail the power of Republican billionaires. But in fact the rich have quite different priorities from average Americans. Dueling billionaires are no substitute for countervailing power.

To take but one example, according to a 2014 Pew Research poll, a large majority of Americans, regardless of party, were worried about jobs. Yet when political scientists Benjamin Page and Larry Bartels surveyed Chicagoans with an average net worth of $14 million, they found that their biggest concerns were either the budget deficit or excessive government spending, ranking these as priorities three times as often as they did unemployment. And—no surprise—these wealthy individuals were also far less willing than other Americans to curb deficits by raising taxes on high-income people and more willing to cut Social Security and Medicare. They also opposed initiatives most other Americans favored, such as increasing spending on schools and raising the minimum wage.

The other thing distinguishing Page and Bartels's wealthy

respondents from the rest of America was their political influence. In the previous twelve months, two-thirds of them had contributed money (averaging $4,633) to political campaigns or organizations. A fifth of them had even bundled contributions from others. That money bought the kind of political access most Americans only dream of. About half of these wealthy people had recently initiated contact with a U.S. senator or representative, and nearly half (44 percent) of those contacts concerned matters of relatively narrow economic self-interest rather than broader national concerns. This is just the wealthy of one city—Chicago. Multiply it across the entire United States and you begin to see the larger picture of whom our elected representatives are listening to, and why. Nor does the survey include the institutionalized wealth and economic clout of Wall Street and large corporations. Multiply the multiplier.

If wealth and income were not concentrated in the hands of a few, and countervailing power had not withered, the Supreme Court's decisions in *Citizens United v. Federal Election Commission* (2010) and *McCutcheon v. Federal Election Commission* (2014), both supported by the five Republican appointees to the court, would not be nearly as worrisome. *Citizens United* declared that corporations are people under the First Amendment, entitled to participate fully in elections through financial contributions. A subsequent federal appeals court ruling, *SpeechNow.org v. Federal Election Commission,* which explicitly relied on *Citizens United* as precedent, allowed corporations and individuals to make unlimited contributions to independent expenditure committees, better known as "super PACs." *McCutcheon* eliminated the $123,200 cap on the amount an individual can contribute to federal candidates and political parties, allowed a presidential candidate to solicit as much as $1.2 million per donor in a two-year election cycle, and permitted a House leader to raise as much as $2.3 million per donor in a two-year election cycle.

By effectively eviscerating campaign finance laws, the Supreme

Court accelerated the vicious cycle to which I have referred, in which large corporations and wealthy individuals pay to shape the rules of the game to their advantage, thereby becoming even richer and having even greater influence over the rules. Even worse, much of this is in secret. In the 2014 midterm election, more than half the advertising aired by outside groups came from organizations that disclosed little or nothing about their donors. Some of these organizations were established specifically to shield the identities of the wealthy individuals and corporations that contributed to them. These groups financed more political advertising than did super PACs.

Economic and political power have thereby been compounded. In 1990, the Supreme Court sensibly viewed corruption as including "the corrosive and distorting effects of immense aggregations of wealth that are accumulated with the help of the corporate form and that have little or no correlation to the public's support for the corporation's political ideas." Twenty years later, the court defined corruption far more narrowly, to mean the exchange of specific money for specific votes—outright bribery. Writing for a majority of the court, Justice Anthony Kennedy simply declared that "independent expenditures, including those made by corporations, do not give rise to corruption or the appearance of corruption."

Small wonder that confidence in political institutions and actors continues to wane. In 1964, just 29 percent of voters believed that government was "run by a few big interests looking out for themselves." But by 2013, that opinion predominated, with 79 percent of Americans agreeing.

The erosion in public trust has been particularly steep in more recent years. In 2006, 59 percent of Americans felt that government corruption was widespread; by 2013, 79 percent of Americans felt that way. In Rasmussen polls undertaken in the fall of 2014, 63 percent thought most members of Congress were willing to sell their vote for either cash or a campaign contribution, and 59 percent thought it likely their own representative already had.

Sixty-six percent believed most members of Congress didn't care what their constituents thought, and 51 percent said even their own representative did not care what they thought.

A large portion of the American public no longer even bothers voting. The largest political party in America is neither the Republican Party nor the Democratic Party; it's the party of nonvoters. Only 58.2 percent of eligible voters cast their ballots in the 2012 presidential election. Turnout in midterm elections is always lower, but in the midterm elections of 2014 a measly 33.2 percent of the voting-age population turned out—the lowest percentage since the midterm elections of 1942, which, not incidentally, occurred in the middle of World War II. Moreover, those who do vote have tended to express their discontent by careening from one wave election to another, each one replacing the dominant or controlling party. Barack Obama and the Democrats were overwhelmingly elected in 2008, only to have the tide turn abruptly in the opposite direction and Republicans take over the House in 2010 and the Senate in 2014.

Other nations, facing a similar divergence between the economic gains of a controlling establishment and the economic precariousness of everyone else, have shown analogous signs of discontent. By 2014, separatist movements were breaking out in many of the world's major economies. In 2014, Scotland came close to seceding from Great Britain, and Catalonians in a straw poll showed a desire to separate from Spain. Earlier that year, in European parliamentary elections, ultranationalist parties gained ground. National movements against global elites and international institutions also surged in Russia, Japan, India, and China.

In the years leading up to the 2016 presidential election in the United States, a perfect storm of a record concentration of income and wealth at the top combined with unprecedented amounts of campaign spending and influence peddling by corporations, Wall Street, and wealthy individuals—much of it in secret—has taken a toll. Countervailing power has all but disappeared in America. Not surprisingly, most Americans feel powerless, disdain politics and politicians, and express cynicism about the possibilities for meaningful change. But powerlessness is also a self-fulfilling prophecy. The only way back toward a democracy and economy that work for the majority is for the majority to become politically active once again, establishing a new countervailing power. The moneyed interests will continue to do what they do best—make money. The rest of us must do what we do best—use our voice, our vigor, and our votes to wrest back economic and political control.

19

Restoring Countervailing Power

If we are able to rid ourselves of the notions that the "free market" exists separately from government, and that people earn what they are worth to society, it will be possible for Americans to view more clearly the underlying choice: not more or less government, but a government responsive either to the demands of a wealthy minority becoming ever wealthier or to the needs of a majority that is becoming relatively poorer and less economically secure. We could then move beyond the ideological brawls that have consumed so much of the political right and left and attend instead to the central challenge of our time—restoring countervailing power to our political-economic system.

Moneyed interests do not want the curtain of the "free market" lifted because that would expose their influence over the rules of the capitalist game and reveal potential alliances that could countervail that power. They would prefer the bottom 90 percent continue to preoccupy themselves with tendentious battles over government's size (or that it war over noneconomic issues such as same-sex marriage, abortion, guns, race, and religion) than find common economic cause.

It is therefore necessary to lift the curtain. When a majority of Americans are becoming poorer while a small and privileged minority is becoming richer than ever—and when the rules of the game redistribute economic gains upward—there exist possibilities for new alliances, and a new politics. Some who are now typically on the right of the political spectrum—individual investors, family businesses, entrepreneurs, the inhabitants of rural communities, and the white working class, for example—may discover they have much in common with working women, minorities, and urban professionals, all typically on the left. Among other things, all are paying more for pharmaceuticals, broadband connections, food, credit card debt, and health insurance than they would be were the rules of the market not shaped by big corporations.

Many are also struggling with a financial system whose rules are crafted and enforced by the biggest banks on Wall Street, which have grown bigger after the bailout: small-business owners, who are paying substantially higher interest rates on loans, if they can get loans at all; former students buried under student loan debts; homeowners who owe more on their mortgages than their homes are worth. Others are up against an intellectual property system whose entry barriers are impossibly high: individual inventors trying to bring their ideas to life, lone entrepreneurs trying to start companies, creative artists seeking audiences for their works, consumers merely wanting to share designs or images. Or they are paying through the nose for access to platforms and networks that are costly solely because their corporate owners have created a standard that everyone has to use because so many others are using it—and the corporate owners have been able to hold antitrust enforcers at bay.

Franchisees find themselves trapped in contracts that siphon off almost all their profits, don't allow them access to courts, and can be unilaterally terminated by big franchisors at any time. They are in a similar position to many hourly workers trapped in employment contracts that require them to work long hours or irregular hours at low pay, impose mandatory arbitration, and can be unilaterally terminated by their employers at any time.

Likewise, small creditors, union members, individual shareholders, family farmers, and small contractors are on the same side
when a big corporation that owes them money stonewalls them.
And they're in a similar fix when the corporation enters into
bankruptcy and they find themselves assigned a lower priority
than large creditors because that is how the banks and big creditors have organized the rules.

Consider also the potential linkages between individual investors, salaried employees, and hourly workers, all of whom receive
smaller and smaller portions of the pie as the portions going to
CEOs, other top executives, and portfolio and hedge-fund managers continue to grow. This is because the latter have access to
inside information and the power to set the rules for how and
when such information is distributed.

In all these ways, the bottom 90 percent of Americans—
regardless of whether they are owners of small businesses or working poor, entrepreneurs or student debtors, small investors or
homeowners, white or black or Latino, men or women—have far
more in common, economically, than they do with the top executives of large corporations, the Wall Street crowd, or America's
wealthy. The bottom 90 percent are losing ground in large part
because of upward pre-distributions embedded inside "free market" rules over which those at the top have great influence. If the
smaller players understood this dynamic, presumably they would
seek to gain greater influence by allying themselves. This alliance,
or set of alliances, would form the new countervailing power.

It is impossible to predict how or when this might occur, but it is
already possible to discern the bare beginnings of a movement.
By 2014, antipathy toward Wall Street and large corporations was
at record levels. In a CNBC/Burson-Marstteller international survey, released in September 2014, more than half (51 percent) of
the respondents agreed with the statement "Strong and influential corporations are bad, even if they promote innovation and

growth." Meanwhile, a civil war has raged inside the Republican Party between anti-establishment Republicans who eschew large corporations and Wall Street and establishment Republicans closely tied to them. We "cannot be the party of fat cats, rich people, and Wall Street," said Republican senator Rand Paul, in seeking to position himself for a 2016 presidential run. Republican senator Ted Cruz, another presidential aspirant, has accused the "rich and powerful, those who walk the corridors of power," of "getting fat and happy." Republican David Brat, who, in June 2014, beat House majority leader Eric Cantor in the Republican primary in Virginia's Seventh Congressional District, accused Cantor of "crony capitalism" and charged big corporations with wanting only "cheap labor . . . that's going to lower wages for everybody else."

The sincerity behind these statements might be questioned, but sincerity is not the point. Such statements are uttered because those who make them know they will be received enthusiastically by the voters they are courting. Pollsters and campaign consultants who advise Republican candidates have picked up on an indelible strain of voter anger toward the "rich and powerful" who are "getting fat and happy" and "going to lower wages for everybody else." Polls show, for example, support among self-described Republicans as well as Democrats for cutting the biggest Wall Street banks down to a size where they are no longer too big to fail. In 2014, Republican representative David Camp, House Ways and Means Committee chair, proposed a quarterly tax on the assets of the biggest Wall Street banks in order to give them an incentive to trim down. "There is nothing conservative about bailing out Wall Street," said Rand Paul.

Similarly, rank-and-file Republicans as well as Democrats are in favor of resurrecting the Glass-Steagall Act, which used to separate commercial and investment banking until it was repealed in 1999 by a coalition of congressional Republicans and the Clinton White House. In 2013, when Democratic senator Elizabeth Warren introduced legislation to re-create such an act, Republican senator John McCain co-sponsored it. Tea Party Republicans expressed strong support for the measure, even criticizing establishment Republicans for not getting more fully behind it. "The establishment political class would never admit that their financial donors and patrons must hinder their unbridled trading strategies," wrote the *Tea Party Tribune.* A similar alliance occurred briefly at the end of 2014, brought together by Congress's omnibus spending bill, which contained a provision rolling back the Dodd-Frank financial reform legislation and allowing the big banks to once again gamble with commercial deposits. Several progressive Democratic senators, including Elizabeth Warren, joined Tea Party Republican senator David Vitter of Louisiana in opposing the rollback.

There is also growing bipartisan support for ending "corporate welfare," including subsidies to Big Oil, Big Agribusiness, Big Pharma, Wall Street, and the Export-Import Bank. Progressives on the left have long been urging this, but by 2014 many on the right were joining in. David Camp's proposed tax reforms would have eliminated dozens of targeted tax breaks. Ted Cruz urged that Congress "eliminate corporate welfare and crony capitalism." Finally, as I have noted, grassroots antipathy has grown toward trade agreements crafted by big corporations. In the 1990s, Republicans joined with Democrats to enact the North American Free Trade Agreement, join the World Trade Organization, and support China's membership in the WTO. But after the turn of the new century, rank-and-file Republicans as well as Democrats turned against such agreements. "The Tea Party movement does not support the Trans-Pacific Partnership," stated Judson Phillips, president of Tea Party Nation. "Special interests and big corporations are being given a seat at the table," while average Americans are excluded.

It is likely that in coming years the major fault line in American politics will shift from Democrat versus Republican to anti-establishment versus establishment—that is, to the middle class, working class, and poor who see the game as rigged versus the executives of large corporations, the inhabitants of Wall Street, and the billionaires who do the rigging. By late 2014, big business and Wall Street Republicans were already signaling their preference for a Democratic establishment candidate over a Republican anti-establishment one. Dozens of major GOP donors, Wall Street Republicans, and corporate lobbyists told the Washington journal *Politico* that if the Republican Party did not put forward a candidate supportive of big business and Wall Street—Jeb Bush, Chris Christie, or Mitt Romney—they would support Hillary Clinton. "The darkest secret in the big money world of the Republican coastal elite is that the most palatable alternative to a nominee such as Sen. Ted Cruz of Texas or Sen. Rand Paul of Kentucky would be Clinton," concluded *Politico*'s analyst. A top Republican-leaning Wall Street lawyer told the journal, "If it's Rand Paul or Ted Cruz versus someone like Elizabeth Warren that would be everybody's worst nightmare."

Everybody on Wall Street and in corporate suites, that is. And even if the "nightmare" did not occur in 2016, some such nightmare is likely within the following decade if the economic and political trend we have been examining does not change. There is simply no way the American economy can be sustained if the richest 10 percent continue to reap all the economic gains while the poorest 90 percent grow poorer; there is no way American democracy can be maintained if the voices of the vast majority continue to be ignored.

Unless one or both of the two major parties in the United States shift away from the established centers of political and economic power, the new countervailing power could emerge in the form of a new party that unites the disaffected, anti-establishment elements of both major parties and gives the 90 percent of Americans who have been losing ground their own political voice. This will require, as I have emphasized, eschewing the tired and increasingly irrelevant choice between the "free market" and "government," and focusing instead on the myriad ways the market has been organized to benefit large corporations, Wall Street, and a small and increasingly wealthy minority at the top and on how to make it work instead for the vast majority. The explicit aim of this new party would be to save capitalism by enabling most Americans to benefit from its success.

There appears to be increasing interest in such a third party. In a Gallup poll conducted in September 2014, only 35 percent of Americans believed the two major parties adequately represented them, and 58 percent of Americans thought that the Democratic and Republican parties do such a poor job representing the American people that a third major party is needed. This is one of the highest percentages Gallup found since it first raised the question of a third party a decade before. The prior high point in expressed desire for a third party occurred in October 2013, during the partial federal government shutdown. Interestingly, 46 percent of self-described Republicans as well as 47 percent of self-described Democrats feel a third party is needed.

The professed desire for a third party does not mean one will emerge to become a dominant force in American politics, however. The American political system discourages the formation of strong third parties because the two that predominate at any given time have enormous advantages, not the least of which is the lack of proportional representation. Winners of races for the Senate and House and of state Electoral College races for the presidency represent the entire constituencies. As a result, when third parties have appeared, they usually have done little more than siphon off votes from the dominant party closest to them in ideology or voter preference.

In addition, the two dominant parties have been sufficiently adaptable and gingerly opportunistic enough to take advantage of the electorate's changing views. In the 1932 presidential election, for example, the Democratic Party reinvented itself to create a new coalition of urban ethnic voters, blue-collar unionized workers, white southerners, western voters, Catholics, and Jews, to give Franklin D. Roosevelt a landslide victory and the incipient New Deal a strong electoral foundation. Democrats grew from holding 37.7 percent of the seats in the House of Representatives in 1929 to 72 percent in 1933, and from 40.6 percent of the seats in the Senate to 61.5 percent.

Further evidence of the adaptability of the two dominant parties can be found in the sixteen years commencing with the presidential election of 1896, when Democratic candidate William Jennings Bryan attempted to mobilize western farmers, southerners, and eastern laborers against big business and finance in a putative crusade of working people against the rich, while Republican William McKinley maintained a winning conservative coalition of businessmen, skilled factory workers, and professionals. By the election of 1904, President Theodore Roosevelt and other Republican leaders felt it necessary to respond to deepening public concerns about abuses of economic power by the giant trusts and reoriented the party to include laborers, urban immigrants, and progressive reformers, and they advanced the reforms I have previously mentioned. In the campaign of 1912, Roosevelt sought the presidency under the banner of the Progressive Party, whose platform called for "dissolving the unholy alliance between corrupt business and corrupt politics" through stricter limits on and disclosures of political campaign contributions and the registration of lobbyists; social insurance for the elderly, the unemployed, and the disabled; women's suffrage and a minimum wage for women workers; an eight-hour workday; a federal securities commission; and compensation for workers who were injured on the job. Although rejected by the electorate, who chose Democrat Woodrow Wilson instead, Theodore Roosevelt's Progressive Party platform found its way into the New Deal of his Democratic fifth cousin.

In these instances, one or both of the two major parties adapted to the shifting views and needs of the times. A viable third party is likely to emerge only if both the Democratic and Republican parties are so dependent on big business and Wall Street that neither is able to respond to the emerging views and needs of the vast majority at this juncture in history. Whether it comes about through adaptation by one of the current dominant parties or the emergence of a new third party is less important than that countervailing power be re-established in America.

No one should expect this to occur smoothly or easily. The moneyed interests have too much at stake in the prevailing distribution of income, wealth, and political power to passively allow countervailing power to re-emerge. While they would be wise to support it for all the reasons I have enumerated above—mostly, they will do better with a smaller share of a faster-growing economy whose participants enjoy more of the gains and will be more secure in an inclusive society whose citizens feel they are being heard—they will nonetheless resist. The status quo is too comfortable, and the prospect of countervailing power too risky and unpredictable. Yet its re-emergence is inevitable. We cannot continue in the direction we are now headed.

What would the new countervailing power seek to accomplish? As a first step, it would reform the nation's system of campaign finance in order to get big money out of politics. That would require that the Supreme Court's decisions in *Citizens United* and *McCutcheon* be reversed—either because one justice who had been in the majority sees the folly of his ways and joins with a new majority to reverse it judicially (that happened in the 1930s, when Justice Owen Roberts switched allegiance from his four anti–New Deal colleagues on the court to the four pro–New Dealers), or a new president fills vacancies on the court that thereby create a majority to reverse it, or, far less likely, because the new countervailing power summons enough political force to amend the Constitution to declare that Congress may regulate campaign spending.

Getting big money out of politics would also require full disclosure of the sources of all political expenditures. In addition, it would necessitate public financing of general elections, probably by means of a system in which public funds matched donations from small donors. And it would ban gerrymandered districts that suppress the votes of minorities, as well as voting restrictions imposing disproportionate burdens on minorities.

A closely related set of reforms would reduce or eliminate revolving doors between government service and Wall Street, large corporations, and lobbying firms. At the least, all elected and appointed government officials would be prohibited, for a minimum of five years from the end of their government service, from accepting any form of employment with any corporation, trade association, lobbying firm, or other for-profit organization that they oversaw, monitored, regulated, or had any other official relation with while in government.

Finally, expert witnesses, academics, and inhabitants of think tanks would be required to disclose any and all sources of outside funding for testimony, books, papers, or studies that are put in the public domain. That way, if an "expert" funded by Koch Industries asserts that humans have no part in climate change, for example, or a professor funded by the National Retail Federation finds that raising the minimum wage leads to less employment, the public would have a means of evaluating the neutrality of such claims.

20

Ending Upward Pre-distributions

Countervailing power would also seek to end the upward pre-distributions currently embedded in market rules, such as those we have examined. The lengths of patent and copyright protection would be shortened, for example, and pay-for-delay agreements banned, as they are in most other advanced economies. Patents could not be extended by means of small or cosmetic changes in products or processes, and pharmaceutical companies would be prohibited from advertising their prescription brands, as had been the rule in the United States until Big Pharma insisted otherwise.

Antitrust would be returned to its original purpose, not only achieving market efficiency and maximizing consumer welfare but also reducing the political influence of large aggregates of economic power. Antitrust law would be used to bust up cable monopolies, prevent oligopolies such as now exist in the provision of credit cards, contain the size of giant hospital chains, and limit the market power of large high-tech companies over networks and standard platforms. No firm would be allowed to hold a patent to the key genetic traits of our food chain. Insurers would no longer be exempt from antitrust laws, so they could not fix prices, allocate markets, or collude over terms. At the same time, the size of Wall Street's giant banks would be limited so that none could hold more than 5 percent of the nation's banking assets, have any role in the pricing of commodities, or play a dominant role in initial public offerings of stock. The Glass-Steagall Act would be resurrected, so that investment banking's wagers on stocks and derivatives would be separated from commercial banking's more staid and secure lending of commercial deposits, as they were between 1933 and 1999.

Meanwhile, contract laws and regulations would prohibit corporations from binding their employees, contractors, or franchisees to forced arbitration. No franchisor could terminate the contract of a franchisee for minor violations in order to resell the franchise at a higher price to new owners. Fraud would be defined to prohibit all forms of insider trading, including any use by corporations and their CEOs of corporate buybacks to pump up share prices and cash in on stock options and awards, as had been the rule before 1991. Corporations would also have to disclose to shareholders the timing and extent of their buybacks, as was the case before 1982. Also prohibited would be all stock trades based on information unavailable to the general public. High-frequency trading firms would be required to share their methodologies and technologies with all other traders. Moreover, shareholders would have the right to force an entire corporate board to stand for re-election if a quarter or more of a company's shareholders and stakeholders vote against a CEO pay plan two years in a row (the current rule in Australia). Bankruptcy law would give labor agreements a higher priority than agreements with other creditors. Bankruptcy would allow individuals with unmanageable student debt or mortgage debt on their first homes to reorganize those debts, thereby giving them more bargaining leverage with lenders.

The minimum wage would be raised to half the median wage and thereafter adjusted for inflation. Workers in low-wage industries such as retail chains, fast-food chains, hotels, and hospitals would be able to form a union by a majority up-or-down vote, thereby giving them more bargaining leverage in contract negotiations over their wages and benefits. A more evenhanded approach to international trade agreements would seek to protect not only American corporations' intellectual property and the financial assets of American banks but also the jobs of American workers that might be imperiled. For example, the United States would require that all trading partners to such agreements establish minimum wages equal to half their median wages in order that the gains from trade be widely shared in those countries, thereby generating new customers for American exports and arguably more political stability overall. Meanwhile, a portion of the gains from trade at home would finance a world-class re-employment system including wage insurance, so that job losers who took new jobs paying less than their former jobs would receive 90 percent of the difference for two years and income support of 90 percent of their former wages if they seek to upgrade or change skills in full-time educational programs.

Enforcement resources would be adequate to fully implement all laws and rules; fines and penalties would be sufficiently high to deter corporate or financial law breaking; and private rights of action and class actions would be fully available to supplement government enforcement.

Finally, although not strictly a part of the market mechanism but an important aspect of the prevailing system of upward pre-redistribution, educational resources would no longer be allocated as they are currently. Children in poorer school districts would no longer receive less per-pupil funding than children in wealthier school districts. Given that the nation has segregated by income into different cities and townships, schools would no longer depend on local property taxes as major sources of revenue.

In these and other ways, the new countervailing power would end upward pre-distributions currently baked into market rules. But this modest agenda would only be a start. The centrifugal forces of globalization and technological change require bolder steps if prosperity is to be more widely shared.

21

Reinventing the Corporation

In addition to ending upward pre-distribution inside the market, countervailing power would also seek a *fairer* pre-distribution inside the market, thereby making taxes and transfer payments less necessary. Achieving this would entail reinventing the central organization of modern capitalism—the large corporation.

For the last thirty years, as I have noted, almost all incentives operating on the corporation have resulted in lower pay for average workers and higher pay for CEOs and other top executives. The question is how those incentives can be reversed.

One possibility would be to make corporate tax rates depend on the ratio of CEO pay to the pay of the median worker in the firm. Corporations with low ratios would pay a lower corporate tax rate, and vice versa. A bill introduced in the California legislature in 2014 offers an example. Under it, if a CEO earns 100 times as much as the median worker in the company, the company's tax rate drops from the 8.8 percent corporate tax rate now applied to all firms in California to 8 percent. If the CEO makes 25 times the pay of the typical worker, the tax rate drops to 7 percent. On the other hand, if the CEO earns 200 times that of the typical employee, the tax rate rises to 9.5 percent; 400 times, to 13 percent.

The California Chamber of Commerce has dubbed the bill a "job killer," but the reality is the opposite. CEOs do not create jobs. Their customers create jobs by buying more of what their companies have to sell, giving the companies cause to expand and hire. So pushing companies to put less money into the hands of their CEOs and more into the hands of their average employees creates more purchasing power among people who will buy, and therefore more jobs. The other argument against the bill is the supposed complexity of the computation it requires. But the Dodd-Frank Act already requires companies to publish the ratios of CEO pay to the pay of the company's median worker (at this writing, the Securities and Exchange Commission has not yet issued rules implementing this provision of the law). So the California bill would not force companies to do anything more than they will have to do under federal law. And the tax brackets in the bill are wide enough to make the computation easy. California's proposal is not perfect, but it offers a promising direction. That the largest state in America is seriously considering it tells you something about how top-heavy American business has become, and why—even without countervailing power—political support is growing to do something serious about it.

A variation on this idea, proposed by William Galston of the Brookings Institution, would lower taxes on employers who give their workers wage increases commensurate with the nation's annual productivity growth, while raising taxes on employers who do not. This proposal would go some way to reconnecting worker income to the nation's overall economic gains. One objection might be that companies can game the system by subcontracting low-paying jobs to another company. Both proposals control for this. Under the California proposal, corporations that begin subcontracting more of their low-paying jobs would have to pay a higher tax; under the Galston proposal, employers would be barred from misclassifying employees as independent contractors or outsourcing low-wage work that previously had been done inside the corporation.

Another proposed change would give workers more direct ownership of the corporation by providing additional tax incentives for employee stock ownership and profit sharing, or the formation of employee-owned cooperatives. The idea is hardly new. It dates back to the early years of the Republic, when legislation provided tax credits to owners of fishing trawlers who established "a written, profit-sharing contract with all the sailors . . . covering the entire catch."

All such proposals raise a more basic question, which suggests even more fundamental reform: Why should shareholders take prominence over employees? As I have noted, corporations are nothing more than collections of contracts and property rights. They are not "owned" by shareholders the way ordinary goods are owned. It is common for the individual shareholders of large companies to be blissfully unaware of which specific companies they own, or for how long, because their ownership is through pension funds or mutual funds that tend to move quickly into and out of shares of stock, seeking quick speculative gains. If nothing else, high-frequency trading illustrates the irrelevance of stock ownership to effective corporate governance. Shareholder "ownership" is therefore a legal fiction. So is the idea that CEOs and other corporate executives have a fiduciary duty to maximize the value of corporations' shares of stock. Corporate charters, issued by states, require no such thing. While shareholders select a corporation's directors, the directors are under no legal obligation to put their interests above all others. Indeed, as we've seen, the idea that the sole purpose of a corporation is to maximize shareholder value is relatively new, dating back only to the 1980s. The dominant view in the first decades after World War II was that corporations had responsibilities to all of their stakeholders.

Besides, shareholders are not the only parties who invest in the corporation and bear a risk that their investments will drop in value. Workers who have been with the firm for many years may have developed skills and knowledge unique to it. Others may have moved their families to take a job with the firm, buying homes in the community. The community itself may have invested in roads and other infrastructure to accommodate the corporation. By contrast, most shareholders of a large corporation do not put their money into enlarging its productive capacity because most of the value of the stock market has little to do with new infusions of cash. Stocks are more like a vast collection of baseball cards, repeatedly traded. Apple raised $97 million in its initial public offering in 1980. Since then, those shares have circulated among investors who have bid up their price, but the added value has not gone to Apple; it has gone to investors lucky enough to buy them low and sell them high. Activist investors like Carl Icahn have bought enough shares to demand that the firm raise its stock price even higher by, for example, buying back some of its shares. (As I have noted, Steve Jobs's successor, Timothy D. Cook, was happy to oblige. In 2011 and 2012, during his first two years as CEO, he pocketed $382 million, of which $376 million was in the form of stock awards.) But none of these machinations have anything to do with Apple's capacity to innovate and add real value, or to be successful over the long term.

In 2014, the managers, employees, and customers of a New England chain of supermarkets called Market Basket joined together to oppose the board of directors' decision earlier that year to oust the chain's popular chief executive, Arthur T. Demoulas. Their demonstrations and boycotts emptied most of the chain's seventy stores. What was special about Arthur T., as he was known, was his business model. He kept prices lower than his competitors, paid his employees more, and gave them and his managers more authority. Just before he was ousted he offered customers an additional 4 percent discount, arguing that they could use the money more than the shareholders. In other words, Arthur T. viewed the company as a joint enterprise from which everyone should benefit, not just its shareholders—which was why the board fired him. Eventually, consumers and employees won. The boycott was costing Market Basket so much that the board sold the company to Arthur T.

Market Basket was not a publicly held company at the time, but we are beginning to see Arthur T.'s business model pop up all over the place, even where many shareholders are involved. Patagonia, a large apparel manufacturer based in Ventura, California, for example, has organized itself as a so-called benefit corporation—a for-profit company whose articles of incorporation require it to take into account the interests of workers, the community, and the environment, as well as shareholders. Benefit corporations are certified and their performance is regularly reviewed by nonprofit third-party entities, such as B Lab. By 2014, twenty-seven states had enacted laws allowing companies to incorporate in this manner, thereby giving directors explicit legal protection to consider the interests of all stakeholders rather than just the shareholders who elected them. And by then, more than 1,165 companies in 121 industries had been certified as benefit corporations, including the household-products firm Seventh Generation.

We may be witnessing the beginning of a return to a form of stakeholder capitalism that was taken for granted in America sixty years ago. But some economists claim that shareholder capitalism is more efficient. They argue that under the pressure of shareholders, corporations move economic resources to where they are most productive and thereby enable the entire economy to grow faster. In their view, the midcentury form of stakeholder capitalism locked up resources in unproductive ways and allowed CEOs to be too complacent—employing workers the company didn't need, paying them too much, and becoming too tied to their communities.

Yet when you take a hard look at the consequences of the shareholder capitalism that took root in the 1980s—a legacy that includes flat or declining wages for most Americans, along with growing economic insecurity, outsourced jobs, abandoned communities, CEO pay that has soared into the stratosphere, a myopic focus on quarterly earnings, and a financial sector akin to a casino whose near failure in 2008 imposed collateral damage on most Americans—you might have some doubts about how well shareholder capitalism has worked in practice. Only some of us are corporate shareholders, and a tiny minority of wealthy Americans own most of the shares traded on America's stock exchanges. But we are all stakeholders in the American economy, and most stakeholders have not done particularly well. Perhaps more stakeholder capitalism is in order, and less of the shareholder variety.

Germany's laws and rules on corporate governance illustrate this approach. In Germany, corporate laws require "co-determination," with a management board overseeing day-to-day operations and a supervisory board for more high-level decisions. Depending on the size of the company, up to half of the members of the supervisory board represent employees rather than shareholders. Workers on the shop floor are also represented by works councils, or *Betriebsrate*. This structure has made major German corporations, such as Volkswagen, far more receptive to worker rights than their counterparts in America (as was dramatically illustrated in 2014 when VW workers sought to form a union at their factory in Chattanooga, Tennessee; while VW did not object, state and local politicians worried aloud that unionization would harm the state's economy). It has also limited CEO pay, preserved many high-skill jobs, and resulted in a higher median wage and a far more secure and prosperous working class than in the United States.

With effective countervailing power, the American corporation could be reimagined and reinvented. Laws would require not only that employees be represented but that they receive voting rights proportional to their stakes and would prevent any single person or stakeholder from keeping most voting rights for him- or herself. The legal privileges of incorporation in America— limited liability, life in perpetuity, corporate personhood for the purpose of making contracts and the enjoyment of constitutional rights—would be available only to entities that share the gains from growth with their workers while also taking the interests of their communities and the environment into account.

The long-term agenda for countervailing power would not stop here, however. Reinventing the corporation would move us only part of the way toward a more balanced economy. That is largely because the corporation of the future will need far fewer workers. New technologies will be doing much of the work. The coming challenge will be to develop new market rules that spread the economic gains when robots take over.

22

When Robots Take Over

Technological change has spawned many predictions since the dawn of the industrial age, not all of which have been borne out. In his 1928 essay "Economic Possibilities for Our Grandchildren," John Maynard Keynes foresaw in a century "the discovery of means of economizing the use of labour outrunning the pace at which we can find new uses for labour." He nonetheless predicted that by 2028 the "standard of life" in Europe and the United States would be so improved that no one would need to worry about making money. It would be an age of abundance. "For the first time since his creation man will be faced with his real, his permanent problem—how to use his freedom from pressing economic cares, how to occupy the leisure, which science and compound interest will have won for him, to live wisely and agreeably and well."

The year 2028 hasn't yet arrived, but we don't seem to be on the road to a society resembling Keynes's prediction. Most people, even in advanced economies like the United States, do not feel freed from pressing economic cares. Rather than creating an age of abundance in which most no longer have to worry about money, labor-saving technologies are well on the way to creating a two-tiered society comprising a few with extraordinary wealth and a vast majority getting poorer.

I have made my share of predictions as well. In 1991, in my book *The Work of Nations,* I separated almost all modern work into three categories and then predicted what would happen to each of them. The first category I called "routine production services," which entailed the kind of repetitive tasks performed by the old foot soldiers of American capitalism through most of the twentieth century—done over and over, on an assembly line or in an office. Although often thought of as traditional blue-collar jobs, they also include routine supervisory jobs involving repetitive checks on subordinates' work, enforcement of standard operating procedures, and routine data entry and retrieval. I estimated that such work then constituted about one-quarter of all jobs in the United States but would decline steadily as it was replaced by new labor-saving technologies and by workers in developing nations eager to do it for far lower wages. I also assumed that the pay of remaining routine production workers in America would drop, for similar reasons.

I was not wrong. Using the same methodology I used then, I found that by 2014 routine production work constituted no more than a fifth of all jobs in America, and its median pay, adjusted for inflation, was 15 percent lower than it was two decades before. Indeed, all work that could be codified into software had been replaced by it or was soon to be. Text-mining programs were on the way to displacing many legal jobs; image-processing software was making lab technicians unnecessary; tax software was replacing accountants, and so on.

The second category I called "in-person services." This work had to be provided personally because the human touch was essential to it. It included retail sales workers, hotel and restaurant workers, nursing-home aides, realtors, child-care workers, home health care aides, flight attendants, physical therapists, and security guards, among many others. The essence of this work was to sell one to one; to ensure the personal security of others; or to make sure other people were well taken care of, happy, and at ease. In 1990, by my estimate, such workers accounted for about 30 percent of all employees in America, and I predicted their numbers would grow because—given that their services were delivered in person—neither advancing technologies nor foreign-based workers would be able to replace them. But I also predicted their pay would drop, for two reasons. First, they would be competing with a large number of former routine production workers, who could now only find jobs in the in-person sector. And second, they would also be competing with labor-saving machinery— "automated tellers, computerized cashiers, automatic car washes, robotized vending machines, self-service gas pumps"—and that even retail sales workers would be up against "personal computers linked to television screens" through which "tomorrow's consumers will be able to buy furniture, appliances, and all sorts of electronic toys from their living rooms—examining the merchandise from all angles, selecting whatever color, size, special features, and price seem most appealing, and then transmitting the order instantly to warehouses from which the selections will be shipped directly to their homes. So, too, with financial transactions, airline and hotel reservations, rental car agreements, and similar contracts, which will be executed between consumers in their homes and computer banks somewhere else on the globe."

Here again, my predictions were not far off. By 2014, in-person service work accounted for almost half of all jobs in America, and for most of the new jobs. Moreover, adjusted for inflation, the median pay of such work was below what it had been in 1990. But I did not foresee how quickly advanced technologies would begin to make inroads even on in-person services. By 2014 Amazon was busily wiping out retail jobs, working on how to eliminate humans in its warehouses, and even planning future deliveries by aerial robot drone. Even commercial driving was threatened. In their 2004 book, *The New Division of Labor,* economists Frank Levy and Richard Murnane used driving a truck as an example of the sort of task computers would never be able to perform because it requires complex pattern recognition. But by 2014, Google's self-driving car posed a serious threat to the jobs of some

4.5 million taxi drivers, bus drivers, truck drivers, and sanitation workers.

The third job category I named "symbolic-analytic services." Here I included all the problem solving, problem identifying, and strategic thinking that go into the manipulation of symbols—data, words, oral and visual representations. This category encompasses engineers, investment bankers, lawyers, management consultants, systems analysts, advertising and marketing specialists, professionals in all creative fields such as journalism and film-making, and even university professors. Most are well-educated professionals who tend to work in teams or stare at computer screens. The essence of this work is to rearrange abstract symbols using a variety of analytic and creative tools—mathematical algorithms, legal arguments, financial gimmicks, scientific principles, powerful words and phrases, visual patterns, psychological insights, and other techniques for solving conceptual puzzles. Such manipulations improve efficiency—accomplishing tasks more accurately and quickly—or they better entertain, amuse, inform, or fascinate the human mind.

I estimated in 1990 that symbolic analysts accounted for 20 percent of all American employees, and expected their share to continue to grow, as would their incomes, because the demand for people to do these jobs would continue to outrun the supply of people capable of doing them. This widening disconnect between symbolic-analytic jobs and the other two major categories of work would, I predicted, be the major force driving widening inequality. Here again, I was not too far off, but I had not anticipated how quickly it would happen or how wide the divide would become, or how great a toll inequality and economic insecurity would take. I would never have expected, for example, that the life expectancy of an American white woman without a high school degree would decrease by five years between 1990 and 2008.

I also failed to anticipate how quickly the combination of digital technologies with huge network effects would push the ratio of employees to customers to extraordinary lows. When Instagram, a popular photo-sharing site, was sold to Facebook for about

$1 billion in 2012, it had thirteen employees and thirty million customers. Contrast this with Kodak, which had filed for bankruptcy a few months before. In its prime, Kodak had employed 145,000 people.

The ratio continues to drop. When Facebook purchased WhatsApp for $19 billion in early 2014, WhatsApp had fifty-five employees (including its two young founders) serving 450 million customers. Digitization does not require many workers. It is possible to sell a new idea to hundreds of millions of people without needing many, if any, workers to produce or distribute it. A friend, operating from his home in Tucson, recently designed a machine to determine traces of certain elements in the air, used a 3D printer to make hundreds of copies of the machine, and has been selling them over the Internet to customers all over the world. All he needs is a drone to deliver them and his entire business will depend on just one person—himself.

Consider that in 1964 the four most valuable American companies, with an average market capitalization of $180 billion (in 2011 dollars), employed an average of 430,000 people. Forty-seven years later, the largest American companies were each valued at about twice their former counterparts but were accomplishing their work with less than one-quarter of the number of employees.

We are faced not just with labor-replacing technologies but with knowledge-replacing technologies.* The combination of advanced sensors, voice recognition, artificial intelligence, big data, text mining, and pattern-recognition algorithms is generating smart robots capable of quickly learning human actions, and even of learning from one another. A revolution in life sciences is also under way, allowing drugs to be tailored to a patient's particular condition and genome.

If the current trend continues, many more symbolic ana-

---

* Official productivity data do not yet show the growth in output the new technologies appear to be generating. This could be because the official data don't measure it very well (open-source software, for example, doesn't show up as part of output because it's freely available) and because it often takes years for technological breakthroughs to pervade the overall economy, given how deeply embedded are older technologies.

lysts will be replaced in coming years. The two largest professionally intensive sectors of the United States—health care and education—will be particularly affected because of increasing pressures to hold down costs and, at the same time, the increasing availability of expert machines. We are on the verge of a wave of mobile health applications, for example, directly measuring everything from calories to blood pressure, along with software programs capable of performing for an individual the same functions as costly medical devices run by medical technicians (think ultrasound, CT scans, and electrocardiograms) and diagnostic software that can tell you what it all means and what to do about it. Schools and universities will likewise be reorganized around smart machines (although faculties will scream all the way). Many teachers and university professors are already on the way to being replaced by software—so-called MOOCs (massive open online courses) and interactive online textbooks—along with adjuncts who guide student learning.

Where will this end? Imagine a small box—let's call it an iEverything—capable of producing for you everything you could possibly desire, a modern-day Aladdin's lamp. You would simply tell it what you want, and—presto!—that item would arrive at your feet. The only problem is that no one will be able to buy it, because no one will have any means of earning money, since the iEverything will do it all. This is obviously fanciful, but when more and more can be done by fewer and fewer people, the profits will go to an ever-smaller circle of executives and owner-investors, leaving the rest with less and less money to buy what can be produced because we will either be unemployed or in low-paying jobs. The economic model that predominated through most of the twentieth century was mass production by many for mass consumption by many. That no longer holds. The model of the future seems likely to be unlimited production by a handful for consumption by whoever can afford it.

The underlying problem is not the number of jobs but the allocation of income and wealth. Those who create or invest in blockbuster ideas are earning unprecedented sums and returns. One of the young founders of WhatsApp, CEO Jan Koum, had a 45 percent equity stake in the company when Facebook purchased it, which yielded him $6.8 billion. Co-founder Brian Acton got $3 billion for his 20 percent stake. Each of the early employees reportedly had a 1 percent stake, which would have netted them $160 million each.

If present trends continue, the fortunate creators of blockbuster ideas will earn even more. The corollary, as I have emphasized, is that they will also gain unparalleled political power. But most people will not share in the monetary gains, and their political power will disappear. They will see the dazzling array of products and services spawned by the new technologies but will be unable to buy them because the technologies will supplant their work and drive down their pay.

When I made my predictions almost twenty-five years ago I expected that modern technologies would continue to increase the demand for highly educated workers while reducing demand for the less educated. So I assumed that the remedy for job losses and for declining wages lay in helping more people get more and better education, especially access to higher education. I was only partly correct. Those with college degrees continued to do far better than people without them. In 2013, Americans with four-year college degrees earned 98 percent more per hour on average than people without college degrees. That was a bigger advantage than the 89 percent premium that college graduates earned relative to nongraduates five years before, and the 64 percent advantage they held in the early 1980s.

Yet I was wrong in believing that college degrees would deliver steadily higher wages and a larger share of the economic pie. In fact, the demand for well-educated workers in the United States seems to have peaked around 2000 and then fallen, even as the supply of well-educated workers has continued to grow. As I have noted, since 2000 the vast majority of college graduates have experienced little or no income gains at all. Even those in the top 90th percentile of college graduates increased their cumulative income by only 4.4 percent between 2000 and 2013. Over the same years, the entry-level wages of college graduates actually dropped (a decline of 8.1 percent for women graduates and 6.7 percent for men). To state it another way, while a college education has become a prerequisite for joining the middle class, it is no longer a sure means of gaining ground once admitted to it. The middle class's share of the total economic pie continues to shrink, while the share going to the top continues to grow.

Reversing the upward pre-distributions baked into the rules of the market, getting big money out of politics, reinventing the corporation, and improving the quality of and access to education will all be helpful. Countervailing power should aim for no less. But these changes will not themselves alter the direction in which technological advances are taking us. And yet, as I have shown, no economy, and no society, can sustain itself with a system of production whose revenues and profits overwhelmingly flow to a very few. What, then, is the answer?

Some call for higher taxes on the incomes and the wealth of the few big winners, with the revenues then redistributed to everyone else. It should be possible for countervailing power to raise the top marginal income-tax rate. After all, during the three decades after World War II, when the power of large corporations and Wall Street was effectively countervailed, the top marginal rate never fell below 70 percent (and the effective rate, including all deductions and tax credits, never below 50 percent). But if current trends continue, direct redistribution on the scale necessary to achieve broadly shared prosperity forty or fifty years from now will require more than this. When almost everything can be done by knowledge-replacing technologies owned by a small number of people, not even Thomas Piketty's proposed global tax on wealth will suffice. What will be needed? And how could the market be reorganized to accomplish it?

23

The Citizen's Bequest

Instead of directly taxing the current income or wealth of a few and transferring it to the many, a more sensible approach is to more widely share future wealth. The difference is not merely semantic. As we have seen, current wealth is the outcome of a system of market rules. Presumably the founders of WhatsApp went to the trouble of creating their blockbuster product because they hoped they would win the jackpot with it, as they did. But the size of that prize, and the system of incentives of which it is a part, depend in turn on rules about intellectual property, such as the duration of patents and copyrights; rules about market power, such as when standard platforms violate antitrust laws; rules about contracts, such as when a corporation becomes so powerful that its agreements with consumers and employees become coercive, or when conflicts of interest and insider information result in fraud; rules about who can declare bankruptcy and have their debts reorganized; and rules about enforcing all of these, including the protection of private property and wealth.

If the rules were different—if, for example, the Patent Office defined "new and useful" so strictly that it denied WhatsApp's patent application as being insufficiently novel or useful relative to other messaging services; or Congress decided patents will last only three years instead of twenty; or antitrust laws prohibited any company that controlled a large network or major platform (such as Facebook) from acquiring another company on the way to gaining control of another network (such as WhatsApp); or enforcement of patents was so lax that anyone could freely appropriate WhatsApp's messaging service—WhatsApp would not be worth $19 billion. It would be worth far less, or nothing, which would leave its founders with relatively small rewards or no remuneration at all for their efforts. Is this a good outcome?

The question has to do with the underlying market rules for pre-distributing income and wealth, including providing adequate incentives to innovators such as WhatsApp's founders. As I have pointed out, current market rules are generating increasing returns to the owners of capital assets and decreasing returns to the vast majority who work for a living. With sufficient countervailing power, society has the option of creating rules that will not heap such huge rewards on so few but will still give innovators enough incentive to keep their inventions coming.

What's the appropriate balance between stimulating new inventions and investments that could possibly improve the quality of life for millions of people and not concentrating too much wealth in the hands of a few, thereby impoverishing almost everyone else? There's no correct answer. But with adequate countervailing power we could have more confidence in the ability of our political-economic system to decide. We could better trust that the resulting distribution of income and wealth represents a trade-off society is willing to make.

That doesn't end the matter, because that trade-off would change for wealth handed down to future generations who played no role in the original invention and investment. Even if the market is designed to richly reward WhatsApp's two founders, it need not lavish similar rewards on their descendants in order to give the founders ample incentive. Even if they care about their kids, they are likely to care far less about their great-grandchildren and about subsequent generations whom they will never know and whose genes will be further diluted with the genes of many forebears other than the founders'. This means that the market rules affecting wealth and income in the long term could generate smaller and smaller returns to each succeeding generation of heirs to inventors without reducing the original inventors' motivation. From society's point of view, that would allow the trade-off to tilt ever more in the direction of reducing concentrated wealth and spreading economic gains.

The appropriate analogy is to intellectual property, which poses a similar balance between giving creators adequate incentives and putting their creations into the public's hands—into the "public domain" as it is called—as soon as those incentives are no longer necessary. Extended to the entire process of technological advancement and to all the market rules underlying it, this suggests a principle for deciding on the rules governing future wealth. Just as with intellectual property, at some point that wealth would revert to the public domain.

The absence of countervailing power has moved us in the opposite direction, however. To repeat: By 2014 six of the ten wealthiest Americans were heirs to prominent fortunes. The six Walmart heirs together had more wealth than the bottom 42 percent of Americans combined (up from 30.5 percent in 2007). According to political economist Peter Barnes, interest, dividends, capital gains, and inheritances account for one out of every three dollars of income received by Americans—and almost all of that goes to the richest 1 percent. Meanwhile, the estate tax no longer kicks in until a couple's estate is worth more than $10.68 million, and the laws give ample opportunity for a halfway clever estate attorney to lock away far more in trust funds. In addition, assets that increase in value over the course of a lifetime—homes, stocks and bonds, jewelry, paintings, antiques, land—can go to heirs without the heirs paying capital gains taxes on such increases. The heirs can draw income from the assets through the course of their own lives and then pass them on to their own heirs, without anyone ever paying capital gains taxes.

Put this together with the technological trend I have outlined, which is putting more and more value in fewer and fewer hands while reducing the real wages of most, and the expected transfer by wealthy Americans to their heirs over the next half century of some $36 trillion, and you see why we are lurching toward a capitalism so top-heavy it cannot be sustained.

Countervailing power would not only reverse this but would use the proceeds from the changes in market rules I have suggested to guarantee all citizens a share in the future growth of the economy.

One straightforward way to do this would be to provide all Americans, beginning the month they turn eighteen and continuing each month thereafter, a basic minimum income that enables them to be economically independent and self-sufficient.

This is not as radical as it may sound. In 1979, the conservative economist F. A. Hayek endorsed just such a system:

> The assurance of a certain minimum income for everyone, or a sort of floor below which nobody need fall even when he is unable to provide for himself, appears not only to be a wholly legitimate protection against a risk common to all, but a necessary part of the Great Society in which the individual no longer has specific claims on the members of the particular small group into which he was born.*

Many who call themselves libertarian are also attracted to a basic minimum income because it eliminates the need for welfare or another form of government transfer to the poor that tells them how to spend the funds or otherwise demeans or stigmatizes them. It would likewise reduce people's dependence on private employers, thereby freeing them to express their views without fear of retaliation.

---

* A similar proposal, which would provide every Swiss citizen a stipend of $2,800 per month, was submitted to Swiss voters in October 2013. To date, the proposal has not been enacted.

Some might object that such a system would contravene society's work ethic, robbing citizens of the structure and meaning work provides. The answer is that a basic minimum payment would be only enough to ensure recipients and their families a minimally decent standard of living. Anyone wishing to supplement their basic minimum could of course choose to work, even though most jobs will pay modestly, for reasons already mentioned.

The basic minimum would allow people to pursue whatever arts or avocations provide them with meaning, thereby also enabling society to enjoy the fruits of such artistry or voluntary effort. It seems doubtful that the vast majority would choose idleness over physical and mental activity. Instead, we're likely to see a reversion to a time when many jobs were considered "callings," expressing a deeply personal commitment rather than simply a means of acquiring money. I have met a number of teachers, social workers, doctors, nurses, and—yes—even politicians who still view their work this way. I have not yet found an investment banker who does, but perhaps there are a few.

Similarly, potential artists will be freed to pursue their work. It was once possible for T. S. Eliot to survey land when he wasn't writing poetry, or Walt Whitman to earn money as a copyist in an army paymaster's office, or the young Albert Einstein to develop his theory of relativity while an examiner in a patent office. But in recent decades, for most people, paid work has become more intrusive, occupying more waking hours and even intruding on sleep. How many budding poets or artists or scientific theorists cannot pursue their craft because they are effectively on call almost all hours in order to have enough to live on? A basic minimum income would give them that opportunity.

We would thereby create a future in which robots do most of the work and our people reap the benefits. This would be that kind of society John Maynard Keynes foresaw in 1928, when he claimed that in a century technological advances would create an age of abundance in which no one would need to worry about making money, leaving us with the challenge of how best to use the resulting freedom and leisure. Keynes left out the crucial mechanism for distributing the gains from technological advances in such a way that nearly everyone would have the means of benefitting from them. A basic minimum, financed through reduced property rights for the future heirs of owners of breakthrough technologies, would realize Keynes's vision.

But the true visionary here, as elsewhere, was Thomas Paine, author of *Common Sense,* published in 1776, who authored another essay as prescient and important as the former but that is less remembered. Entitled *Agrarian Justice* and published in 1797, Paine's essay proposed that every American man and woman be paid fifteen pounds when he or she turned twenty-one, a sum that would serve as a basic minimum income. Revenues for this would come from a tax on the inheritance of land. This, Paine reasoned, would foster economic independence, so crucial to the budding democracy. In setting out the argument for his proposal he noted that private property was a human contrivance. When people were hunters and gatherers, the earth was "common property." But with the coming of agriculture, property took the form of the right to exclude others. Such landholdings were useful and inevitable, Paine thought, because of the difficulty of distinguishing improvements to the land from ownership of the land itself. But it was necessary and proper to give every citizen a stake, a "just indemnity" for what was taken.

The analogy is not perfect. The robots of the future, along with other breakthrough technologies, will not exactly take away "common property" for which citizens deserve to be indemnified. But they will take away good jobs that are already dwindling in number and replace opportunities already growing scarce. They will, in short, supplant the middle class that has been the centerpiece of our economy and society and that is already shrinking. New market rules that cause wealth eventually to revert to the public domain rather than compound for future generations that had nothing to do with creating it, and be used instead to finance a minimum guaranteed income for all citizens, is one way to avoid this fate.

An alternative would be to provide every citizen a tiny share of all intellectual property awarded by the patent office and protected by the government. As the worth of the nation's stock of intellectual capital grew, all citizens would reap the dividends. Another alternative would be to give every child at birth a basic minimum endowment of stocks and bonds—a "share" in the future economy, which, as the economy grew and the value of the endowment compounded, would become a nest egg capable of producing a minimum basic income.

However it is accomplished, the rules must be adapted toward creating a more inclusive economy. Absent some means for sharing the increasingly large rewards that will otherwise go to a few people and their heirs fortunate enough to possess ownership rights to these robots and related technologies, the middle class will disappear, and capitalism as we know it will not survive.

24

New Rules

As I hope I've made clear, there is much cause for optimism. We are on the cusp of a wave of inventions and innovations that can vastly improve our lives. Although these inventions and innovations will also replace countless jobs and thereby drive down the wages of the vast majority—a process that has already started in the United States and other advanced nations—we have the capacity to reorganize capitalism so the gains are shared widely.

The larger cause for optimism is that we need not be victims of impersonal "market forces" over which we have no control. The market is a human creation. It is based on rules that human beings devise. The central question is who shapes those rules and for what purpose. Over the last three decades, the rules have been shaped by large corporations, Wall Street, and very wealthy individuals in order to channel a large portion of the nation's total income and wealth to themselves. If they continue to have unbridled influence over the rules, and they gain control of the assets at the core of the new wave of innovations, they will end up with almost all the wealth, all the income, and all the political power. That result is no more in their interest than in the interests of the rest of the population, because under such conditions an economy and a society cannot endure.

The coming challenge is not to technology or to economics. It is a challenge to democracy. The critical debate for the future is not about the size of government; it is about whom government is *for*. The central choice is not between the "free market" and government; it is between a market organized for broadly based prosperity and one designed to deliver almost all the gains to a few at the top. The pertinent issue is not how much is to be taxed away from the wealthy and redistributed to those who are not; it is how to design the rules of the market so that the economy generates what most people would consider a fair distribution on its own, without necessitating large redistributions after the fact.

The vast majority of the nation's citizens do have the power to alter the rules of the market to meet their needs. But to exercise that power, they must understand what is happening and where their interests lie, and they must join together. We have done so before. If history is any guide and common sense has any sway, we will do so again.

Acknowledgments

This book is the product of several years of research, observations, and discussions, undertaken with many people whose insights appear throughout. It is impossible to thank all of them adequately. My colleagues at the Goldman School of Public Policy at the University of California, Berkeley have been founts of intellectual provocation and nurturance. I am particularly indebted to Henry Brady, Sean Farhang, Alex Gelber, Hilary Hoynes, David Kirp, Amy Lerman, Paul Pierson, Jesse Rothstein, and Eugene Smolensky for their valuable comments on earlier drafts. I am also grateful to several friends and former colleagues whose candid and constructive criticisms kept me on track. Richard Parker, Jacob Kornbluth, John Isaacson, Steve Silberstein, Michael Pertschuk, Paul Starr, Laura Tyson, and Erik Tarloff deserve special mention. The eminent political economist Charles Lindblom added valuable perspective, for which I'm especially grateful. Three exceptional graduate students—Liz Gross, Sonja Petek, and Taylor Smiley—provided superb assistance tracking down hard-to-find facts and examples. Technical assistance was deftly furnished by Manuel Castrillo and Sergey Shevtchenko. My ever-cheerful and remarkably efficient assistant, Rebecca Boles, helped in ways too numerous to mention. I have appreciated the research support provided by the Goldman School and the Blum Center for Developing Economies. My literary agent, Rafe Sagalyn, offered valuable advice, as he has done so many times before, and my editor, Jonathan Segal, was a source of wisdom and common sense, as has been his custom. Not the least, I am grateful to my wife and partner, Perian Flaherty, whose passion for authenticity and social truth is an enduring inspiration.

Notes

INTRODUCTION

xv Then, the CEOs of large corporations: See Lawrence Mischel and Alyssa Davis, *CEO Pay Continues to Rise as Typical Workers Are Paid Less,* Issue Brief #380, Economic Policy Institute website, 2014.

xv In those years, the richest 1 percent: See, for example, A. Atkinsin, T. Piketty, and E. Saez, "Top Incomes in the Long Run of History," *Journal of Economic Literature* 49, no. 1 (2011): 3–71.

xvi Confidence in the economic system: While in 2001 a Gallup poll found 76 percent of Americans satisfied with opportunities to get ahead by working hard and only 22 percent dissatisfied, by 2013, only 54 percent were satisfied and 45 percent were dissatisfied. See Rebecca Riffkin, "In U.S., 67% Dissatisfied with Income, Wealth Distribution," Gallup website, January 20, 2014 (http://www.gallup.com/poll/166904/dissatisfied -income-wealth-distribution.aspx).

xvi The apparent arbitrariness: According to Pew, the percentage of Americans who feel most people who want to get ahead can do so through hard work had dropped by fourteen points since 2000. See Pew Research Center for the People and the Press/USA Today, "January 2014 Political Survey, Final Topline," Pew Research Center website, January 15–19, 2014 (http:// www.people-press.org/files/legacy-questionnaires/1-23-14%20Poverty _Inequality%20topline%20for%20release.pdf).

xvi the economic and political systems seem rigged: Sixty-three percent of Americans believe most members of Congress are willing to sell their vote for either cash or a campaign contribution, and 59 percent think it likely their own representative already has. Sixty-six percent think most members of Congress do not care what their constituents think. See "Americans

Don't Think Incumbents Deserve Reelection," Rasmussen Reports website, October 2, 2014.

xvi The threat to capitalism: See "Views of Government: Key Data Points," Pew Research Center website, October 22, 2013 (http://www.pewresearch.org/key-data-points/views-of-government-key-data-points/).

xix While this book focuses: See European Commission, *Standard Eurobarometer 81, Spring 2014: Public Opinion in the European Union, First Results*, European Commission website, July 2014.

1 THE PREVAILING VIEW

4 "[in nature] there is no place": See Thomas Hobbes, *Leviathan, or the Matter, Forme, and Power of a Commonwealth, Ecclesiastical and Civil* (1651), ch. 13, "Of the Natural Condition of Mankind as Concerning Their Felicity, and Misery."

5 As the economic historian Karl Polanyi recognized: See Karl Polanyi, *The Great Transformation: The Political and Economic Origins of Our Time* (New York: Farrar & Rinehart, 1944).

2 THE FIVE BUILDING BLOCKS OF CAPITALISM

10 Accordingly, the "free market": See John Rawls, *A Theory of Justice*, rev. ed. (Cambridge, MA: Belknap Press, 1999), pp. 102–68.

3 FREEDOM AND POWER

11 In 2010, a majority of the Supreme Court: *Citizens United v. Federal Election Commission*, 558 U.S. 310 (2010).

11 Therefore, said the court: Ibid.

12 In *Carter v. Carter Coal Company* (1936): *Carter v. Carter Coal Co. et al.*, 298 U.S. 238 (1936), p. 311.

12 *Carter* was subsequently overruled: See, for example, *United States v. Darby*, 312 U.S. 100 (1941).

14 Allowing Internet service providers: See Nick Russo and Robert Morgus with Sarah Morris and Danielle Kehl, *The Cost of Connectivity 2014*, Open Technology Institute at New America website, October 30, 2014. See also Claire Cain Miller, "Why the U.S. Has Fallen Behind in Internet Speed and Affordability," *New York Times*, October 30, 2014.

14 Permitting drug companies: See Valerie Paris, "Why Do Americans Spend So Much on Pharmaceuticals?" *PBS NewsHour* website, February 7, 2014.

4 THE NEW PROPERTY

16 Garrett Hardin warned: Garrett Hardin, "The Tragedy of the Commons," *Science* 162, no. 3859 (1968): 1243–48.

17 slaves far outnumbered free persons: Adam Hochschild, *Bury the Chains* (New York: Houghton Mifflin, 2005), p. 2.

17 The Republican Party in the United States: See Heather Cox Richardson, *To Make Men Free: A History of the Republican Party* (New York: Basic Books, 2014), pp. 6–12.

17 By the end of the nineteenth century: Hochschild, *Bury the Chains,* p. 3.

17 It was not officially banned: Constance Johnson, "Mauritania: United Nations: Plan to End Slavery Expected," Law Library of Congress website, March 11, 2014.

17 Even in twenty-first-century America: See Shared Hope International, *National Colloquium 2012 Final Report,* Shared Hope International website, May 2013, p. 80.

17 beginning with the Land Ordinance of 1785: "Teaching with Documents: The Homestead Act of 1862," National Archives website.

18 Henry George, in his book *Progress and Poverty:* Henry George, *Progress and Poverty,* 25th ann. ed. (Garden City, NY: Doubleday, Page & Company, 1912), p. 9.

18 The book sold two million copies: Ibid., p. x.

19 airlines with overbooked flights: See Julian L. Simon, "The Airline Over-sales Auction Plan: The Results," *Journal of Transport Economics and Policy* 28, no. 3 (1994): 319–23.

20 The framers of the Constitution: U.S. Constitution, art. I, sec. 8.

21 The first patent law in America: Patent Act of 1790, 1 Stat. 109–12 (1790).

21 Congress has extended patent protection: The Patent Act of 1793 said patents could be obtained for "any new and useful art." See Patent Act of 1793, 1 Stat. 318–23 (1793).

21 almost ten thousand employees: U.S. Patent and Trademark Office, *Performance and Accountability Report Fiscal Year 2009,* Patent and Trademark Office website, p. 11.

21 and the federal courts included: See Administrative Office of the U.S. Courts, "Caseload Statistics 2014: Caseload Analysis," table "Federal Circuit Filings, Percent Change Over Time," U.S. Courts website (http://www.uscourts.gov/Statistics/FederalJudicialCaseloadStatistics/caseload-statistics-2014/caseload-analysis.aspx). See also PricewaterhouseCoopers LLP, *2013 Patent Litigation Study,* PricewaterhouseCoopers website, 2013, p. 6.

21 Amazon, for example: Peri Hartman, Jeffrey P. Bezos, Shel Kaphan, and Joel Spiegel, Method and System for Placing a Purchase Order via a Communications Network, U.S. Patent 5,960,411, filed September 12, 1997, and issued September 28, 1999.

21 Apple received a patent: Casey Maureen Dougherty and Melissa Breglio Hajj, Embedding an Autograph in an Electronic Book, U.S. Patent 8,880,602, filed March 23, 2012, and issued November 4, 2014.

22 IBM and Microsoft: See Timothy B. Lee, "Software Patent Reform Just Died in the House, Thanks to IBM and Microsoft," *Washington Post,* November 20, 2013.

22 By purchasing Motorola Mobility: See Phillip Elmer-DeWitt, "Is Google Buying Motorola for Its 24,000 Patents?" *Forbes,* August 15, 2011.

22 White House intellectual property advisor: Colleen Chien, "Reforming Software Patents," *Houston Law Review* 50, no. 2 (2012): 323–88.

22 America spends far more on medications: OECD, *Health at a Glance 2013: OECD Indicators* (OECD Publishing, 2013), pp. 160–61. See also Valerie Paris, "Why Do Americans Spend So Much on Pharmaceuticals?" *PBS NewsHour* website, February 7, 2014.

22 Of the $3.1 trillion: National Center for Health Statistics, *Health, United States, 2013: With Special Feature on Prescription Drugs,* National Center for Health Statistics website, 2014, tables 112 and 114.

23 Drug prices are high in America: Robert Pear, "Bill to Let Medicare Negotiate Drug Prices Is Blocked," *New York Times,* April 18, 2007.

23 applications for patents on vaccines: Elisabeth Rosenthal, "The Price of Prevention: Vaccine Costs Are Soaring," *New York Times,* July 2, 2014.

23 Pfizer raked in nearly $4 billion: Ibid.

23 The capsules were simply: Ed Silverman, "Actavis Is Ordered to Continue Selling the Namenda Alzheimer's Pill," *Wall Street Journal,* December 11, 2014.

24 America is one of the few advanced nations: C. Lee Ventola, "Direct-to-Consumer Pharmaceutical Advertising: Therapeutic or Toxic?" *Pharmacy & Therapeutics* 36, no. 10 (2011): 669–84.

24 The ostensible reason: "Food and Drug Administration Safety and Innovation Act (FDASIA)," U.S. Food and Drug Administration website.

24 Yet the real threat: Sara R. Collins, Ruth Robertson, Tracy Garber, and Michelle M. Doty, *Insuring the Future: Current Trends in Health Coverage and the Effects of Implementing the Affordable Care Act,* Commonwealth Fund website, April 2013, pp. 9–10.

24 Over a five-month period in 2013: Katie Thomas, Agustin Armendariz, and Sarah Cohen, "Detailing Financial Links of Doctors and Drug Makers," *New York Times,* September 30, 2014.

24 Some doctors pocketed: Ibid.

25 The tactic costs Americans: "Pay-for-Delay: When Drug Companies Agree Not to Compete," Federal Trade Commission website.

25 But that argument neglects: Marc-André Gagnon and Joel Lexchin, "The Cost of Pushing Pills: A New Estimate of Pharmaceutical Promotion Expenditures in the United States," *PLoS Med* 5, no. 1 (2008): 0029–0033.

25 their lobbying tab came to $225 million: Center for Responsive Politics, "Influence and Lobbying: Pharmaceuticals/Health Products: Industry Profile: Summary, 2013," OpenSecrets.org website (https://www.open secrets.org/lobby/indusclient.php?id=H04&year=2013).

25 In 2012 it shelled out more than $36 million: Center for Responsive Politics, "Pharmaceuticals/Health Products Summary," OpenSecrets.org website (https://www.opensecrets.org/industries/indus.php?cycle=2014&ind =H04).

26 When the nation was founded: Copyright Act of 1790, 1 Stat. 124 (1790).

26 This change operated retroactively: For the discussion of copyright history in the United States, see "United States Copyright Office: A Brief Introduction and History," U.S. Copyright Office website.

27 Most of those old copyrights: For a discussion of the Disney case, see Timothy B. Lee, "15 Years Ago, Congress Kept Mickey Mouse out of the Public Domain. Will They Do It Again?" *Washington Post,* October 25, 2013.

5 THE NEW MONOPOLY

30 Between 1978 and 2011: Ian Hathaway and Robert E. Litan, "Declining Business Dynamism in the United States: A Look at States and Metros," Brookings Institution website, p. 1.

30 The decline transcends the business cycle: Ibid.

30 And that trend has been immune: Ibid., figure 1.

31 The average peak Internet connection speed: Akamai Technologies, *Akamai's State of the Internet,* Akamai Technologies website, 2014, figures 12 and 22.

31 many lower-income Americans: Just 52 percent of those with household incomes under $30,000 had broadband Internet access at home in 2013 compared with 91 percent of those earning $75,000 or more. Pew Research Internet Project, "Broadband Technology Fact Sheet," Pew Research Center website, data from 2013.

31 The costs are so high: See Susan Crawford, *Captive Audience: The Telecom Industry and Monopoly Power in the New Gilded Age* (New Haven, CT: Yale University Press, 2013), p. 65.

31 When it comes to fiber connections: For speeds, see "Global Broadband: Household Download Index," Ookla website. For prices, see "OECD Broadband Portal," section 4.01, "Range of Broadband Prices per Megabit per Second of Advertised Speed," OECD website, figure 7.17.

32 The project quickly recouped its costs: Susan Crawford, "Government Should Invest in Fiber Optics," *New York Times,* July 14, 2014.

32 prohibiting cities from laying fiber cables: Allan Holmes, "How Big Telecom Smothers City-Run Broadband," Center for Public Integrity website, August 28, 2014, updated September 15, 2014.

32 "Cable's pretty much a monopoly now": David Lieberman, "Liberty Media's John Malone Says Cable Is 'Pretty Much a Monopoly' in Broadband," *Deadline Hollywood,* May 6, 2011.

32 more than 80 percent of Americans had no choice: Prepared remarks of FCC chairman Tom Wheeler, "The Facts and Future of Broadband Competition," 1776 Headquarters, Washington, DC, September 4, 2014.

32 Since none of the cable companies: Susan Crawford, "Let America's Cities Provide Broadband to Their Citizens," *Bloomberg View,* February 14, 2012.

32 By 2014, Comcast: Stephen Seufert, "Chattanooga v. Kabletown," Philly .com, June 29, 2014.

33 Comcast and other cable operators: Center for Responsive Politics, "Influence and Lobbying: Lobbying: Top Spenders, 2014." See also "Comcast Corp.: Profile for 2014 Election Cycle," OpenSecrets.org website (https:// www.opensecrets.org/orgs/summary.php?id=D000000461&lname=Com cast+Corp).

33 Michael Powell, who chaired the Federal Communications Commission: See "Michael Powell," National Cable and Telecommunications Association website.

33 The National Cable and Telecommunications Association: Center for Responsive Politics, "Influence and Lobbying: Lobbying: Top Spenders, 2014," OpenSecrets.org website (https://www.opensecrets.org/lobby/top .php?indexType=s&showYear=2014).

33 Of its 126 lobbyists: Center for Responsive Politics, "Comcast Corp.: Lobbyists Representing Comcast Corp., 2014," OpenSecrets.org website (http:// www.opensecrets.org/lobby/clientlbs.php?id=D000000461&year=2014).

33 Meredith Attwell Baker: "Tying Up the Cable Business," *The Economist,* October 4, 2014.

33 Comcast's in-house lobbyists: See Alex Rogers, "Comcast Has About 76 Lobbyists Working Washington on the Time-Warner Cable Merger. This Is Why," *Time,* April 29, 2014.

34 Monsanto, the giant biotech corporation: Food and Water Watch, *Monsanto: A Corporate Profile,* Food and Water Watch website, April 2013.

34 To ensure its dominance: For the discussion of Monsanto seeds, see Donald L. Barlett and James B. Steele, "Monsanto's Harvest of Fear," *Vanity Fair,* May 2008.

35 in less than fifteen years: Ibid.

35 Monsanto has more than doubled the price: See William Neuman, "Rapid Rise in Seed Prices Draws U.S. Scrutiny," *New York Times,* March 11, 2010.

35 The average cost of planting: See Center for Food Safety & Save Our Seeds, *Seed Giants v. U.S. Farmers,* Center for Food Safety website, 2013. See also Rachel Tepper, "Seed Giants Sue U.S. Farmers over Genetically Modified Seed Patents in Shocking Numbers: Report," *Huffington Post,* February 13, 2013.

35 This increases the risk: Richard Schiffman, "Seeds of the Future," Truthout

website, December 4, 2014. See also Center for Food Safety & Save Our Seeds, *Seed Giants v. U.S. Farmers.*

35 A third consequence: Center for Food Safety & Save Our Seeds, *Seed Giants v. U.S. Farmers*, p. 5.

35 the Plant Variety Protection Act of 1970: Kristina Hubbard, "Monsanto's Growing Monopoly," *Salon*, May 30, 2013.

35 It has successfully fought off: Mina Nasseri and Daniel J. Herling, "Ho Ho Ho GMO! The 2014 GMO Legislation Scorecard," *National Law Review*, December 23, 2014. See also Connor Adams Sheets, "GMO Labeling Debate Headed to Congressional Committee," *International Business Times*, December 4, 2014.

35 They've sued other companies: See Barlett and Steele, "Monsanto's Harvest of Fear."

35 Monsanto's lawyers: See Union of Concerned Scientists, "Eight Ways Monsanto Fails at Sustainable Agriculture," no. 7, "Suppressing Research," Union of Concerned Scientists website.

35 it succeeded in putting an end: See Monsanto, "Monsanto Notified That U.S. Department of Justice Has Concluded Its Inquiry," Monsanto website, November 16, 2012. See also Tom Philpott, "DOJ Mysteriously Quits Monsanto Antitrust Investigation," *Mother Jones*, December 1, 2012.

35 Monsanto has the distinction: Center for Responsive Politics, "Agricultural Services/Products: Summary, 2012," OpenSecrets.org website (https://www.opensecrets.org/lobby/indusclient.php?id=A07&year=2012).

35 Monsanto's former (and future) employees: See Center for Responsive Politics, "Monsanto Co.: Lobbyists Representing Monsanto Co., 2014," OpenSecrets.org website (https://www.opensecrets.org/lobby/clientlbs.php?id=D000000055&year=2014), and Janie Boschma, "Monsanto: Big Guy on the Block When It Comes to Friends in Washington," OpenSecrets.org website, February 19, 2013. See also Food and Water Watch, *Monsanto: A Corporate Profile*, figure 3, p. 10, and Janice Person, "I Heard Monsanto Employees Control USDA, FDA, etc.," *Beyond the Rows* blog, February 15, 2012.

37 Apple says it wants: Apple says its "business strategy leverages its unique ability to design and develop its own operating systems, hardware, application software and services to provide its customers products and solutions with innovative design, superior ease-of-use and seamless integration." See U.S. Securities and Exchange Commission, Apple Inc. Proxy Statement, part 1, item 1, "Business Strategy," p. 1 (http://files.shareholder.com/downloads/AAPL/3750879716x0x789040/ed3853da-2e3f-448d-adb4-34816c375f5d/2014_Form_10_K_As_Filed.PDF).

37 Microsoft settled the case: *United States v. Microsoft Corporation*, U.S. District Court for the District of Columbia, civil action no. 98-1232 (CKK), 2002.

37 Apple spent $3,370,000 on lobbying: Center for Responsive Politics, "Cli-

ent Profiles: Summary, 2013," for Apple, Amazon, Facebook, Microsoft, and Google, and "Influence and Lobbying: Lobbying: Top Spenders, 2013," OpenSecrets.org website (https://www.opensecrets.org/lobby/top.php?showYear=2013&indexType=s).

37 "conduct . . . that will result in real harm": Brody Mullins, Rolfe Winkler, and Brent Kendall, "Inside the U.S. Antitrust Probe of Google," *Wall Street Journal*, March 19, 2015.

37 Google's increasing political clout: Tom Hamburger and Matea Gold, "Google, Once Disdainful of Lobbying, Now a Master of Washington Influence," *Washington Post*, April 12, 2014.

38 Google and Facebook were the first stops: See, for example, Frédéric Filloux, "Do the Media Really Have an Alternative to Distribution via Facebook and Google?" *Quartz*, October 20, 2014.

38 The newer the media company: Ibid.

38 Amazon has become the first stop: "Fifty Favorite Retailers (2013)," National Retail Federation website.

38 the top ten websites: See Astra Taylor, *The People's Platform: Taking Back Power and Culture in the Digital Age* (Toronto: Random House Canada, 2014), p. 37.

39 In 2014, Amazon: Nick Statt, "Amazon Facing United Front of Authors in Hachette E-book Dispute," *CNET*, July 25, 2014.

39 Amazon said this was only fair: David Streitfeld, "Amazon, a Friendly Giant as Long as It's Fed," *New York Times*, July 12, 2014.

39 Amazon eventually agreed: David Streitfeld, "Amazon and Hachette Resolve Dispute," *New York Times*, November 13, 2014.

39 Large retailers including Borders: Jeremy Greenfield, "How the Amazon-Hachette Fight Could Shape the Future of Ideas," *The Atlantic*, May 28, 2014.

40 Perhaps it was pure coincidence: David Streitfeld, "Amazon Is Not Holding Back on Paul Ryan," *New York Times*, September 30, 2014.

40 In France, for example: Elaine Sciolino, "The French Still Flock to Bookstores," *New York Times*, June 10, 2012.

40 The French government classifies books: Pamela Druckerman, "The French Do Buy Books. Real Books," *New York Times*, July 9, 2014.

40 The firm's annual lobbying expenditures: Center for Responsive Politics, "Amazon.com, Client Profile: Summary, 2008," OpenSecrets.org website (https://www.opensecrets.org/lobby/clientsum.php?id=D000023883&year=2008), and "Summary, 2012," OpenSecrets.org website (https://www.opensecrets.org/lobby/clientsum.php?id=D000023883&year=2012).

40 the firm beefed up its presence: Paul Farhi, "Washington Post Closes Sale to Amazon Founder Jeff Bezos," *Washington Post*, October 1, 2013.

40 By 2014, Wall Street's five largest banks: Federal Deposit Insurance Corporation, "Top 100 Banks and Thrifts, Nationally by Asset Size," December 31,

2000, and September 30, 2014, and "FDIC—Statistics on Depository Institutions Report," Assets and Liabilities, December 31, 2000, and September 30, 2014.

41 the financial sector grew six times as fast: Thomas M. Hoenig, "Statement by Thomas M. Hoenig, Vice Chairman, FDIC on the Credibility of the 2013 Living Wills Submitted by First Wave Filers," Federal Deposit Insurance Corporation website, August 4, 2014.

41 In the 2008 presidential campaign: Center for Responsive Politics, Contributions to Presidential Candidates, "Barack Obama (D): Top Industries, 2008," OpenSecrets.org website (https://www.opensecrets.org/pres08/indus .php?cycle=2008&cid=N00009638).

41 John McCain, at $9.3 million: Center for Responsive Politics, Contributions to Presidential Candidates, "John McCain (R): Top Industries, 2008." OpenSecrets.org website (https://www.opensecrets.org/pres08/indus.php ?cycle=2008&cid=N00006424).

41 The employees of Goldman Sachs: Center for Responsive Politics, Contributions to Presidential Candidates, "Barack Obama (D): Top Contributors, 2008." OpenSecrets.org website (https://www.opensecrets.org/pres08/ contrib.php?cycle=2008&cid=N00009638).

41 In the presidential campaign of 2012: Center for Responsive Politics, Contributions to Presidential Candidates, "Mitt Romney (R): Top Industries, 2012," OpenSecrets.org website (https://www.opensecrets.org/pres12/indus .php?cycle=2012&id=N00000286).

41 The Treasury secretaries under Bill Clinton: CBS Investigates, "Goldman Sachs' Revolving Door," CBS News website, April 8, 2010. See also Eric Dash and Louise Story, "Rubin Leaving Citigroup; Smith Barney for Sale," *New York Times,* January 9, 2009.

41 Timothy Geithner had been handpicked: Center for Responsive Politics, Employment History, "Geithner, Timothy, Bio," OpenSecrets.org website (http://www.opensecrets.org/revolving/rev_summary.php?id=78265).

41 As a member of the House Financial Services Committee: Josh Israel, "After 30 Years of Fighting for Wall Street, Eric Cantor Will Make Millions at an Investment Bank," *ThinkProgress,* September 2, 2014.

42 Cantor joined the Wall Street investment bank: See U.S. Securities and Exchange Commission, Moelis & Company, Form 8-K, September 2, 2014, Item 5.02 (d) (http://www.sec.gov/Archives/edgar/data/1596967/000 110465914064087/a14-20284_18k.htm).

42 Cantor would run: Dana Cimilluca and Patrick O'Connor, "Eric Cantor to Join Wall Street Investment Bank," *Wall Street Journal,* September 2, 2014.

42 "I have known Ken": Moelis & Company, "Moelis & Company Announces the Appointment of Eric Cantor as Vice Chairman and Member of the Board of Directors," press release, September 2, 2014.

42 three leading private-equity firms: William Alden, "K.K.R., Blackstone and

TPG Private Equity Firms Agree to Settle Lawsuit on Collusion," *New York Times*, August 7, 2014.

42 Evidence showed: Ibid.

43 Libor (short for "London interbank offered rate"): Halah Touryalai, "Libor Explained: How Manipulated Rates Could Be Hurting (Or Helping) You," *Forbes*, July 9, 2012.

43 Evidence shows that bankers: "Timeline: Libor-Fixing Scandal," BBC News website, February 6, 2013.

43 The scandal initially focused: Ibid.

43 The health care sector: It is estimated that health care expenditures are 17.9 percent of GDP. See Global Health Observatory Data Repository, "United States of America Statistics Summary (2002–present)," World Health Organization website.

43 In 1945, they wangled from Congress: McCarran-Ferguson Act of 1945, 15 U.S.C. §§ 1011–1015 (2011).

45 "What do I care about the law?": H. W. Brands, *American Colossus: The Triumph of Capitalism, 1865–1900* (New York: Anchor Books, 2011), p. 8.

45 Forty-eight of the seventy-three men: Jack Beatty, *Age of Betrayal: The Triumph of Money in America, 1865–1900* (New York: Vintage Books, 2008), p. 192.

45 "The enterprises of the country": Chief Justice Edward G. Ryan quoted in James Truslow Adams, *The Epic of America* (New York: Triangle Books, 1931), pp. 297–98.

45 "Wall Street owns the country": Mary K. Lease, quoted in Bruce Levine, *Who Built America?* (New York: Harper & Bros., 1947), p. 147.

45 "Liberty produces wealth": Henry Demarest Lloyd, *Wealth Against Commonwealth* (New York: Harper & Bros., 1902), pp. 2, 494.

46 "If we will not endure a king": Winfield Scott Kerr, *John Sherman: His Life and Public Services*, vol. 2 (Boston: Sherman, French & Co., 1908), p. 215.

46 Sherman's Antitrust Act passed the Senate: Sherman Antitrust Act, 15 U.S.C. §§ 1–7 (1890). See also Kerr, *John Sherman*, p. 204.

46 "malefactors of great wealth": Kathleen Dalton, *Theodore Roosevelt: A Strenuous Life* (New York: Vintage Books, 2004), pp. 208, 224–26, 253.

46 As Roosevelt later recounted: Doris Kearns Goodwin, *The Bully Pulpit: Theodore Roosevelt, William Howard Taft, and the Golden Age of Journalism* (New York: Simon & Schuster, 2013), p. 299.

46 Antitrust lawsuits were also brought: Marc Winerman, "The Origins of the FTC: Concentration, Cooperation, Control, and Competition," *Antitrust Law Journal* 71, no. 1 (2003): 1–97.

46 President William Howard Taft broke up: Ibid., p. 12.

46 President Woodrow Wilson explained: Woodrow Wilson, *The New Freedom* (BiblioBazaar, 2007).

47 even Franklin D. Roosevelt encouraged businesses to cooperate: See Spen-

cer Weber Waller, *Thurman Arnold: A Biography* (New York: New York University Press, 2005), ch. 6.

47 The giant AT&T Bell System monopoly: "AT&T Breakup II: Highlights in the History of a Telecommunications Giant," *Los Angeles Times*, September 21, 1995.

6 THE NEW CONTRACTS

49 Sales of organs are banned: The National Organ Transplant Act of 1984, 1984 Pub. L. 98–507; see Title III—Prohibition of Organ Purchases, sec. 301.

49 The ban dates back to 1984: Laura Meckler, "Kidney Shortage Inspires a Radical Idea: Organ Sales," *Wall Street Journal*, November 13, 2007.

49 you can sell your blood: U.S. Food and Drug Administration, "CPG Sec. 230.150 Blood Donor Classification Statement, Paid or Volunteer Donor," U.S. Food and Drug Administration website, last updated September 18, 2014.

49 You can rent out your womb: Tamar Lewin, "Coming to U.S. for Baby, and Womb to Carry It," *New York Times*, July 5, 2014. See also Surrogacy Arrangements Act 1985, 1985 ch. 49.

50 Studies find that most prostitutes: See Heather J. Clawson, Nicole Dutch, Amy Solomon, and Lisa Goldblatt Grace, *Human Trafficking Into and Within the United States: A Review of the Literature*, Office of the Assistant Secretary for Planning and Evaluation, U.S. Department of Health and Human Services website, August 2009.

50 the pharmaceutical giant GlaxoSmithKline settled: Office of Public Affairs, "GlaxoSmithKline to Plead Guilty and Pay $3 Billion to Resolve Fraud Allegations and Failure to Report Safety Data," U.S. Department of Justice website, July 2, 2012.

50 Congress enacted the Fair Sentencing Act: Fair Sentencing Act of 2010, Pub. L. No. 111–220, 124 Stat. 2372 (2010). See also Gary G. Grindler, "Memorandum for All Federal Prosecutors," U.S. Department of Justice website, August 5, 2010.

50 America's National Rifle Association has gone to great lengths: Ruth Levush, "Firearms-Control Legislation and Policy: Comparative Analysis," Law Library of Congress website, last updated September 16, 2014. See also Philip Alpers, Amélie Rossetti, Daniel Salinas, and Marcus Wilson, "United States—Gun Facts, Figures and the Law," Sydney School of Public Health, University of Sydney, GunPolicy.org website, August 20, 2014.

51 Before the twentieth century: Zephyr Teachout, *Corruption in America: From Benjamin Franklin's Snuff Box to Citizens United* (Cambridge, MA: Harvard University Press, 2014), p. 154.

51 In the 1874 case *Trist v. Child*: *Trist v. Child*, 88 U.S. 441 (1874).

51 "If any of the great corporations": Ibid., p. 451.

51 That logic obviously failed to impress: *Citizens United v. Federal Election Commission,* 558 U.S. 310 (2010).

51 Indentured servitude is banned: Beth Akers, "How Income Share Agreements Could Play a Role in Higher Ed Financing," Brookings Institution website, October 16, 2014.

51 Price gouging is also prohibited: Joe Coscarelli, "The Uber Hangover: That Bar Tab Might Not Be the Only Thing You'll Regret in the Morning," *New York Magazine,* December 27, 2013.

52 High-frequency stock trading: Bart Chilton, "No Need to Demonize High-Frequency Trading," *New York Times,* July 7, 2014.

52 a practice presumably banned in the Securities Exchange Act of 1934: Securities Exchange Act of 1934, Pub. L. 73–291, 48 Stat. 881.

52 Over the years, commissioners at the SEC: "Insider Trading," U.S. Securities and Exchange Commission website.

52 Anthony Chiasson claimed he didn't know: Floyd Norris, "Loosening the Rules on Insider Trading," *New York Times,* April 24, 2014.

54 Employees who invest part of their paychecks: Anya Kamenetz, "Is Your 401(k) Plan Is [*sic*] Ripping You Off?" *Chicago Tribune,* July 8, 2014.

54 One contractual provision: "Commission on the Future of Worker-Management Relations," ch. 4, "Employment Litigation and Dispute Resolution," U.S. Department of Labor website.

55 employees complaining of job discrimination: Alexander Colvin, "An Empirical Study of Employment Arbitration: Case Outcomes and Processes," Cornell University, Digital Commons@ILR website, February 2011. See also David Benjamin Oppenheimer, "Verdicts Matter: An Empirical Study of California Employment Discrimination and Wrongful Discharge Jury Verdicts Reveals Low Success Rates for Women and Minorities," *U.C. Davis Law Review* 37 (2003): 511–66.

55 when consumers sued several hotels: For discussion of online terms-of-service agreements, see Jeremy B. Merrill, "One-Third of Top Websites Restrict Customers' Right to Sue," *New York Times,* October 23, 2014. See also "In re. Online Travel Company (OTC) Hotel Booking Antitrust Litigation," Consol. Civil Action No. 3:12-cv-3515-B (http://s3.amazonaws.com/cdn.orrick.com/files/Order-re-Motion-for-Leave-to-Amend.pdf).

55 When the owner of a small restaurant: *American Express Co. et al. v. Italian Colors Restaurant et al.,* 570 U.S. ____ (2013).

55 The case went to the Supreme Court: Ibid.

55 "The monopolist gets to use its monopoly power": Ibid.

56 Purchasers who check "I accept": Aleecia M. McDonald and Lorrie Faith Cranor, "The Cost of Reading Privacy Policies," *I/S: A Journal of Law and Policy for the Information Society* 4, no. 3 (2008): 540–65.

56 "You are solely responsible": "iCloud Terms and Conditions," Apple website, last revised October 20, 2014.

57 lawmakers in several states: Michael Corkery, "States Ease Interest Rate Laws That Protected Poor Borrowers," *New York Times,* October 21, 2014.

57 Citigroup's OneMain Financial unit: Ibid.

57 "There was simply no need": Ibid.

57 Meanwhile, employees of large corporations: Steven Greenhouse, "Noncompete Clauses Increasingly Pop Up in Array of Jobs," *New York Times,* June 8, 2014.

57 "an overarching conspiracy": David Streitfeld, "Court Rejects Deal on Hiring in Silicon Valley," *New York Times,* August 8, 2014.

57 Court papers showed: Ibid.

57 Not only did Google back down: Ibid.

7 THE NEW BANKRUPTCY

59 On the day Trump Plaza opened: "Trump Plaza: 4th Atlantic City Casino Shutdown," Associated Press, September 16, 2014.

59 Thirty years later: "Trump Plaza to Close, Costing Atlantic City 1,000 Jobs," Bloomberg News, July 14, 2014.

59 Trump, meanwhile, was on Twitter: Vicki Hyman, "Donald Trump Crows about Casino Woes: Atlantic City 'Lost Its Magic After I Left,'" NJ.com website, September 16, 2014.

60 In the late nineteenth century: Todd Zywicki, "The Auto Bailout and the Rule of Law," *National Affairs,* no. 7 (2011): 66–80.

61 "uniform Laws on the subject of Bankruptcies": U.S. Constitution, art. I, sec. 8, cl. 4. See also "The Evolution of U.S. Bankruptcy Law: A Timeline," Federal Judicial Center (http://www.rib.uscourts.gov/newhome/docs/the _evolution_of_bankruptcy_law.pdf).

61 The credit card industry spent more than $100 million: Timothy Egan, "Newly Bankrupt Raking in Piles of Credit Offers," *New York Times,* December 11, 2005.

61 every major U.S. airline: "The Last Great American Airline Merger . . . and the Last Great American Airline Bankruptcy?" *The Economist,* January 12, 2013.

61 Carty preached the necessity: Richard Finger, "Why American Airlines Employees Loathe Management," *Forbes,* April 29, 2013.

61 The corporation then promptly rejected: Gregory Karp, "American Airlines Parent Will Freeze, Not Terminate, Pensions," *Chicago Tribune,* March 7, 2012.

61 American's stock rose even further: For the discussion of American's emergence from bankruptcy, see Jack Nicas, "American Airlines Delivers Rich Payout," *Wall Street Journal,* April 8, 2014.

62 To top it off: Nick Brown, "American Airlines–US Airways Merger Gets Court Approval," Reuters, March 27, 2013.

62 Everyone came out ahead: Finger, "Why American Airlines Employees Loathe Management."

62 When the debt bubble exploded: U.S. Financial Crisis Inquiry Commission, *The Financial Crisis Inquiry Report* (Washington, DC: U.S. Government Printing Office, 2011).

62 Some commentators (including yours truly): See Robert Reich, "The Coming Bailout of All Bailouts: A Better Alternative," *Robert Reich* blog, September 18, 2008.

62 When Lehman Brothers went into bankruptcy: Jon Hilsenrath, Deborah Solomon, and Damian Paletta, "Paulson, Bernanke Strained for Consensus in Bailout," *Wall Street Journal*, November 10, 2008.

62 The banks also received an estimated $83 billion: Bob Ivry, "Fed Gave Banks Crisis Gains on Secretive Loans Low as 0.01%," Bloomberg News, May 26, 2011.

62 Yet Chapter 13 of the bankruptcy code: James C. Duff, *Bankruptcy Basics*, rev. 3rd ed., Administrative Office of the U.S. Courts, April 2010 (http:// www.uscourts.gov/uscourts/FederalCourts/BankruptcyResources/bank basics.pdf).

63 When the financial crisis hit: Helping Families Save Their Homes in Bankruptcy Act of 2008, S. 2136 (110th).

63 The bill passed the House: Dick Durbin, "Durbin's Bankruptcy Amendment to Help Homeowners in Foreclosure," remarks delivered on the floor of the U.S. Senate, April 29, 2009 (http://www.durbin.senate.gov/ public/index.cfm/statementscommentary?ID=5f256057-e6ed-442b-a866 -396a16735b0a).

63 The bill garnered only forty-five Senate votes: See Anne Flaherty, "Senate Votes Down Foreclosure Mortgage Relief Bill," *USA Today*, April 30, 2009.

63 student loans constituted 10 percent of all debt: Federal Reserve Bank of New York, "Quarterly Report on Household Debt and Credit," August 2014, p. 3 (http://www.newyorkfed.org/householdcredit/2014-q2/data/pdf/ HHDC_2014Q2.pdf).

63 But the bankruptcy code does not allow: Josh Mitchell, "Trying to Shed Student Debt," *Wall Street Journal*, May 3, 2012.

63 If debtors cannot meet their payments: Annamaria Andriotis, "Student Debt Takes a Bite Out of More Paychecks," *Wall Street Journal*, June 13, 2014.

63 If people are still behind: Ibid.

63 The only way graduates can reduce their student debt: Federal Student Aid, "Forgiveness, Cancellation, and Discharge: Discharge in Bankruptcy," Federal Student Aid website.

64 This is a stricter standard: Tim Donovan, "Student Loan Debt Should Be Treated Like Detroit's," *Salon*, July 24, 2013.

64 Congress and its banking patrons: Ibid.

64 the investors holding 2005 certificates: For the discussion of the Detroit

bankruptcy, see Monica Davey and Mary Williams Walsh, "Plan to Exit Bankruptcy Is Approved for Detroit," *New York Times,* November 7, 2014.

65 Greater Detroit: "Detroit: Economy; Major Industries and Commercial Activity," City-Data.com website, 2009. See also Automation Alley, *Automation Alley's 2013 Technology Industry Report,* Anderson Economic Group website.

65 The median household in the region: U.S. Census Bureau, 2008–12 American Community Survey, Detroit-Warren-Livonia, MI, Metro Area, table DP-03 5-Year Estimates, American FactFinder website.

65 The median household in Birmingham, Michigan: U.S. Census Bureau, 2009–13 American Community Survey, Birmingham and Bloomfield Hills, 5-Year Estimates, "Community Facts," American FactFinder website.

65 between 2000 and 2010, Detroit lost a quarter of its population: U.S. Census Bureau, "Profile of General Population and Housing Characteristics: 2010 Demographic Profile," table DP-1, and "Profile of General Demographic Characteristics: Census 2000 Summary File 1 (SF 1) 100-Percent Data," table DP-1, Detroit, MI, American FactFinder website.

65 By the time of the bankruptcy: Sixty-four percent were below 200 percent of the federal poverty level. See U.S. Census Bureau, 2009–13 American Community Survey, Detroit, MI, 5-Year Estimate, "Poverty Status in the Past 12 Months," table S1701, American FactFinder website.

65 Its median household income: U.S. Census Bureau, 2009–13 American Community Survey, Detroit, MI, 5-Year Estimate, "Community Facts," American FactFinder website.

65 More than half of its children were impoverished: Fifty-five percent were living below the federal poverty level. See U.S. Census Bureau, 2009–13 American Community Survey, Detroit, MI, 5-Year Estimate, "Children Characteristics," table S0901, American FactFinder website.

65 Forty percent of its streetlights didn't work: "Proposal for Creditors," City of Detroit website, June 14, 2013, p. 12.

65 Two-thirds of its parks: Ibid., p. 15.

65 monthly water bills in Detroit: Rick Cohen, "UN Declares Detroit Water Shutoffs Violate Human Rights," *Nonprofit Quarterly,* June 26, 2014.

65 "Now, all of a sudden, they're having problems": Paige Williams, "Drop Dead, Detroit!" *New Yorker,* January 27, 2014.

8 THE ENFORCEMENT MECHANISM

68 the National Vaccine Injury Compensation Program: For a discussion of the Vaccine Injury Compensation Program history in the United States, see "Vaccine Injury Compensation Programs," College of Physicians of Philadelphia, History of Vaccines website. For a discussion of pharmaceutical action that prompted the creation of the VICP, see "History of Vaccine

Safety," Centers for Disease Control and Prevention website, last updated November 4, 2014.

68 the National Rifle Association went into action: See Gregg Lee Carter, *Gun Control in the United States* (Santa Barbara: ABC-CLIO Inc., 2006), pp. 193–94.

68 Congress enacted the Protection of Lawful Commerce in Arms Act: Protection of Lawful Commerce in Arms Act, House Report 109-124, June 14, 2005.

68 the dangers associated with the Mark 1 reactor: Tom Zeller, Jr., "Experts Had Long Criticized Potential Weakness in Design of Stricken Reactor," *New York Times*, March 15, 2011. See also "U.S. Boiling Water Reactors with 'Mark 1' and 'Mark 2' Containments," U.S. Nuclear Regulatory Commission website.

68 Harold Denton: Zeller, "Experts Had Long Criticized Potential Weakness in Design of Stricken Reactor."

69 A follow-up report: Paul Gunter, "Hazards of Boiling Water Reactors in the United States," Nuclear Information and Resource Service website, last updated March 2011.

69 In the presidential election year of 2012: Center for Responsive Politics, "General Electric: Profile for 2012 Election Cycle," OpenSecrets.org website (https://www.opensecrets.org/orgs/summary.php?id=D000000125&cycle =2012).

69 104 of its 144 lobbyists: Center for Responsive Politics, "Influence and Lobbying: Lobbyists Representing General Electric, 2012," OpenSecrets.org website (http://www.opensecrets.org/lobby/clientlbs.php?id=D000000125 &year=2012).

69 BP failed to adequately supervise: See National Commission on the BP *Deepwater Horizon* Oil Spill and Offshore Drilling, *Deep Water: The Gulf Oil Disaster and the Future of Offshore Drilling,* U.S. Government Publishing Office website, January 2011. See also Stephen Power and Ben Casselman, "White House Probe Blames BP, Industry in Gulf Blast," *Wall Street Journal,* January 6, 2011.

69 the Minerals Management Service: Stephen Power, "Regulators Accepted Gifts from Oil Industry, Report Says," *Wall Street Journal,* May 25, 2010.

69 the National Highway Traffic Safety Administration: "Chronology: A Regulatory Free Ride? NHTSA and the Hidden History of the SUV," PBS website (http://www.pbs.org/wgbh/pages/frontline/shows/rollover/unsafe/cron .html).

70 "You didn't hear that": See "The Secret Recordings of Carmen Segarra," radio broadcast, *This American Life,* Chicago Public Media, September 26, 2014.

70 the West, Texas, chemical and fertilizer plant: Daniel Gilbert, Alexandra Berzon, and Nathan Koppel, "Deadly Explosion Prompts Fresh Look at Regulation," *Wall Street Journal,* April 19, 2013.

70 only 2,200 inspectors: "Statement of David Michaels, PHD, MPH, Assistant Secretary Occupational Safety and Health Administration U.S. Department of Labor Before the Committee on Education and the Workforce Subcommittee on Workforce Protections," October 5, 2011 (https://www.osha.gov/pls/oshaweb/owadisp.show_document?p_table =TESTIMONIES&p_id=1482).

70 Its $134 million budget for 2013: For the NHTSA budget, see "National Highway Traffic Safety Administration Budget Information: Fiscal Year 2015 Budget Overview," NHTSA website, p. 14. For the cost of protecting the Baghdad embassy, see U.S. Department of State and the Broadcasting Board of Governors, *Inspection of Embassy Baghdad and Constituent Posts, Iraq,* U.S. State Department, Office of Inspector General website, May 2013.

71 the IRS lost more than ten thousand staff: John Koskinen, speech at the National Press Club, April 2, 2014 (https://www.youtube.com/watch?v=M uIMC7syoXo&feature=youtu.be).

71 For every dollar that goes into IRS enforcement: "IRS Releases FY 2012 Data Book," Internal Revenue Service website, March 25, 2013.

71 This was the case when the food industry: Rob Nixon, "Funding Gap Hinders Law for Ensuring Food Safety," *New York Times,* April 8, 2015.

72 The commission thereafter considered fifteen thousand comments: Commissioner Michael V. Dunn, "Opening Statement, Public Meeting on Final Rules Under the Dodd-Frank Act," U.S. Commodities Futures Trading Commission website, October 18, 2011.

72 Its lawyers then filed a lawsuit: *SIFMA v. U.S. CFTC,* 1:11-cv-02146-RLW (2011) (http://www.scribd.com/doc/74545374/Financial-industry-groups-lawsuit -against-the-C-F-T-C).

72 Wall Street sued the SEC: *Business Roundtable and Chamber of Commerce v. U.S. Securities and Exchange Commission,* U.S. Chamber Litigation Center website. See also Christopher Doering, "Wall St. Sues CFTC Over Commodity Trading Crackdown," Reuters, December 2, 2011.

74 the bank lost $6.2 billion: U.S. Senate Permanent Subcommittee on Investigations, "JPMorgan Chase Whale Trades: A Case History of Derivatives Risks and Abuses," U.S. Senate Committee on Homeland Security and Government Affairs website, March 15, 2013, p. 1.

74 All this caused the Justice Department: Jessica Silver-Greenberg and Ben Protess, "JPMorgan Caught in Swirl of Regulatory Woes," *New York Times,* May 2, 2013.

74 JPMorgan's financial report: "Form 10-Q, Quarterly Report," JPMorgan, filed August 7, 2013, pp. 198–206 (http://investor.shareholder.com/jp morganchase/secfiling.cfm?filingID=19617-13-354). See also Stephen Gandel, "JP Morgan's Legal Problems Continue to Mount," *Fortune,* August 19, 2013.

74 Yet $6.8 billion was a pittance: Floyd Norris, "The Perils When Megabanks Lose Focus," *New York Times,* September 5, 2013.

75   Not even JPMorgan's $13 billion settlement: Francesco Guerrera, "The J.P. Morgan Settlement: Misconceptions Debunked," *Wall Street Journal*, November 25, 2013.

75   Citigroup's $7 billion settlement: Michael Korkery, "Citigroup Settles Mortgage Inquiry for $7 Billion," *New York Times*, July 14, 2014.

75   in the days leading up to the Bank of America settlement: Christina Rexrode and Andrew Grossman, "Record Bank of America Settlement Latest in Government Crusade," *Wall Street Journal*, August 21, 2014.

75   At least $7 billion of Bank of America's $16.65 billion settlement: "Bank of America to Pay $16.65 Billion in Historic Justice Department Settlement for Financial Fraud Leading Up to and During the Financial Crisis," U.S. Department of Justice website, August 21, 2014.

75   Bank of America's pretax income: *Bank of America Corporation 2013 Annual Report*, Bank of America website, table 2, p. 23.

75   "This case shows": James Kwak, "Why Is Credit Suisse Still Allowed to Do Business in the United States?" *The Atlantic*, May 20, 2014.

75   financial markets shrugged off: "Credit Suisse Pleads Guilty, Pays $2.6 Billion to Settle U.S. Tax Evasion Charges," *Forbes*, May 20, 2014.

75   the bank's shares rose: Katharina Bart, Karen Freifeld, and Aruna Viswanatha, "Credit Suisse Guilty Plea Has Little Immediate Impact as Shares Rise," Reuters, May 20, 2014.

75   "Our discussions with clients": John Cassidy, "Credit Suisse Got Off Lightly," *New Yorker*, May 20, 2014.

76   "What GM did was break the law": Jonathan Berr, "GM's Pain Will Exceed That $35 Million Fine," CBS News website, June 1, 2014.

76   The firm also agreed: Clifford Krauss, "Halliburton Pleads Guilty to Destroying Evidence After Gulf Spill," *New York Times*, July 25, 2013.

76   Halliburton's revenues in 2013: Halliburton, "Halliburton Announces Fourth Quarter Income," press release, January 21, 2014, p. 1.

77   This was a carefully crafted fraud: "Court-Appointed Lehman Examiner Unveils Report," *New York Times*, March 11, 2010.

78   Thirty-two states hold elections for judges: Adam Liptak, "Rendering Justice with One Eye on Re-election," *New York Times*, May 25, 2008.

78   "No other nation in the world does that": Ibid.

78   In the 2012 election cycle: Alicia Bannon, Eric Velasco, Linda Casey, and Lianna Reagan, *The New Politics of Judicial Elections 2011–12*, New York University, Brennan Center for Justice, October 2013, p. 5 (http://newpolitics report.org/report/2012-report/).

78   A 2013 study by Professor Joanna Shepherd: Joanna Shepherd, "Justice at Risk: An Empirical Analysis of Campaign Contributions and Judicial Decisions," American Constitution Society for Law and Policy website, June 2013.

78   "In the span of a few short years": Billy Corriher, "No Justice for the Injured," Center for American Progress website, May 2013.

79 major law firms were funneling: Eric Lipton, "Lobbyists, Bearing Gifts, Pursue Attorneys General," *New York Times,* October 28, 2014.

79 AT&T was a major contributor: Ibid.

80 in *AT&T Mobility v. Concepcion: AT&T Mobility LLC v. Concepcion et ux.,* 563 U.S. 321 (2011).

80 according to a survey by Carlton Fields Jorden Burt: Jeremy B. Merrill, "One-Third of Top Websites Restrict Customers' Right to Sue," *New York Times,* October 23, 2014.

80 in their 2013 decision *Comcast v. Behrend: Comcast v. Behrend,* 569 U.S. ____ (2013).

9 SUMMARY: THE MARKET MECHANISM AS A WHOLE

83 In 2014, corporate profits before taxes: Floyd Norris, "Corporate Profits Grow and Wages Slide," *New York Times,* April 4, 2014.

83 Between 2000 and 2014: "Corporate Profits After Tax with Inventory Valuation Adjustment (IVA) and Capital Consumption Adjustment (CCAdj)," Federal Reserve Bank of St. Louis Economic Research website, updated December 23, 2014.

84 labor's share of nonfarm business income: Robert J. Samuelson, "Robert Samuelson: Capitalists Wait, While Labor Loses Out," *Washington Post,* September 8, 2013.

84 In 2013, it was 57 percent: Ibid.

84 Piketty posits: Thomas Piketty, *Capital in the Twenty-First Century,* trans. Arthur Goldhammer (Cambridge, MA: Harvard University Press, 2014), p. 25.

10 THE MERITOCRATIC MYTH

89 "I say for these people making their millions": See *Inequality for All,* dir. Jacob Kornbluth, 72 Productions, 2014.

90 During his twenty years at the helm of SAC Capital Advisors: See Agustino Fontevecchia, "Steve Cohen Personally Made $2.3B in 2013 Despite Having to Shut Down SAC Capital," *Forbes,* March 13, 2014.

90 "Private hedge fund people": Quoted in Joshua Rhett Miller, "Ex-Clinton Official Robert Reich Delivers Lecture on Greed While Earning $240G to Teach One Class," FoxNews.com website, August 10, 2014. (For the record, the statement in this Fox News headline was, and still is, false.)

90 insider trading at SAC Capital under Cohen's leadership: See U.S. District Court Southern District of New York, sealed indictment, *United States of America v. SAC Advisors L.P., et al.,* July 25, 2013 (http://www.justice.gov/usao/nys/pressreleases/July13/SACChargingAndSupportingDocuments.php).

90 Had the firm's insider trading been discovered: See John Cassidy, "The Great Hedge Fund Mystery: Why Do They Make So Much?" *New Yorker,* May 12, 2014.

91 One of the most broadly held assumptions: See Stephen J. McNamee and Robert K. Miller, Jr., *The Meritocracy Myth* (Lanham, MD: Rowman & Littlefield, 2009).

91 "If we are very generous with ourselves": See Herbert Simon, "Public Administration in Today's World of Organizations and Markets," *PS: Political Science & Politics* 33, no. 4 (2000): 749–56.

91 This "enormously productive social system": See Anthony B. Atkinson, Thomas Piketty, and Emmanuel Saez, "Top Incomes in the Long Run of History," *Journal of Economic Literature* 49, no. 1 (2011): 3–71.

92 By 2010, the richest 1 percent of Americans: See Edward N. Wolff, "The Asset Price Meltdown of the Middle Class," panel paper, 2012 APPAM Fall Research Conference, presented November 10, 2012, National Bureau of Economic Research website.

92 In 2014, more than two-thirds of Americans: See "Getting Paid in America 2014," American Payroll Association, 2014 (http://www.nationalpay rollweek.com/documents/2014GettingPaidInAmericaSurveyResults _FINAL_000.pdf).

93 good teachers increase the average present value: See Raj Chetty, John N. Friedman, and Jonah E. Rockoff, "Measuring the Impacts of Teachers II: Teacher Value Added and Student Outcomes in Adulthood," NBER Working Paper No. 19424, National Bureau of Economic Research website, September 2013.

93 According to research by sociologist Lauren Rivera: See Amy J. Binder, "Why Are Harvard Grads Still Flocking to Wall Street?" *Washington Monthly,* September 2014.

93 At Princeton: See Catherine Rampell, "Out of Harvard, and into Finance," *New York Times,* December 21, 2011.

94 the median wage of the bottom 90 percent: See Thomas Piketty and Emmanuel Saez, "Income Inequality in the United States, 1913–1998," *Quarterly Journal of Economics* 118, no. 1 (2003): 1–39 (tables and figures updated to 2012, September 2013, table A6).

94 CEOs of big companies: See Lawrence Mischel and Alyssa Davis, *CEO Pay Continues to Rise as Typical Workers Are Paid Less,* Issue Brief #380, Economic Policy Institute website, 2014.

95 A growing portion of the compensation of top corporate executives: For a discussion of the occupations of the top 0.1 percent, see Jon Bakija, Adam Cole, and Bradley Heim, "Jobs and Income Growth of Top Earners and the Causes of Changing Income Inequality: Evidence from U.S. Tax Return Data," Department of Economics Working Papers 2010-22, Williams College, Department of Economics website, 2008, revised January 2012.

11 THE HIDDEN MECHANISM OF CEO PAY

97 Anyone who still believes people are paid: See Lawrence Mischel and Alyssa Davis, *CEO Pay Continues to Rise as Typical Workers Are Paid Less,* Issue Brief #380, Economic Policy Institute website, 2014.

97 Consider that in 1992: See William Lazonick, *Taking Stock: Why Executive Pay Results in an Unstable and Inequitable Economy,* white paper, Roosevelt Institute website, June 5, 2014.

97 Comcast CEO Brian L. Roberts's total compensation: See Comcast Corporation, Schedule 14A Definitive Proxy Statement, April 5, 2013, p. 42 (http://www.sec.gov/Archives/edgar/data/1166691/000119312513144100/d496632ddef14a.htm). See also Karl Russell, "Executive Pay by the Numbers," *New York Times,* June 29, 2013.

98 The share of corporate income: Lucian A. Bebchuk and Yaniv Grinstein, "The Growth of Executive Pay," *Oxford Review of Economic Policy* 21, no. 2 (2005): 283–303.

98 almost all of it was deducted: See Scott Klinger and Sarah Anderson, *Fleecing Uncle Sam,* Center for Effective Government and Institute for Policy Studies websites, 2014.

98 "The most natural explanation": See N. Gregory Mankiw, "Yes, the Wealthy Can Be Deserving," *New York Times,* February 16, 2014.

99 the average compensation for a board member: Jeff Green and Hideki Suzuki, "Board Director Pay Hits Record $251,000 for 250 Hours," Bloomberg News, May 29, 2013.

100 "Say on pay" votes: U.S. Securities and Exchange Commission, "SEC Adopts Rules for Say-on-Pay and Golden Parachute Compensation as Required Under Dodd-Frank Act," press release, January 25, 2011.

100 Billionaire Larry Ellison: Aaron Ricadela, "Oracle Investors Reject CEO Ellison's Pay at Annual Meeting," *Bloomberg Business,* October 31, 2013.

100 In Australia, by contrast: See Julie Walker, "Australia Has Had Three Years with the Two-Strikes Law and Executive Pay Pain Won't Go Away," *Business Insider Australia,* October 17, 2013.

100 That rule has contributed: Trevor Chappell, "Pay Packets for Top Bosses Hit $4.8m," *The Australian,* September 18, 2014.

100 a steadily larger portion of CEO pay: See Kevin J. Murphy, "Executive Compensation: Where We Are, and How We Got There," *Handbook of the Economics of Finance,* ed. George Constantinides, Milton Harris, and René Stulz (Oxford: Elsevier Science North Holland, 2013), pp. 211–356.

100 Professor William Lazonick of the University of Massachusetts Lowell: See Lazonick, *Taking Stock,* p. 5.

101 the Securities and Exchange Commission regarded stock buybacks: Ibid., p. 8.

101 Adding to the allure of stock options: Ibid., p. 9.

101 in 1993, the Clinton administration decided: See Steven Balsam, *Taxes and*

Executive Compensation, Briefing Paper #344, Economic Policy Institute website, August 14, 2012.

102 Between 2003 and 2012: William Lazonick, "Profits Without Prosperity," *Harvard Business Review,* September 2014.

102 companies in the Standard & Poor's 500 index repurchased: "The Repurchase Revolution," *The Economist,* September 13, 2014.

102 S&P 500 companies put most of their net earnings: Lazonick, "Profits Without Prosperity."

102 it spent $108 billion buying back its own shares: IBM, *What Will We Make of This Moment? 2013 IBM Annual Report,* IBM website, 2013, p. 7.

103 "all these 'shareholder friendly' maneuvers": Andrew Ross Sorkin, "The Truth Hidden by IBM's Buybacks," *New York Times,* October 20, 2014.

103 the strategy had paid off for IBM's CEOs: Lazonick, *Taking Stock,* p. 12.

103 It, too, had a lifelong employment policy: William Lazonick, "Innovative Enterprise and Shareholder Value," AIR Working Paper #14-03/01, Academic-Industry Research Network website, March 2014, p. 16.

103 Hewlett-Packard's CEOs received: Lazonick, *Taking Stock,* p. 12.

103 Apple borrowed $17 billion: Charles Mead and Sarika Gangar, "Apple Raises $17 Billion in Record Corporate Bond Sale," Bloomberg News, April 30, 2013.

103 Apple CEO Tim Cook: Gary Strauss, Barbara Hansen, and Matt Krantz, "Millions by Millions, CEO Pay Goes Up," *USA Today,* April 4, 2014; see chart "2013 CEO Compensation, Realized Compensation."

103 Stock options and restricted stock grants: Murphy, "Executive Compensation," pp. 211–356.

103 Time Warner chief executive Jeff Bewkes: William Launder, "Time Warner CEO Bewkes's 2013 Compensation Up 26%," *Wall Street Journal,* April 21, 2014.

103 Facebook's Mark Zuckerberg: Facebook, Inc., Schedule 14A Definitive Proxy Statement, March 31, 2014, pp. 21, 32 (http://www.sec.gov/Archives/edgar/data/1326801/000132680114000016/facebook2014proxystatement.htm).

103 Michael J. Cooper of the University of Utah: On the relationship between CEO pay and performance, see Michael J. Cooper, Huseyin Gulen, and P. Raghavendra Rau, "Performance for Pay? The Relation Between CEO Incentive Compensation and Future Stock Price Performance," working paper series, Social Science Research Network website, October 1, 2014. See also Susan Adams, "The Highest-Paid CEOs Are the Worst Performers, New Study Says," *Forbes,* June 16, 2014.

104 Sony CEO Kazuo Hirai: Gavin J. Blair, "Sony CEO, Top Execs to Return $10 Million in Bonuses Amid Electronics Unit Losses," *Hollywood Reporter,* May 13, 2014.

104 Martin Sullivan: Michael B. Dorff, *Indispensable and Other Myths: How the*

CEO Pay Experiment Failed and How to Fix It (Berkeley and Los Angeles: University of California Press, 2014), pp. 1–2.

105 Hank A. McKinnell, Jr.: Gary Rivlin, "New Study Shows How Golden Parachutes Are Getting Bigger," *Daily Beast,* January 11, 2012.

105 Douglas Ivester of Coca-Cola: Liz Moyer, "Supersize That Severance!" *Forbes,* October 31, 2007.

105 Donald Carty: Richard Finger, "Why American Airlines Employees Loathe Management," *Forbes,* April 29, 2013.

105 If anything, pay for failure: Paul Hodgson and Greg Ruel, *Twenty-One U.S. CEOs with Golden Parachutes of More Than $100 Million,* GMI Ratings website, January 2012.

105 Howard Schultz, CEO of Starbucks: Sarah Anderson and Marjorie Wood, *Restaurant Industry Pay: Taxpayers' Double Burden,* Institute for Policy Studies website, April 22, 2014, p. 5.

105 "It was well-intentioned": Senator Chuck Grassley, "Executive Compensation: Backdating to the Future/Oversight of Current Issues Regarding Executive Compensation Including Backdating of Stock Options; and Tax Treatment of Executive Compensation, Retirement and Benefits," closing statement, Finance Committee hearing, September 6, 2006 (http://www.finance.senate.gov/newsroom/chairman/release/?id=fa3 baac7-174f-4e3e-b16d-2edaob6cec87).

106 The Economic Policy Institute estimated: Steven Balsam, *Taxes and Executive Compensation,* Briefing Paper #344, Economic Policy Institute website, August 14, 2012.

106 Capital gains are taxed at a lower rate: "Topic 409—Capital Gains and Losses," Internal Revenue Service website, August 19, 2014.

12 THE SUBTERFUGE OF WALL STREET PAY

108 Wall Street's five largest banks: Hester Peirce and Robert Greene, "The Decline of US Small Banks (2000–2013)," Mercatus Center website, February 24, 2014.

109 Kenichi Ueda of the International Monetary Fund: Kenichi Ueda and Beatrice Weder di Mauro, "Quantifying Structural Subsidy Values for Systemically Important Financial Institutions," IMF Working Paper no. 12/28, International Monetary Fund website, May 2012, p. 4.

109 This may not sound like much: "Why Should Taxpayers Give Big Banks $83 Billion a Year?" editorial, *Bloomberg View,* February 20, 2013.

109 This estimate, by the way, is consistent: See International Monetary Fund, "Global Financial Stability Report: Moving from Liquidity- to Growth-Driven Markets," World Economic and Financial Surveys, International Monetary Fund website, April 2014, p. 104; U.S. Government Accountability Office, *Large Bank Holding Companies: Expectations of Government*

Support, GAO-14-621, U.S. Government Accountability website, July 2014, pp. 50–51.

109 Economists from New York University: See Viral V. Acharya, Deniz Anginer, A. Joseph Warburton, "The End of Market Discipline? Investor Expectations of Implicit State Guarantees," Minneapolis Federal Reserve Bank, Social Science Research Network website, June 2014.

109 The lion's share of that subsidy: "Why Should Taxpayers Give Big Banks $83 Billion a Year?"

110 After reviewing these wills: Board of Governors of the Federal Reserve System and Federal Deposit Insurance Corporation, "Agencies Provide Feedback on Second Round Resolution Plans of 'First-Wave' Filers," joint press release, August 5, 2014.

110 Thomas Hoenig: Statement by Thomas M. Hoenig, Vice Chairman, Federal Deposit Insurance Corporation, "Credibility of the 2013 Living Wills Submitted by First Wave Filers," FDIC website, August 5, 2014, p. 2.

110 the $26.7 billion distributed to Wall Street bankers: Sarah Anderson, "Wall Street Bonuses and the Minimum Wage," Institute for Policy Studies website, March 12, 2014.

111 The remainder of the $83 billion: "Rewarding Work Through State Earned Income Tax Credits," policy brief, Institute on Taxation and Economic Policy website, April 2014.

111 That year the top twenty-five hedge-fund managers: Nathan Vardi, "The 25 Highest-Earning Hedge Fund Managers and Traders," *Forbes*, February 26, 2014.

111 Even run-of-the-mill portfolio managers: Brendan Conway, "Entry Level Hedge Fund Pay: $353,000," *Barron's*, October 31, 2013.

111 "The portfolio managers know the best price": Eric Falkenstein, "Righteous Bonuses," *Falkenblog*, February 2, 2009.

112 SAC Capital managed so much money: For a discussion of SAC Capital, see Marcia Vickers, "The Most Powerful Trader on Wall Street You've Never Heard Of," *Bloomberg Businessweek*, July 20, 2003.

112 His firm was fined $1.8 billion: Agustino Fontevecchia, "Steve Cohen Personally Made $2.3B in 2013 Despite Having to Shut Down SAC Capital," *Forbes*, March 13, 2014.

112 But Cohen's treatment: Peter H. Stone and Michael Isikoff, "Hedge Funds Bet Heavily on Republicans at End of Election," Center for Public Integrity website, January 5, 2011.

113 If confidential information is indeed: Floyd Norris, "Loosening the Rules on Inside Trading," *New York Times*, April 24, 2014.

113 Michigan congressman Sander M. Levin: See Monica Vendituoli, "Hedge Funds: Background," OpenSecrets.org website, updated September 2013 (http://www.opensecrets.org/industries/background.php?ind=F2700).

13 THE DECLINING BARGAINING POWER
OF THE MIDDLE

115 For three decades after World War II: See Susan Fleck, John Glaser, and Shawn Sprague, "The Compensation-Productivity Gap: A Visual Essay," *Monthly Labor Review,* January 2011.

115 By 2013, the median household: U.S. Census Bureau, "Historical Income Tables: Households," table H-6 (https://www.census.gov/hhes/www/income/data/historical/household/).

116 Job security also declined: See Henry S. Farber, "Job Loss and the Decline in Job Security in the United States," in *Labor in the New Economy,* ed. Katharine G. Abraham, James R. Spletzer, and Michael Harper (Chicago: University of Chicago Press, 2010). See also U.S. Bureau of Labor Statistics, "Seasonally Adjusted Employment-Population Ratio" (http://data.bls.gov/timeseries/LNS12300000).

116 In 2013, an American household: U.S. Census Bureau, "Historical Income Tables: Households," table H-6.

116 Their average pay: Drew DeSilver, "For Most Workers, Real Wages Have Barely Budged for Decades," *Fact Tank,* Pew Research Center website, October 9, 2014.

117 the median income in Germany: David Leonhardt, "The German Example," *New York Times,* June 7, 2011.

117 the standard explanation doesn't tell us why: Heidi Shierholz, *Six Years from Its Beginning, the Great Recession's Shadow Looms Over the Labor Market,* Issue Brief #374, Economic Policy Institute website, January 9, 2014.

117 the real average hourly wages: Heidi Shierholz, Alyssa Davis, and Will Kimball, *The Class of 2014: The Weak Economy Is Idling Too Many Young Graduates,* Briefing Paper #377, Economic Policy Institute website, May 1, 2014.

117 according to the Federal Reserve Bank of New York: Jaison R. Abel and Richard Deitz, "Are the Job Prospects of Recent College Graduates Improving?" *Liberty Street Economics,* Federal Reserve Bank of New York website, September 4, 2014.

118 "Generation Limbo": Jennifer 8. Lee, "Generation Limbo: Waiting It Out," *New York Times,* August 31, 2011.

119 As early as 1914: Walter Lippmann, *Drift and Mastery* (Englewood Cliffs, NJ: Prentice Hall, 1914; reprinted 1961), pp. 22, 23.

119 "in their own interest": Adolf A. Berle and Gardiner C. Means, *The Modern Corporation and Private Property* (New York: Macmillan, 1932), p. 302.

119 The solution, Berle and Means concluded: Ibid., p. 312.

119 "The job of management": Frank Abrams, "Management's Responsibilities in a Complex World," *Harvard Business Review* 29, no. 3 (1951): 29–34.

120 *Fortune* magazine urged CEOs: See *Fortune* 40, no. 4 (October 1951): 98–99.

120 "the majority of Americans support private enterprise": For a discussion of General Electric and corporate stewardship, see Rick Wartzman, "Whatever

Happened to Corporate Stewardship?" *Harvard Business Review,* August 29, 2014. See also "Business: The New Conservatism," *Time,* November 26, 1956.

121 The 1974 act changed that: See Michael McCarthy, "Why Pension Funds Go to Risky Investments," *Washington Post,* October 19, 2014.

121 In 1982, another large pool of capital became available: See Garn–St. Germain Depository Institutions Act of 1982, Pub. L. No. 97-320. See also Marcia Millon Cornett and Hassan Tehranian, "An Examination of the Impact of the Garn–St. Germain Depository Institutions Act of 1982 on Commercial Banks and Savings and Loans," *Journal of Finance* 45, no. 1 (March 1990): 95–111.

121 The convenient fact: Timothy Curry and Lynn Shibut, "The Cost of the Savings and Loan Crisis: Truth and Consequences," *FDIC Banking Review* 13, no. 2 (2000): 26–35.

121 Between 1979 and 1989: Tim Opler and Sheridan Titman, "The Determinants of Leveraged Buyout Activity: Free Cash Flow v. Financial Distress Costs," *Journal of Finance* 48, no. 5 (1993): 1985–99.

121 The party was temporarily halted: See Jesse Kornbluth, *Highly Confident: The Crime and Punishment of Michael Milken* (New York: William Morrow, 1992).

122 "We have one job": Ian Somerville and D. Quinn Mills, "Leading to a Leaderless World," *Leader to Leader* 1999, no. 13 (1999): 30–38.

122 When Jack Welch took the helm of GE: See Jack Welch, *Jack: Straight from the Gut* (New York: Warner, 2001).

122 "Chainsaw" Al Dunlap: John Byrne, *Chainsaw: The Notorious Career of Al Dunlap in the Era of Profit-at-Any-Price* (New York: HarperBusiness, 2003).

122 When Dunlap moved to Sunbeam: Ibid., pp. 123–24.

123 the nation's productivity has risen 65 percent: Josh Bivens, Elise Gould, Lawrence Mishel, and Heidi Shierholz, *Raising America's Pay: Why It's Our Central Economic Policy Challenge,* Briefing Paper #378, Economic Policy Institute website, June 4, 2014.

124 During the Clinton administration: Lawrence Mishel, *The Wedges Between Productivity and Median Compensation Growth,* Issue Brief #330, Economic Policy Institute website, April 26, 2012.

125 Nearly one out of every five working Americans: U.S. Bureau of Labor Statistics, *The Employment Situation—November 2014,* U.S. Bureau of Labor Statistics website, December 5, 2014.

126 By 2014, 66 percent of American workers: American Payroll Association, "2013 Getting Paid in America Survey Results," 2013 (http://www.national payrollweek.com/documents/2013GettingPaidInAmericaSurveyResults2 _JW_001.pdf).

126 more than 80 percent of large and medium-sized firms: Employee Benefit Research Institute, "EBRI Databook on Employee Benefits," ch. 4, "Par-

ticipation in Employee Benefit Programs," table 4.1a, Employee Benefit Research Institute website, March 2011.

126 Today, a third of all workers: Ruth Helman, Nevin Adams, and Jack Van-Derhei, *The 2014 Retirement Confidence Survey: Confidence Rebounds—For Those with Retirement Plans*, Issue Brief No. 397, Employee Benefit Research Institute website, March 2014, p. 18.

126 the portion of workers with any pension: Rebecca Thiess, *The Future of Work: Trends and Challenges for Low-Wage Workers*, Briefing Paper #341, Economic Policy Institute website, April 27, 2012.

126 In MetLife's 2014 survey: MetLife, *Benefits Breakthrough: How Employees and Their Employers Are Navigating an Evolving Environment*, 2014 (https://benefittrends.metlife.com/assets/downloads/benefits-breakthrough-summaries-2014.pdf).

126 the Panel Study of Income Dynamics at the University of Michigan: Jacob S. Hacker, *The Great Risk Shift: The New Economic Insecurity and the Decline of the American Dream* (New York: Oxford University Press, 2008), p. 31.

126 In the 1970s, the typical drop: Ibid.

126 By the mid-2000s: Ibid., p. 32.

127 America's largest employer was Walmart: Brianna Cardiff-Hicks, Francine Lafontaine, and Kathryn Shaw, "Do Large Modern Retailers Pay Premium Wages?" NBER Working Paper No. 20313, National Bureau of Economic Research website, July 2014, p. 9.

127 average hourly wage of Walmart workers: Shelly Banjo, "Pay at Wal-Mart: Low at the Checkout But High in the Manager's Office," *Wall Street Journal*, July 23, 2014.

127 And because more than a third of workers: See David Madland and Keith Miller, "Latest Census Data Underscore How Important Unions Are for the Middle Class," Center for American Progress Action Fund website, September 17, 2013.

127 fewer than 7 percent: U.S. Bureau of Labor Statistics, "Union Members Summary," economic news release, January 24, 2014, p. 1.

127 real average hourly pay in Germany: Leonhardt, "The German Example."

127 the percentage of total income going to the top 1 percent: See Anthony B. Atkinson, Thomas Piketty, and Emmanuel Saez, "Top Incomes in the Long Run of History," *Journal of Economic Literature* 49, no. 1 (2011): 41–42.

128 When railroad workers went on strike: See Robert E. Weir, *Workers in America* (Santa Barbara, CA: ABC-CLIO, 2013), p. 365.

128 President Grover Cleveland dispatched: U.S. Strike Commission, *Report on the Chicago Strike of June–July 1894*, 53rd Congress, 3rd sess., Sen. exec. doc. no. 4. (Washington, DC: Government Printing Office, 1895), pp. 18, 19.

128 "organized labor knows but one law": Quoted in "Facing the Issue," editorial, *Public Policy* 8, no. 24 (2013): 376; D. M. Perry, "Labor Unions Denounced," *Public Policy* 8, no. 20 (1903): 319.

128 Congress passed the Clayton Antitrust Act of 1914: 15 U.S. Code § 17, "Antitrust Laws Not Applicable to Labor Organizations," October 15, 1914.

128 Congress finally and forever legalized them: See "Labor and the Sherman Act," *Yale Law Journal* 49, no. 3 (January 1940): 518–37.

128 The National Labor Relations Act of 1935: See Frank Levy and Peter Temlin, "Inequality and Institutions in 20th Century America," NBER Working Paper No. 13106, National Bureau of Economic Research website, June 27, 2007, p. 16.

129 After the legendary Treaty of Detroit: Ibid.

129 Ronald Reagan's notorious firing: See Harold Meyerson, "Class Warrior," *Washington Post*, June 9, 2004.

129 In what would become a repeating nightmare: Greg J. Bamber, Jody Hoffer Gittell, Thomas A. Kochan, and Andrew von Nordenflycht, *Up in the Air: How Airlines Can Improve Performance by Engaging Their Employees* (Ithaca, NY: Cornell University Press, 2009), p. 125.

130 Northwest Airlines threatened bankruptcy: See Peter Rachleff, "Workers Rights and Wrongs," *Dallas Morning News*, November 4, 2007.

130 the airline outsourced most of their jobs: Ibid.

130 In 2002, United Airlines entered bankruptcy: "Court OKs UAL Wage Cuts," *Los Angeles Times*, February 1, 2005.

130 the Taft-Hartley Act of 1947: See Elise Gould and Heidi Shierholz, *The Compensation Penalty of "Right-to-Work" Laws*, Issue Brief #299, Economic Policy Institute website, February 17, 2011.

130 even the old heartland industrial states: See "2012 Right-to-Work Legislation," National Conference of State Legislatures website.

131 the board imposed minuscule penalties: For a discussion of the weakening of the National Labor Relations Board, see Dean Baker, *The End of Loser Liberalism: Making Markets Progressive* (Washington, DC: Center for Economic and Policy Research, 2011), p. 29.

131 that decline parallels the decline in the share: Madland and Miller, "Latest Census Data Underscore How Important Unions Are for the Middle Class."

14 THE RISE OF THE WORKING POOR

134 the poor have "this idea": See Paul Krugman, "Those Lazy Jobless," *New York Times*, September 21, 2014.

134 America's poor work diligently: U.S. Bureau of Labor Statistics, *A Profile of the Working Poor, 2010*, U.S. Bureau of Labor Statistics website, March 2012.

134 One-fourth of all American workers: Rebecca Thiess, *The Future of Work: Trends and Challenges for Low-Wage Workers*, Briefing Paper #341, Economic Policy Institute website, April 27, 2012, p. 4.

134 average incomes for the bottom fifth dropped 8 percent: Jesse Bricker, Lisa J. Dettling, Alice Henriques, Joanne W. Hsu, et al., "Changes in U.S. Fam-

ily Finances from 2010 to 2013: Evidence from the Survey of Consumer Finances," *Federal Reserve Bulletin* 100, no. 4 (September 2014): 9, 12.

134 According to a study by Oxfam America: Oxfam America, *From Paycheck to Pantry: Hunger in Working America,* Oxfam America website, p. 3.

134 Low-paying industries such as retail: National Employment Law Project, *The Low-Wage Recovery: Industry Employment and Wages Four Years into the Recovery,* Data Brief, National Employment Law Project website, April 2014, p. 1.

134 they generated 44 percent of the jobs: Ibid.

135 By 2014, its real value ($7.25 an hour): U.S. Department of Labor, "History of Federal Minimum Wage Rates Under the Fair Labor Standards Act, 1938–2009," U.S. Department of Labor website. Figures were adjusted for inflation using the CPI.

135 it would be $10.86 an hour: Ibid.

135 "The big danger of minimum wage": Elias Isquith, "Koch Brothers' Top Political Strategist: The Minimum Wage Leads to Fascism!" *Salon,* September 3, 2014.

135 "the main recruiting ground for totalitarianism": Ibid.

136 "we could potentially virtually wipe out unemployment": Antoine Gara, "Would Killing the Minimum Wage Help?" *Bloomberg Businessweek,* June 30, 2011.

136 Research by Arindrajit Dube: Arindrajit Dube, T. William Lester, and Michael Reich, *Minimum Wage Effects Across State Borders: Estimates Using Contiguous Counties,* IRLE Working Paper No. 157-07, Institute for Research on Labor and Employment website, November 2010.

136 Other researchers who found contrary results: Ibid.

137 Dube, Lester, and Reich also found: Arindrajit Dube, T. William Lester, and Michael Reich, *Minimum Wage Shocks, Employment Flows and Labor Market Frictions,* IRLE Working Paper No. 149-13, Institute for Research on Labor and Employment website, October 2014.

137 52 percent of fast-food workers were dependent: Sylvia Allegretto, Marc Doussard, Dave Graham-Squire, Ken Jacobs, et al., *Fast Food, Poverty Wages: The Public Cost of Low-Wage Jobs in the Fast-Food Industry,* U.C. Berkeley Labor Center website, October 15, 2013, p. 1.

137 Big Macs cost only thirty-five cents more: William Finnegan, "Dignity: Fast-Food Workers and a New Form of Labor Activism," *New Yorker,* September 15, 2014.

137 According to the National Employment Law Project: National Employment Law Project, "Big Business, Corporate Profits, and the Minimum Wage," National Employment Law Project website, July 2012, p. 1.

137 Three-quarters of these employers: Ibid.

137 an average of $24 million a year: Catherine Ruetschlin, *Fast Food Failure: How CEO-to-Worker Pay Disparity Undermines the Industry and the Overall Economy,* Demos website, 2014, p. 2.

137 Walmart's CEO received $20.7 million: Jessica Wohl, "Wal-Mart CEO's Pay Jumps 14.1 Percent to $20.7 Million," Reuters, April 22, 2013.

138 the wealth of the Walton family: Josh Bivens, "Inequality, Exhibit A: Walmart and the Wealth of American Families," *The Economic Policy Institute Blog,* July 17, 2012.

138 only 26 percent of jobless Americans: Josh Bivens, "Poverty Reduction Stalled by Policy, Once Again: Unemployment Insurance Edition," *The Economic Policy Institute Blog,* September 16, 2014.

138 The share of recipients with earnings: See Dorothy Rosenbaum, *The Relationship Between SNAP and Work Among Low-Income Households,* Center on Budget and Policy Priorities website, January 2013.

138 The poverty rate in 2013: Office of the Assistant Secretary for Planning and Evaluation, "Information on Poverty and Income Statistics: A Summary of 2014 Current Population Survey Data," ASPE Issue Brief, U.S. Department of Health and Human Services website, September 16, 2014, p. 3.

139 "How do we help people at the bottom": "Piketty v. Mankiw on Economic Challenges and Inequality," *On Point with Tom Ashbrook,* radio broadcast, April 29, 2014.

139 Once the middle class exhausted all its methods: For a full discussion of middle-class coping mechanisms, see Robert B. Reich, *Supercapitalism: The Transformation of Business, Democracy, and Everyday Life* (New York: Alfred A. Knopf, 2007).

139 Shortly after World War II: See Daniel Aaronson and Bhashkar Mazumder, "Intergenerational Economic Mobility in the U.S., 1940 to 2000," *Journal of Human Resources* 43, no. 1 (2005): 139–72.

139 43 percent of children born into poverty: Pew Charitable Trusts, "Moving On Up: Why Do Some Americans Leave the Bottom of the Economic Ladder, but Not Others?" Pew Charitable Trusts website, November 2013, p. 1.

140 the average gap on SAT-type tests: Sean F. Reardon, "No Rich Child Left Behind," *New York Times,* April 27, 2013.

140 On their reading skills: Program for International Student Assessment, "Reading Literacy: School Poverty Indicator," National Center for Education Statistics website, 2012.

140 The achievement gap: Kelsey Hill, Daniel Moser, R. Sam Shannon, and Timothy St. Louis, *Narrowing the Racial Achievement Gap: Policy Success at the State Level,* University of Wisconsin–Madison, Robert M. La Follette School of Public Affairs website, May 2013.

140 According to the Pew Research Center's analysis: Richard Fry and Paul Taylor, "The Rise of Residential Segregation by Income," Pew Research Center Social and Demographic Trends website, August 1, 2012.

140 The federal government provides: Mark Dixon, *Public Education Finances: 2012,* U.S. Census Bureau website, May 2014, p. xi.

140 Most states do try to give more money: See Michael Leachman and Chris

Mai, "Most States Funding Schools Less Than Before the Recession," Center on Budget and Policy Priorities website, revised May 20, 2014.

140 The result is widening disparities: See Andrew Ujifusa and Michele McNeil, "Analysis Points to Growth in Per-Pupil Spending—and Disparities," *Education Week*, January 22, 2014.

140 The wealthiest, highest-spending districts: The Equity and Excellence Commission, *For Each and Every Child—A Strategy for Education Equity and Excellence*, U.S. Department of Education website, 2013, p. 18.

141 "Parents' foundations": "Keeping Schools Local," *Wall Street Journal*, August 24, 1998.

141 the United States is one of only three: Eduardo Porter, "In Public Education, Edge Still Goes to Rich," *New York Times*, November 5, 2013.

141 Their national governments provide 54 percent of funding: Ibid.

141 "The vast majority of OECD countries": Ibid.

15 THE RISE OF THE NON-WORKING RICH

144 Six of today's ten wealthiest Americans: See "Forbes 400," *Forbes*, September 12, 2014. See also "America's Richest Families: 185 Clans with Billion Dollar Fortunes," *Forbes*, last edited July 8, 2014.

144 the Walmart heirs have more wealth: Josh Bivens, "Inequality, Exhibit A: Walmart and the Wealth of American Families," *The Economic Policy Institute Blog*, July 17, 2012.

144 A study from the Boston College Center on Wealth and Philanthropy: John J. Havens and Paul G. Schervish, *A Golden Age of Philanthropy Still Beckons: National Wealth Transfer and Potential for Philanthropy Technical Report*, Boston College, Center on Wealth and Philanthropy website, May 28, 2014. (http://www.bc.edu/content/dam/files/research_sites/cwp/pdf/A%20 Golden%20Age%20of%20Philanthropy%20Still%20Bekons.pdf).

144 A U.S. Trust bank poll: U.S. Trust, "Insights on Wealth and Worth," Key Findings, U.S. Trust website, 2013, p. 4.

144 For the rich under the age of thirty-five: Ibid.

144 This is the dynastic form of wealth: See Thomas Piketty, *Capital in the Twenty-First Century*, trans. Arthur Goldhammer (Cambridge, MA: Harvard University Press, 2014).

144 the compounded result of these capital investments: See Emmanuel Saez and Gabriel Zucman, "Wealth Inequality in the United States Since 1913: Evidence from Capitalized Income Tax Data," NBER Working Paper No. 20625, National Bureau of Economic Research website, October 2014.

145 in 1978, the richest 1 percent of households: Supplementary data provided by Congressional Budget Office, *The Distribution of Household Income and Federal Taxes, 2011*, table 7, "Sources of Income for All Households, by Market Income Group, 1979 to 2011," Congressional Budget Office website, November 2014.

145 By 2007 they accounted for 49 percent: Ibid.

145 They were also taking in 75 percent: Andy Nicholas, "Richest 1 percent get 75 percent of all capital gains," Washington State Budget and Policy Center, *Schmudget Blog,* January 17, 2012.

145 family trusts used to be limited: See Ray D. Madoff, "America Builds an Aristocracy," *New York Times,* July 11, 2010.

145 While the top tax rate: Curtis S. Dubay, "The Bush Tax Cuts Explained: Where Are They Now?" Issue Brief no. 3855, Heritage Foundation website, February 20, 2013, pp. 1–2.

145 Before George W. Bush was president: Roberton Williams, "Resurrecting the Estate Tax as a Shadow of Its Former Self," Tax Policy Center, *TaxVox* blog, December 14, 2010.

145 By 2014, it applied only to assets in excess of $10 million: Ibid.

145 Representative Paul Ryan's so-called road map: Representative Paul D. Ryan, "A Roadmap for America's Future: Version 2.0," January 2010 (http:// paulryan.house.gov/uploadedfiles/rfafv2.0.pdf).

145 only 1.4 out of every 1,000 estates: Chye-Ching Huang and Nathaniel Frentz, "Myths and Realities About the Estate Tax," Center on Budget and Policy Priorities website, August 29, 2013.

145 the tax rate paid by America's wealthy on their capital gains: "Federal Capital Gains Tax Rates, 1988–2013," Tax Foundation website, June 13, 2013.

146 They now account for more than half: Huang and Frentz, "Myths and Realities About the Estate Tax."

146 "the second golden age": Rob Reich, "What Are Foundations For?" *Boston Review,* March 1, 2013.

147 they totaled an estimated $54 billion: Ibid.

147 To put this into some perspective: U.S. Office of Management and Budget, *Analytical Perspectives: Budget of the U.S. Government* (Washington, DC: U.S. Government Printing Office, 2012), pp. 309, 320, 326.

147 A 2005 analysis by Indiana University's Center on Philanthropy: Center on Philanthropy at Indiana University, summer 2007, p. 28 (http://www .philanthropy.iupui.edu/files/research/giving_focused_on_meeting _needs_of_the_poor_july_2007.pdf).

147 New York's Lincoln Center held a fund-raising gala: See Jenny Anderson, "Fund Managers Raising the Ante in Philanthropy," *New York Times,* August 3, 2005.

147 The University of California, Berkeley: University of California, Berkeley, "Pell Grant Awards as a Peer Metric," May 2013 (http://opa.berkeley.edu/ sites/default/files/2011-12PellGrantComparison.pdf).

148 Private university endowments in 2014: "NACUBO-Commonfund Study of Endowments," National Association of College and University Business Officers website.

148 Harvard's endowment: National Association of College and University Business Officers and Commonfund Institute, *U.S. and Canadian Insti-*

tutions Listed by Fiscal Year 2013 Endowment Market Value and Change in Endowment Market Value from FY 2012 to FY 2013, February 2014, p. 2 (http://www.nacubo.org/Documents/EndowmentFiles/2013NCSEEndow mentMarket%20ValuesRevisedFeb142014.pdf).

148 Harvard launched a capital campaign: Alvin Powell, "Harvard Kicks Off Fundraising Effort," Harvard Gazette, September 21, 2013.

148 A few years back, Meg Whitman: Richard Vedder, "Princeton Reaps Tax Breaks as State Colleges Beg," Bloomberg View, March 18, 2012.

148 The annual government subsidy: Ibid.

148 Dean Henry Brady: See also Sandy Baum, Jennifer Ma, and Kathleen Payea, Trends in Public Higher Education: Enrollment, Prices, Student Aid, Revenues, and Expenditures, College Board Advocacy & Policy Center, College Board website, May 2012, p. 1.

148 State and local financing for public higher education: Eduardo Porter, "Why Aid for College Is Missing the Mark," New York Times, October 7, 2014.

148 more students attend public universities now: Ibid.

149 the average annual government subsidy: "Undergraduate Enrollment," National Center for Education Statistics website, May 2014.

16 REPRISE

154 inequality after taxes: See International Monetary Fund, Fiscal Policy and Income Inequality, policy paper, figure 6, January 23, 2014 (http://www.imf .org/external/np/pp/eng/2014/012314.pdf).

17 THE THREAT TO CAPITALISM

158 "It is a fixed principle": Samuel Tyler, Memoir of Roger Brooke Taney, LL.D.: Chief Justice of the Supreme Court of the United States (Baltimore: J. Murphy & Co., 1872), p. 212.

159 "We can have a democracy": See Irving Dillard, Mr. Justice Brandeis, Great American: Press Opinion and Public Appraisal (St. Louis: The Modern View Press, 1941), p. 42.

159 "malefactors of great wealth": Theodore Roosevelt, "Address of President Roosevelt on the Occasion of the Laying of the Corner Stone of the Pilgrim Memorial Monument," Provincetown, MA, August 20, 1907 (Washington, DC: Government Printing Office, 1907), p. 47.

159 "all contributions by corporations": Theodore Roosevelt, "State of the Union Message," December 5, 1905 (http://www.theodore-roosevelt.com/ images/research/speeches/sotu5.pdf).

160 "Never before in all our history": Franklin D. Roosevelt, address at Madison Square Garden, New York City, October 31, 1936. See Gerhard Peters and John T. Woolley, The American Presidency Project website.

160 the real median household income stagnated: See Carmen Denavas-Walt,

Bernadette D. Proctor, and Jessica C. Smith, *Income, Poverty, and Health Insurance Coverage in the United States: 2012*, U.S. Census Bureau Current Population Reports P60-245 (Washington, DC: Government Printing Office, September 2013), figure 1, p. 5.

160   debt reached 135 percent: See Alberto Chong, "Inequality and Institutions," *The Review of Economics and Statistics* 89, no. 3 (September 22, 2014): 2.

160   It is not coincidental that 1928 and 2007: See Emmanuel Saez, "Striking It Richer: The Evolution of Top Incomes in the United States (Update with 2007 Estimates)," University of California, Department of Economics, August 5, 2009 (http://escholarship.org/uc/item/8dp1f91x). Their calculation is before paying taxes, and it includes income from capital gains.

161   The richest four hundred Americans: See analysis by Lawrence Mishel, Josh Bivens, Elise Gould, and Heidi Shierholz, *The State of Working America*, 12th ed. (Ithaca, NY: Cornell University Press, 2014).

161   the wealthiest 1 percent: See ibid.

161   the share of wealth held by the lower half: See Janet L. Yellin, "Perspectives on Inequality and Opportunity from the Survey of Consumer Finances," speech at the Conference on Economic Opportunity and Inequality, Federal Reserve Bank of Massachusetts, Boston, October 17, 2014.

161   By 2012, the household at the top: See A. Bonica, N. McCarty, K. Poole, and H. Rosenthal, "Why Hasn't Democracy Slowed Rising Inequality," *Journal of Economic Perspectives* 27, no. 3 (Summer 2013): 103–24.

161   Since 2000, adjusted for inflation: See Drew DeSilver, "For Most Workers, Real Wages Have Barely Budged for Decades," *Fact Tank*, Pew Research Center website, October 9, 2014.

162   As Thomas Piketty has shown: See Thomas Piketty, *Capital in the Twenty-First Century*, trans. Arthur Goldhammer (Cambridge, MA: Harvard University Press, 2013).

162   Figure 8 puts the current era into context: See Pavlina R. Tcherneva, "Growth for Whom?," Levy Economics Institute of Bard College, October 6, 2014, figure: "Distribution of Average Income Growth During Expansions" (http://www.levyinstitute.org/pubs/op_47.pdf).

163   In 2001 a Gallup poll found: See Rebecca Riffkin, "In U.S., 67% Dissatisfied with Income, Wealth Distribution," Gallup website, January 20, 2014 (http://www.gallup.com/poll/166904/dissatisfied-income-wealth-distribution.aspx).

163   According to the Pew Research Center: See Pew Research Center for the People and the Press/USA Today, "January 2014 Political Survey, Final Topline," January 15–19, 2014 (http://www.people-press.org/files/legacy-questionnaires/1-23-14%20Poverty_Inequality%20topline%20for%20release.pdf).

165   most Americans were opposed to the Trans-Pacific Partnership: See Hart Research Associates, "National Survey on Fast-Track Authority for TPP

Trade Pact," January 27, 2014 (http://fasttrackpoll.info/docs/Fast-Track
-Survey_Memo.pdf).

166 most Americans no longer supported trade-opening agreements: "Trans-
Pacific Partnership (TPP) Poll: Only the Strongest Obama Supporters
Want Him to Have Fast-Track Authority," *International Business Times,*
January 30, 2014.

167 Consumers in China: See Tom Orlik and Bob Davis, "China Falters in
Effort to Boost Consumption," *Wall Street Journal,* July 16, 2013. Also see
Yu Xie and Xiang Zhou, "Income Inequality in Today's China," *Proceedings
of the National Academy of Sciences,* May 13, 2014.

18 THE DECLINE OF COUNTERVAILING POWER

168 A study published in the fall of 2014: See Martin Gilens and Benjamin Page,
"Testing Theories of American Politics: Elites, Interest Groups, and Average Citizens," *Perspectives on Politics* 12, no. 3 (2014): 564–81.

168 "The preferences of the average American": Ibid., p. 575.

169 Walter Lippmann argued in his 1922 book: See Walter Lippmann, *Public
Opinion* (New York: Harcourt, Brace & Company, 1922).

169 "It is no longer possible": Ibid., pp. 248–49.

169 "The principal balancing force": David Truman, *The Governmental Process*
(New York: Alfred A. Knopf, 1951), p. 535.

169 Yale political scientist Robert A. Dahl: See Robert A. Dahl, *A Preface to
Democratic Theory* (Chicago: University of Chicago Press, 1956).

170 passage of the GI Bill of 1944: See Theda Skocpol, *Diminished Democracy*
(Norman: University of Oklahoma Press, 2003).

171 dubbed all this "countervailing power": See John Kenneth Galbraith, *American Capitalism: The Concept of Countervailing Power* (Boston: Houghton
Mifflin, 1952).

171 "In fact, the support of countervailing power": Ibid., p. 122.

171 "Given the existence of private market power": Ibid., p. 147.

171 It wasn't just that big corporations: See Gilens and Page, "Testing Theories
of American Politics," pp. 564–81.

172 As sociologist Robert Putnam has documented: See Robert D. Putnam,
Bowling Alone: The Collapse and Revival of American Community (New
York: Simon & Schuster, 2000).

173 the Koch brothers' political network: See Matea Gold, "Koch-Backed Political Network, Built to Shield Donors, Raised $400 Million in 2012 Elec-
tions," *Washington Post,* January 5, 2014.

173 This sum was more than twice: See analysis from Center for Responsive
Politics, "Heavy Hitters: Top All Time Donors, 1989–2014," OpenSecrets
.org website.

173 That same year corporations spent: See Lee Drutman, *The Business of America Is Lobbying* (New York: Oxford University Press, 2015), p. 17.

173 In 2012, the richest 0.01 percent: A. Bonica, N. McCarty, K. Poole, and H. Rosenthal, "Why Hasn't Democracy Slowed Rising Inequality?" *Journal of Economic Perspectives* 27, no. 3 (2013): 113.

174 "Business has to deal with us": Gregg Easterbrook, "The Business of Politics," *The Atlantic,* October 1986.

175 Under Obama's watch: See Federal Reserve Bank of St. Louis, "Dow Jones Industrial Average," Federal Reserve Economic Data website (http://research.stlouisfed.org/fred2/series/DJIA/).

175 corporate profits rose to the highest portion: See Floyd Norris, "Corporate Profits Grow and Wages Slide," *New York Times,* April 4, 2014.

176 only about 3 percent of retiring members of Congress: Elliot Gerson, "To Make America Great Again, We Need to Leave the Country," *The Atlantic,* July 10, 2012.

176 "You spend a lot of time on the phone": Listen to Senator Murphy's comments in the opening remarks of the video "Purchasing Power: Money, Politics, and Inequality: Post-Conference," Yale Institution for Social and Policy Studies (http://isps.yale.edu/node/21022#.VJIBCYrF92c).

177 political contributions by the richest one-hundredth of 1 percent: Bonica, McCarty, Poole, and Rosenthal, "Why Hasn't Democracy Slowed Rising Inequality?," p. 112.

177 In 1980, the top 0.01 percent: Ibid.

177 their campaign donations soared to 40 percent: Ibid.

178 the two biggest donors were Sheldon and Miriam Adelson: Ibid., pp. 112–13.

178 Out of the 4,493 board members and CEOs: Ibid., p. 113.

178 according to a 2014 Pew Research poll: "Economy, Jobs, Terrorism Rank High Across Partisan Groups," Pew Research Center website, January 24, 2014. (www.people-press.org/2014/01/27/deficit-reduction-deadlines-or-policy-priority/1-25-2014_05/).

178 political scientists Benjamin Page and Larry Bartels: Benjamin I. Page, Larry M. Bartels, and Jason Seawright, "Democracy and the Policy Preferences of Wealthy Americans," *Perspectives on Politics* 11, no. 1 (March 2013): 55.

179 two-thirds of them had contributed money: Ibid., p. 54.

179 *Citizens United* declared that corporations are people: *Citizens United v. Federal Election Commission,* 558 U. S. 310 (2010).

179 A subsequent federal appeals court ruling: See *Speechnow.org v. FEC,* 599 D.C. Cir. F.3d 686 (D.C. Cir. 2010). See also "Recent Developments in the Law," Federal Election Commission website.

179 *McCutcheon* eliminated the $123,200 cap: *McCutcheon et al. v. Federal Election Commission,* 572 U.S. (2014).

180 In the 2014 midterm election: Nicholas Confessore, "Secret Money Fueling a Flood of Political Ads," *New York Times,* October 10, 2014.

180 These groups financed more political advertising: Ibid.

180 "the corrosive and distorting effects": *Austin v. Michigan Chamber of Commerce*, 494 U.S. 652 (1990).

180 "independent expenditures": *Citizens United v. Federal Election Commission*, 558 U.S. 310 (2010), p. 5.

180 In 1964, just 29 percent of voters: See "The ANES Guide to Public Opinion and Electoral Behavior," American National Election Studies website. See also Thomas B. Edsall, "The Value of Political Corruption," *New York Times*, August 5, 2014.

180 59 percent of Americans felt that government corruption was widespread: Jon Clifton, "Americans Less Satisfied with Freedom" (http://www.gallup.com/poll/172019/americans-less-satisfied-freedom.aspx).

180 In Rasmussen polls undertaken in the fall of 2014: "Voters Think Congress Cheats to Get Reelected," Rasmussen Reports website, September 3, 2014.

181 Sixty-six percent believed: "Americans Don't Think Incumbents Deserve Reelection," Rasmussen Reports website, October 2, 2014.

181 Only 58.2 percent of eligible voters: Drew DeSilver, "Voter Turnout Always Drops Off for Midterm Elections, but Why?" Pew Research Center website, July 24, 2014.

181 Turnout in midterm elections is always lower: "2014 November General Election Turnout Rates," U.S. Election Project website, updated December 16, 2014.

181 the lowest percentage since the midterm elections of 1942: Philip Bump, "We Probably Just Saw One of the Lowest-Turnout Elections in American History," *Washington Post*, November 11, 2014.

181 Catalonians in a straw poll: Raphael Minder, "Catalonia Overwhelmingly Votes for Independence from Spain in Straw Poll," *New York Times*, November 9, 2014.

19 RESTORING COUNTERVAILING POWER

185 In a CNBC/Burson-Marsteller international survey: Donald A. Baer, "The West's Bruised Confidence in Capitalism," *Wall Street Journal*, September 22, 2014.

186 "cannot be the party of fat cats": Rand Paul, speech at the Freedom Summit, Manchester, NH, April 12, 2014.

186 Republican senator Ted Cruz: "The Tea Party's New Koch-Flavored Populism," *Daily Beast*, April 15, 2014.

186 "cheap labor ... that's going to lower wages": Michael Laris and Jenna Portnoy, "Meet David Brat, the Man Who Brought Down House Majority Leader Eric Cantor," *Wall Street Journal*, June 10, 2014.

186 Polls show, for example, support among self-described Republicans: See "2013 Lake Poll Questions and Data," Americans for Financial Reform website, 2013.

186 Republican representative David Camp: Jim Nunns, Amanda Eng, and Lydia Austin, *Description and Analysis of the Camp Tax Reform Plan*, Urban-Brookings Tax Policy Center website, July 8, 2014, p. 18.

186 "There is nothing conservative": Rand Paul, speech at the Conservative Political Action Conference, Washington, D.C., March 6, 2014.

187 "The establishment political class": See "Repeal of Glass-Steagall and the Too Big to Fail Culture," *Tea Party Tribune*, April 23, 2014.

187 "The Tea Party movement": Judson Phillips, "Trade and the Tea Party: Washington Insiders Remain Clueless," *The Hill,* February 24, 2014.

188 "The darkest secret": Ben White and Maggie Haberman, "Wall Street Republicans' Dark Secret: Hillary Clinton 2016," *Politico,* April 28, 2014.

188 "If it's Rand Paul or Ted Cruz": Ibid.

189 In a Gallup poll conducted in September 2014: Jeffrey M. Jones, "Americans Continue to Say a Third Political Party Is Needed," September 24, 2014 (http://www.gallup.com/poll/177284/americans-continue-say-third-political-party-needed.aspx).

189 46 percent of self-described Republicans: Ibid.

190 Democrats grew from holding 37.7 percent of the seats: "Party Division in the Senate, 1789–Present," U.S. Senate website; also see "Party Divisions of the House of Representatives, 1789–Present," U.S. House of Representatives website.

190 In the campaign of 1912: Theodore Roosevelt, *Progressive Covenant with the People,* motion picture, Broadcasting and Recorded Sound Division, Library of Congress, August 1912.

21 REINVENTING THE CORPORATION

196 A bill introduced in the California legislature: See Corporation Taxes: Tax Rates: Publicly Held Corporations: Credits, Cal. SB-1372, February 21, 2014.

197 The California Chamber of Commerce: See "CalChamber Releases 2014 Job Killer List," CalChamber Advocacy website, April 10, 2014.

197 A variation on this idea: William A. Galston, "Closing the Productivity and Pay Gap," *Wall Street Journal,* February 18, 2014.

198 It dates back to the early years of the Republic: See Joseph R. Blasi, Richard B. Freeman, and Douglas L. Kruse, *The Citizen's Share: Putting Ownership Back into Democracy* (New Haven, CT: Yale University Press, 2013), p. 5.

199 Apple raised $97 million: William Lazonick, Marina Mazzucato, and Öner Tulum, "Apple's Changing Business Model: What Should the World's Richest Company Do with All Those Profits?" *Accounting Forum* 37, no. 4 (2013): 249–67.

199 Steve Jobs's successor: U.S. Securities and Exchange Commission, "Definitive Proxy Statement Apple Corporation," Summary Compensation Table—2012, 2011, and 2010, p. 31 (http://www.sec.gov/Archives/edgar/data/320193/000119312513005529/d450591ddef14a.htm).

199   In 2014, the managers, employees, and customers: Jena McGregor, "An Ousted CEO So Popular Employees Are Protesting to Get His Job Back," *Washington Post,* July 22, 2014.

200   By 2014, twenty-seven states had enacted laws: See "State by State Legislative Status," Benefit Corporation website.

200   more than 1,165 companies: See B Corps Fellows (http://www.bcorporation .net/).

201   corporate laws require "co-determination": See Rebecca Page, "Codetermination in Germany—A Beginner's Guide," *Arbeitspapier* 33 (June 2009).

201   as was dramatically illustrated in 2014: Amanda Becker, "Auto Union Forms Branch for Workers at VW Plant in Tennessee," Reuters, July 10, 2014.

22   WHEN ROBOTS TAKE OVER

203   "the discovery of means of economizing": John Maynard Keynes, *Essays in Persuasion* (New York: W. W. Norton & Co., 1963), pp. 358–73.

204   in my book *The Work of Nations:* See Robert B. Reich, *The Work of Nations: Preparing Ourselves for 21st Century Capitalism* (New York: Vintage Books, 1992).

204   Using the same methodology I used then: Ibid.

204   In 1990, by my estimate: Ibid., p. 177.

205   I also predicted their pay would drop: For discussion of "in-person services" wage predictions, see ibid., pp. 215–16.

205   the median pay of such work: U.S. Department of Commerce, Bureau of Labor Statistics, various issues.

205   By 2014 Amazon was busily wiping out retail jobs: Greg Bensinger, "Amazon Robots Get Ready for Christmas," *Wall Street Journal,* updated November 19, 2014. See also Stacy Mitchell, "The Truth About Amazon and Job Creation," *Huffington Post,* July 30, 2013.

205   In their 2004 book, *The New Division of Labor:* Frank Levy and Richard J. Murnane, *The New Division of Labor: How Computers Are Creating the Next Job Market* (Princeton, NJ: Princeton University Press, 2004), p. 48.

205   Google's self-driving car posed a serious threat: Alex Davies, "Google's Self-Driving Car Hits Roads Next Month—Without a Wheel or Pedals," *Wired,* December 23, 2014. See also U.S. Bureau of Labor Statistics, "Occupational Outlook Handbook, 2014–15 Edition," U.S. Bureau of Labor Statistics website, January 8, 2014.

206   Such manipulations improve efficiency: For a discussion of "symbolic-analytic services," see Reich, *The Work of Nations,* pp. 170–240.

206   the life expectancy of an American white woman: S. Jay Olshansky et al., "Differences in Life Expectancy Due to Race and Educational Differences Are Widening, and Many May Not Catch Up," *Health Affairs* 31, no. 8 (2012): 1803–13.

206   Instagram, a popular photo-sharing site: See Shayndi Raice and Spencer E.

Ante, "Insta-Rich: $1 Billion for Instagram," *Wall Street Journal,* April 10, 2012. See also Steve Cooper, "Instagram's Small Workforce Legitimizes Other Small Start-Ups," *Forbes,* April 7, 2012.

207 Contrast this with Kodak: See Eric Savitz, "Kodak Files Chapter 11," *Forbes,* January 19, 2012.

207 In its prime, Kodak had employed: Dana Mattioli, "Their Kodak Moments," *Wall Street Journal,* January 6, 2012.

207 When Facebook purchased WhatsApp: Adam Hartung, "Three Smart Lessons from Facebook's Purchase of WhatsApp," *Forbes,* February 24, 2014.

207 Forty-seven years later, the largest American companies: Derek Thompson, "This Is What the Post-Employee Economy Looks Like," *The Atlantic,* April 20, 2011.

209 Co-founder Brian Acton: Parmy Olson, "Exclusive: The Rags-to-Riches Tale of How Jan Koum Built WhatsApp into Facebook's New $19 Billion Baby," *Forbes,* February 19, 2014.

209 That was a bigger advantage: David Leonhardt, "Is College Worth It? Clearly, New Data Says," *New York Times,* May 27, 2014.

210 the entry-level wages of college graduates: For the discussion of wage stagnation of college graduates since 2000, see Josh Bivens, Elise Gould, Lawrence Mishel, and Heidi Shierholz, *Raising America's Pay: Why It's Our Central Economic Policy Challenge,* Briefing Paper #378, Economic Policy Institute website, June 4, 2014.

210 the top marginal rate never fell below 70 percent: Tax Foundation, "US Federal Individual Income Tax Rates History, 1862–2013 (Inflation-Adjusted 2013 Dollars)," Tax Foundation website, October 17, 2013. See also Andrew Fieldhouse, *Rising Income Inequality and the Role of Shifting Market-Income Distribution, Tax Burdens, and Tax Rates,* Issue Brief #365, Economic Policy Institute website, June 14, 2013.

23 THE CITIZEN'S BEQUEST

213 By 2014 six of the ten wealthiest Americans: See "Forbes 400," *Forbes,* September 12, 2014. See also "America's Richest Families: 185 Clans with Billion Dollar Fortunes," *Forbes,* last edited July 8, 2014.

213 The six Walmart heirs together: Josh Bivens, "Inequality, Exhibit A: Walmart and the Wealth of American Families," *The Economic Policy Institute Blog,* July 17, 2012.

213 According to political economist Peter Barnes: Peter Barnes, "Why You Have the Right to a $5K Dividend from Uncle Sam," *PBS NewsHour* website, August 27, 2014.

214 the expected transfer by wealthy Americans: For discussion of the expected transfer of wealth, see John J. Havens and Paul G. Schervish, *A Golden Age of Philanthropy Still Beckons: National Wealth Transfer and Potential for Phi-*

lanthropy Technical Report, Boston College, Center on Wealth and Philanthropy website, May 28, 2014.

214 One straightforward way to do this: Variations on this suggestion have been made by several thoughtful researchers. See, for example, Bruce Ackerman and Anne Alstoff, *The Stakeholder Society* (New Haven, CT: Yale University Press, 1999), and Peter Barnes, *With Liberty and Dividends for All* (Oakland, CA: Berrett-Koehler, 2014).

214 "The assurance of a certain minimum income": Friedrich A. Hayek, *Law, Legislation, and Liberty*, vol. 3: *The Political Order of a Free People* (Chicago: University of Chicago Press, 1979), p. 55.

215 This would be that kind of society: John Maynard Keynes, *Essays in Persuasion* (New York: W. W. Norton & Co., 1963).

216 Such landholdings were useful: Thomas Paine, *The Writings of Thomas Paine*, vol. 3, ed. Moncure Daniel Conway (New York: G. P. Putnam's Sons, 1895).

Index

A NOTE ABOUT THE AUTHOR

ROBERT REICH is Chancellor's Professor of Public Policy at the Richard and Rhoda Goldman School of Public Policy at the University of California, Berkeley, and senior fellow at the Blum Center for Developing Economies. He has served in three national administrations and has written fourteen books, including the bestsellers *Supercapitalism* and *Locked in the Cabinet*. His articles have appeared in the *New Yorker*, *Atlantic*, *New York Times*, *Washington Post*, and *Wall Street Journal*. He is co-creator of the award-winning 2013 film *Inequality for All*.

A NOTE ON THE TYPE

This book was set in Minion, a typeface produced by the Adobe Corporation specifically for the Macintosh personal computer and released in 1990. Designed by Robert Slimbach, Minion combines the classic characteristics of old-style faces with the full complement of weights required for modern typesetting.